THE MYTH OF THE
ELECTRONIC LIBRARY

The Myth of the Electronic Library

Librarianship and Social Change in America

WILLIAM F. BIRDSALL

CONTRIBUTIONS IN LIBRARIANSHIP AND INFORMATION SCIENCE, NUMBER 82

Greenwood Press
Westport, Connecticut • London _____

Library of Congress Cataloging-in-Publication Data

Birdsall, William F.
　　The myth of the electronic library : librarianship and social
change in America / William F. Birdsall.
　　　　p. cm.—(Contributions in librarianship and information
science, ISSN 0084–9243 ; no. 82)
　　Includes bibliographical references and index.
　　ISBN 0–313–29210–8 (alk. paper)
　　　1. Libraries—United States—Automation.   2. Information
technology—United States.   3. Library science—United States.
4. Libraries—United States—Aims and objectives.   5. Libraries and
society—United States. I. Title. II. Series.
Z678.9.A4U619   1994
025′.00285—dc20　　　93–49534

　British Library Cataloguing in Publication Data is available.

Library of Congress Catalog Card Number: 93–49534
ISBN: 0–313–29210–8
ISSN: 0084–9243

First published in 1994

Greenwood Press, 88 Post Road West, Westport, CT 06881
An imprint of Greenwood Publishing Group, Inc.

Printed in the United States of America

∞™

The paper used in this book complies with the
Permanent Paper Standard issued by the National
Information Standards Organization (Z39.48–1984).

10 9 8 7 6 5 4 3 2

To Ann

Contents

Preface

We are moving toward a more electronic library, but what does electronic library mean—information *paradise*?

John Tongate

The twentieth century is over: History will not wait for the year 2000. We are repeatedly told we live in a "post-" society of one kind or another: post-bourgeois, post-capitalist, post-modern, post-civilized, post-economic, post-Protestant, post-ideological, post-historic, post-industrial.[1] Some claim we are experiencing the information society, the knowledge society, the on-line society, the technological society, the electronic society, or the cybernetic society. With so much emphasis on change, perhaps we should stick to poet W. H. Auden's "Age of Anxiety" as the most appropriate descriptor. A television series calls upon leading intellectuals of the Western world to address the questions: "Why do people living in the most affluent and dynamic societies the world has ever known seem so worried about the present, so frightened about the future? Why does the social, political, and economic landscape seem to be changing so fast? What is the world coming to?[2] Many librarians wonder what the world is coming to, specifically: Will it be a post-library society?

One library conference speaker exclaims that "anybody who isn't scared just isn't thinking about what's happening."[3] On the Internet electronic communications network, anxious librarians call on their colleagues to formulate a new vision for librarianship that promotes an electronic "virtual library," a "library without walls," to serve "information seekers" in an information age.

When Archibald MacLeish, noted American poet and former Librarian of Congress, gave an address exploring the mystery of libraries in 1971 at the dedication of a new library at York University, Toronto, Ontario, he declared the library, with the structuring of knowledge embodied in its orderly arrangement of books and catalogs, one of the greatest achievements of humankind, above all, "the fact that it exists. . . . It is *there*."[4] Only twenty years later Charles Robinson, director of the Baltimore County Public Library, charges librarians in a 1992 *Library Journal* article with wasting the taxpayers' dollars by constructing outmoded central city libraries. Librarians must grasp the opportunities offered by the world of the electronic book, abandon the name of librarian and their identification with the library, and become "information consultants."[5] Similarly, prominent library educator Margaret Steig claims

Librarians have ceased to identify themselves with the building in which they labor. The former identification is coming to be seen as a historical accident; the library was the place where the tools with which the librarian worked were housed and only for that reason the locus of their efforts. Now librarianship is perceived as a process, and its real business defined as fulfilling information needs. It has been divorced from the physical form of the book, as well as from the location in which books were placed. One no longer hears much about its role as preserver of culture.[6]

I was startled to read that it is just a "historical accident" that librarians are found in libraries, that in freeing ourselves from that encumbrance, we can forget about culture and get on with our "real business" of fulfilling "information needs." However, as the year 2000 draws near, generating ever-more theorizing about the future, I believe many librarians long for a new vision of librarianship to carry them into the twenty-first century and see the "electronic library" as that new vision. There are two contending myths within librarianship. The first, the myth of the library as place, emerged in the last quarter of the nineteenth century and is in decline. The second, the myth of the electronic library, emerged in the last quarter of the twentieth century and is becoming more prominent.

Why have librarians adopted the electronic library as their new vision? Where did this idea come from? How does it differ from the way librarians traditionally viewed themselves? Is the electronic library the only option? Why are librarians so eager to abandon the library? As I explored these questions I concluded that the vision of the electronic library is a myth formulated to help librarians adapt to social change.

I refer to the "myth" of the electronic library because the cluster of values, images, and concepts constituting the myth is a largely subjective system of beliefs offering, as myth should, an explanation of change, a new rationale for librarianship, the prospect of a better future. Bryan Pfaffenberger, a scholar of technology studies, reminds us that "a myth grabs and holds our attention because it contains a significant amount of truth and, often, deep insights into the nature of things." But Pfaffenberger also notes "we tend to subscribe to its assumptions without question" and we do so "without making any inquiry into their veracity."[7] As much can be said of the myth of the electronic library. However, to proceed to act on the myth of the electronic library without examining it may result in unfortunate consequences for librarianship. Far from being a radical break from the past, an electronic revolution, the myth of the electronic library represents an effort to incorporate social change into a neo-conservative framework. I wish to explore the myth-making process of the myth of the electronic library and to examine the myth's implications for librarianship.

The electronic library is not a technological issue alone. There is no denying the importance of the technological impact on libraries and the opportunities information technologies offer to enhancing library services. The danger is to ignore the political and cultural implications of the electronic library, which, in the long term, have far more serious consequences for libraries, librarians, and the users of libraries. The technological foundation of the electronic library serves as a magnet, drawing to it a cluster of social, cultural, and political values, beliefs, images, and concepts that forms a distinct alternative to the traditional conception of the library and of librarianship. Therefore, in addition to the literature in library and information studies, my debt to work in the humanities and social sciences is evident in the extensive footnotes in this book.

Portions of this book are based on material that originally appeared in the following publications:

"Community, Individualism, and the American Public Library." *Library Journal*, 110 (November 1, 1985), 21–24.

"Librarians: Personal Service Professionals?" *Argus* 11 (May–August 1982), 53–56.

"Librarianship, Professionalism, and Social Change." *Library Journal*, 107 (February 1, 1982), 223–26.

"The Political Persuasion of Librarianship." *Library Journal*, 113 (June 1, 1988), 75–79.

"Public Libraries and Political Culture." *Public Library Quarterly*, 8 (3/4, 1988), 55–65.

I would like to express my thanks to Bonita Boyd and Elizabeth Hamilton for their reading of early drafts of portions of this work and for their many helpful suggestions. I would also like to express my appreciation to Dalhousie University for granting me a six-month special leave. I am indebted to the Atlantic Provinces Library Association for a research grant through its Memorial Award Fund and to the Dalhousie University Faculty of Graduate Studies for a grant from the Research Development Fund.

I especially appreciate the patience and time Janice Slauenwhite devoted to the numerous drafts and revisions that I endlessly generated.

Several years ago I was attempting to write a paper on the electronic library. I was having a frustrating time until my wife, Ann, observed that I was trying to put too many ideas into one paper. She suggested I write a book. I recognized at once that she was right. It gives me great satisfaction to be able now to thank her for her support and to be able to dedicate this book to her.

THE MYTH OF THE
ELECTRONIC LIBRARY

Introduction: The Myth of the Library

If we succeed, we are heroes, and if we fail we are merely visionaries who were ahead of our time.

Edwin B. Parker

Those who grapple with trying to explain the phenomenon of change describe what is happening as a "paradigm shift." The concept of a paradigm derives from the immensely influential study of the history of science by Thomas Kuhn, *The Structure of Scientific Revolutions*. Kuhn rejects the traditional view that scientific progress is an incremental process, an accumulation of knowledge through individual research and discovery. Instead, he formulated the concept of paradigms, "universally recognized scientific achievements that for a time provide model problems and solutions to a community of practitioners."[1] Scientists attack problems and adjust theories within the generally accepted assumptions of the paradigm. However, in time a sufficient challenge to the prevailing paradigm results in a new paradigm. Such paradigm shifts are of a magnitude representing an entirely new way of viewing and even thinking about the world.

Many other disciplines have adopted the notion of paradigm shifts to represent a profound change in the world view held by a group within society. There has been such widespread use of the term "paradigm" as a way of analyzing change that it has been said Kuhn's idea itself caused a paradigm shift. One often sees references to a paradigm shift in librarianship. But it is too restrictive a concept to capture the intellectual and emotional pressures born of change. I believe myth, constituted as it is of images, heroes, truth, and fable, is a more useful concept than paradigm in understanding the contending values, perceptions, and assumptions currently found in librarianship.

We moderns often associate myths with earlier cultures. We prefer to put our faith in history as a more objective interpretation of the past and guide to the future. Nevertheless, we continue to invent myths as a means of explaining a changing world to ourselves. While we may think myth is more false than history, historian William H. McNeill suggests "mythistory" best describes much of what we believe because "the same words that constitute truth for some are, and always will be, myth for others, who inherit or embrace different assumptions and organizing concepts about the world."[2] According to McNeill, there are myth-breakers and myth-makers always trying to improve our way of perceiving the world and adjusting to change. They attempt to formulate new vocabularies, concepts, and images toward the creation of new myths. For about half a century, myth-breakers and makers have been formulating the myth of the electronic library to replace the myth of the library as place, until recently the prevailing myth of modern librarianship.

Organizations such as the library have then not only a history but a myth. Students of organizations are aware of the need to study the "sensuous, the mythical, the aesthetic, the cultural features of organizations."[3] In this context myth is not a negative quality, something to be dispelled. Rather, examining the myths of librarianship can help us understand the place of the library in history and in society and the role of librarianship as they are perceived by those within and outside of librarianship. Myth may be understood to be "*any set of shared beliefs*, whether they manifest themselves in stories and histories, in the way inquiry is conducted, in the way work is done, or in any other human endeavour."[4] Organizational mythology is part of an hierarchy of myth extending from an individual organization up to the general culture of which it is a part. For example, a specific public library can have a myth—a cluster of symbols, a history, a cast of heroes that are unique to that library. But this library will share with other public libraries a larger myth of the American public library. And the myth of the public library consists of elements contributing to the myth of libraries in general. Finally, libraries at all levels of the hierarchy encompass elements of the metamyths embodied in the macroculture, the "extraorganizational beliefs expressed in language, stories, ritual, and other symbolic forms that transcend the idiosyncrasies of any particular organization but that inform the symbol systems of all of them."[5]

This hierarchy of myth and metamyth is illustrated by the public library of Peterborough, New Hampshire, a library with a rich mythical texture. The history of the Peterborough library has all the elements of myth: its origin in a social library established in the 1790s; an early hero in the person of the newly arrived minister, Dr. Abiel Abbot, who promoted the formation of the Peterborough Library Company; a list of notable benefactors throughout the nineteenth and twentieth centuries; the community's continued proud commitment to the library as expressed through citizen participation as trustees and in town meetings.[6] But its own myth constitutes an important component of the larger myth of the public library movement. Established in 1833, it is considered the first modern public library. According to Jesse Shera's history on the emergence of the public library, its formation "possesses all the elements that make for popular fable—romantic beauty of natural setting, uncertainty as to precise detail, nostalgic longing for a vanishing small-town life, and popular conviction that American leadership finds its greatest expression when it is nurtured by the homespun simplicity of a rustic environment."[7] The elements of the Peterborough myth are embodied in the myth of the public library movement, the story of American library development as a whole, and the American metamyth of heroic democratic institution-building, the creation of an "arsenal of democracy."

Organizational myth becomes an important component of the identity of any profession associated with the organization. An occupational title is also an important part of a profession's identity because the title carries implications promoted by the profession and recognized by its clientele. The combined importance of organizational myth and occupational title to professional identity is particularly true in the case of librarians, whose occupational title and identity stem directly from a specific organization: the library. When the myth-makers advocate a new myth that no longer conceives of the library as a place, they present a fundamental challenge to the identity of librarianship. To understand this challenge we must examine first the myth of the library as place.

An organizational myth embodies ideals and values often captured by specific images in the mind of the general public. Two images embody many of the ideals and values surrounding the traditional perception of the library as place. The first image is well established in the iconography of both American popular culture and librarianship: the small-town public library with its porticoed entrance of Greek columns facing the town square. Its very design and location confirm its identification with values rooted in the communal New England town. This image reflects a deep-seated social need for objective symbols of community; thus, in that respect the library is a profoundly conservative institution. The library, along with the school, post office, town hall, and church says, even to those who do not use it, "This community exists." But another long-standing powerful image is part of the myth of the library as place: the urban public library. It too has symbolic significance, not as a bulwark of community, but as a testament to urban individualism and liberal rationality. It is not surprising that a standard periodical in the public library field features on its cover an illustration based on the lions in front of the New York Public Library, thereby clearly identifying the public library as a powerful urban institution.

These two images are important elements of the myth of the library. The Peterborough Public Library and the Boston Public Library, two landmarks in the history of the public library, are representative of these two images. The library is projected as a stalwart component of the rural, conservative, communal small American town, in short, a repository of all that is virtuous in America. But it is also projected as an urban window to the cosmopolitan world, a source of new ideas free from local restraint, a vehicle for individualism and self-development. Because the myth of the library as place allows for many interpretations, it has been effective in generating a vision and support for all types of libraries. Furthermore, the factor giving these traditional images such mythic potency is their very concreteness, their assuring solidity. As Archibald MacLeish stated, "It is *there*."

In addition to these familiar images of the library, there are other elements of the myth of the library as place. The organizational basis of the myth is the public library. Although there are libraries of many types, the history of modern librarianship and the fundamental issues about which it has been concerned, such as intellectual freedom, first arose and are often most acutely at stake in the sphere of public library development. It was the proliferation of public libraries in the nineteenth century that provided the institutional foundation for the emergence of modern librarianship as a profession—a profession, as we have already noted, intimately bound to a specific organization as distinct from the usual stereotype of the autonomous professional. We have also noted two images of the library that are shot through with paradox: conservatism/liberalism, rural/urban, community/individualism. Because of these paradoxes, the roles of the library and of librarianship itself have always been ambiguous. Throughout its history, the role of the public library has been a constant source of concern to librarians.[8] Regardless of this ambiguity, a fundamental focus of its objectives has been knowledge, and a primary objective of this focus has been the organization of knowledge into coherent systems of classification. The core resource of the library around which its services revolved has been its collection, largely of print material. The emphasis on a local collection and services allowed each library to operate with a considerable degree of autonomy.

The political ideology of the library has been most closely akin to liberalism, with its emphasis on promoting the informed, autonomous individual and its commitment to free library service to all as a means of ensuring individual self-development. This commitment to the individual has been coupled with the perception of the library as a community resource, indeed, as noted above, one of the institutions that define a community. Therefore, while there is specialization of services within individual libraries and among types of libraries, the myth says libraries are committed to serving the entire community.

The knowledge base of the profession of librarianship has been the humanities and, especially during the last fifty years or so, the social sciences. Out of this orientation, the history of libraries and librarianship has concentrated on the importance of social and cultural change in the development of libraries.

To summarize, the characteristics of the myth of the library as place are:

- The organizational base is the public library.
- The core resource is a collection of predominantly print material.
- Each library is primarily an autonomous unit.
- The library serves as the institutional base of the profession of librarianship.
- The objectives of the library are multiple and ambiguous.
- The political ideology is liberalism.
- The social orientation is the community.
- The user orientation is service to everyone.
- The social need being fulfilled is the organization of knowledge.
- This body of knowledge is a public good that should be available at no cost.
- The knowledge base of librarianship is the humanities and social sciences.
- Social and cultural factors provide the impetus for change.

A myth so institutionally anchored now strikes many librarians as anachronistic for a profession wanting to play an important role in the transformation to an electronic information society. As the turbulent 1960s drew to a close, it was observed in a major national study of libraries that "the image of the library has been as immutable as the shape of the steeple in a village landscape. Time has given these forms the stamp of authenticity. Within the past decade, however, cracks have been appearing in the library's facade—and they are growing wider."[9] In the 1990s, many claim the walls of the library are crumbling, if not collapsing altogether. As librarians cope with change they respond to an image far more abstract than the library as place: the electronic library on an electronic super highway.[10]

2

Breaking the Myth of the Library as Place

> The most dramatic predictions about the future of books, libraries, and information technology tend to be made by men of thought rather than men of action—by writers, professors, and committees that do not have to implement their ideas in the marketplace and take personal responsibility for the results.
>
> Richard De Gennero

The origin of a myth is obscure by the very nature of myth, and there can be many variations of a myth. Through retelling, however, elements emerge as a distinct core of the myth, allowing the sources of the myth to be discerned. Although it is not until the middle of the 1970s that there are explicit references to the "electronic library," the core elements of the myth of the electronic library were evident long before then. We find early on it was not very long before the discourse on solving the "information problem" assumed a fairly consistent pattern. To be familiar with this emerging pattern helps us to recognize and understand more clearly the myth of the electronic library.

The sources of the myth of the electronic library are varied and complex, however. Elements attached to the electronic library were previously evident in what I would identify as the myth of the microlibrary. The microlibrary represents an early shift away from the library as place to a focus on a specific technology—microphotography. These elements presage and become incorporated into the myth of the electronic library. Furthermore, the myth-makers of the microlibrary play their part as well in the creation of the later myth.

During World War I scientists were drawn into the war effort in a systematic way, resulting in the establishment of the National Research Council by President Woodrow Wilson in 1916.[1] As never before, science was perceived as a necessary component in the attainment of national objectives. The scientific community was spurred on to greater self-promotion. After the war there were numerous initiatives by scientists and science research administrators to provide an infrastructure to promote a national science research effort. These initiatives included efforts to popularize science for the instruction of the general public. Also important in efforts to disseminate scientific research was the bibliographic control of the rapidly expanding body of increasingly specialized research publications. These became important objectives for an organization called Science Service, which was established jointly by the American Association for the Advancement of Science, the National Academy of Sciences, and the National Research Council in 1921. In 1928, Watson Davis, a civil engineer and previously an editor at Science Service, became its director. He remained its director until his retirement in 1966. Davis became an active promoter of microfilm as a medium for the distribution of research.

The idea of using microfilm for the storage and distribution of documents dates from the middle of the nineteenth century in Europe.[2] By the 1920s, microphotography was a technology attracting the interest of many of the most innovative librarians, scholars, scientists, and engineers in the United States and Europe. These early myth-makers identified microfilm as the most significant innovation in publishing since the invention of movable type in the fifteenth century. Microfilm would revolutionize library services. It would free scholars from the limitations of the printed text and overcome the barriers created by the geographic distribution of printed material. No longer would the book and journal be the sole means of distributing the intellectual record. Furthermore, this technological revolution would lead to a cultural revolution. The ability to distribute information on microfilm at a nominal cost would promote, according to one of its strongest advocates, the "cultural revival of the small town as against the monopoly of the metropolis, and the democratization and 'deprofessionalization' of scholarship" and "lead the whole population toward participation in a new cultural design."[3]

In the 1930s, the idea of combining microfilm storage with some type of workstation providing access to specific documents became widespread. Various initiatives to design a "rapid selector" of microfilm documents were undertaken. Pursuing this goal, Davis met in 1932 with Vannevar Bush at the Massachusetts Institute of Technology. Bush, an electrical engineer, was recently appointed vice president of the institute and dean of the engineering school. At MIT since 1919, he had developed a research program on computational machines. One of the results was the differential analyzer, a forerunner of the computer. Davis hoped Bush could assist in the development of microphotographic equipment for the retrieval of documents. Indeed, Bush published an article in 1933 describing a machine occupying only a few cubic feet that could hold the collection of a university library, and prior to World War II Bush did develop a "rapid selector" machine. It is not clear that Davis had any direct influence on Bush but they evidently shared an interest in using machines to facilitate the dissemination of scientific information. As we will see shortly, Bush's further efforts would establish him as the father of the electronic library.

Davis and others promoted new services based on microphotography technology. He envisioned using microfilm for interlibrary loans and the delivery of research results directly to scientists, concepts that would later be recognized as selective dissemination of information (SDI) and document delivery services. The distribution of microfilm documents directly to researchers was initiated in 1934 by the Department of Agriculture Library in Washington, D.C. This Bibliofilm Service was shortly taken over by the Science Service and formed the foundation for an effective network for the dissemination of information.[4]

Among many other activities arising out of his interest in microphotography and the distribution of research, Davis was instrumental in the formation of the American Documentation Institute (ADI) in 1953, later to become, in 1968, the American Society for Information Science (ASIS). The ADI was a heterogeneous group of individuals coming together around a vague concept of "documentation" and the potential of new technologies. Some notable librarians were involved in ADI, but most of its active members were scholars, scientists, science administrators, archivists, administrators, and inventors. Although it was not entirely clear to the members of ADI what precisely "documentation" meant, there was clearly an emphasis on the provision of access to information regardless of its format. Furthermore, unlike the American Library Association or the Special Library Association, the ADI was not identified with any particular institutional structure.

However, there was a librarian directing his attention to the problem of handling the mass of publications using microphotography. Fremont Rider, the librarian at Wesleyan University, was exploring various ideas for reducing costs associated with the acquisition, physical preparation, cataloging, and storage of library materials. These costs were increasing, according to Rider, because of the growth in the material acquired by research libraries. Rider compiled statistical evidence showing that research libraries were doubling in size every sixteen years. He presented this evidence along with his proposed solution in his now-classic book, *The Scholar and the Future of the Research Library*, published in 1944.[5]

To reduce library costs and provide greater access to research material, Rider proposed the microcatalog, a concept that married two tools familiar to libraries, the card catalog and microphotography. The recent development of microprint gave Rider the idea of putting books and journal articles on the back of catalog cards, bringing together the bibliographic record and the document itself. Rider's conception of the microcatalog had a number of advantages. A scholar could have a microlibrary in his or her office. Students and other users could gain access to the catalog at microreader machines distributed throughout a campus. Collections of material could be assembled to meet the specific needs of the scholar and other professional groups. Rider believed that recent developments in microphotography signaled the beginning of the "micro-card era" and offered libraries for the first time in 2,000 years the opportunity to start again. To enter this new era, however, librarians would have to shift their thinking away from treating microtext like books and, instead, explore its potential for providing new ways of enhancing access to recorded research. Certainly, he felt, moderate changes in current library practices would not suffice; radical solutions, such as the microcatalog, were required to provide access to the growing mass of material.

Rider, along with Davis and Bush, represents those themes taken up later in the myth of the electronic library: the need to respond in a radical way to the growth in research material, the orientation of his proposal to the needs of scholars, the turning to technology as the solution, the provision of access to research material at the scholars' workplace. With his reference to the "micro-card era," we can also place Rider among those who feel obliged to denote a particular epoch with a specific moniker. Microphotography technology formed a nucleus for a cluster of values and ideas that would, like a second wave, arise again after World War II. Most important, the myth of the microlibrary shifted the focus from providing access to information through an institution, specifically the library, to its provision by means of a technology divorced from any institutional framework. This microform technology fostered an utopian rhetoric as to its benefits for society and provided a focus for the emergence of a professional association, the ADI, outside of librarianship.

The potential of microphotography remained a focus for those looking for means of facilitating the storage of and access to research material. However, if there is to be only one hero among our myth-makers of the electronic library, it is Vannevar Bush. During the 1930s, Bush continued to think about how machines could facilitate the human thinking process. In 1939, he wrote a draft article on "Mechanization and the Record" in which he describes a machine he called "Memex," a mechanical indexing device that would assist the memory (hence "Mem(ory-)ex").[6] He was undecided about the best place to publish this article to reach the desired audience of scientists and science policy makers. It was finally published in the July 1945, issue of *Atlantic Monthly*, titled "As We May Think."[7] While the general ideas embodied in Memex were familiar to many by the late 1930s, Bush's article, perhaps because of his own prestige as adviser to the president and director of the office of Scientific Research and Development during the war, combined with the status of the *Atlantic Monthly*, established Memex as the touchstone for almost all subsequent developments in information retrieval. Upon its publication *Time* magazine and the Associated Press printed stories on it. *Life* magazine published a condensed illustrated version. It has been reprinted numerous times and cited in hundreds of articles, books, and reports.[8] Since 1945, any new development in information technology generates a new wave of references to Memex. Almost a half-century later, a Memex Research Institute was established at California State University in Chico, California, for the purpose of developing the electronic library.

According to Bush, the growing mountain of research combined with increased specialization made traditional means of transmitting the results of research, including the library, obsolete. "There may be," according to Bush, "millions of fine thoughts . . . all encased within stone walls of acceptable architectural form; but if the scholar can get at only one a week by diligent search, his syntheses are not likely to keep up with current science."[9] Bush did not see the solution to this problem in libraries, where he felt there was "a lag in the adoption of mechanisms" to address the problem. He proposed a "mechanized private file and library." Memex would store an individual's books, records, and communications. He envisioned a desk that could be accessible remotely, consisting of a keyboard, buttons, and levers, and a screen for the display of information stored in the desk on microfilm.[10] The use of microform would permit the reduction of the *Encyclopedia Britannica* to the size of a matchbox. The user of Memex could also input directly on a translucent platen longhand notes, memoranda, and photographs.

Items would be indexed so that they could be easily retrieved simply by entering the appropriate code on the keyboard. The combining of mechanical access and storage with index and coding would enhance access through "associated indexing, . . . a provision whereby any item may be caused at will to select immediately and automatically another."[11] Entering an index term would automatically link it to associated terms, thereby providing a trail of interconnected research and ideas. The ability to link items together was considered by Bush the primary feature of Memex. He believed that associated indexing would encourage the publication of all kinds of encyclopedic collections consisting of trails of linked information. Such files would be available to the lawyer requiring a patent search, to the physician diagnosing a patient, to a chemist experimenting with a synthesis of an organic compound, to the historian tracing a chronology. Bush could foresee the emergence of a new profession dedicated to formulating useful compilations of associated trails, but it would be the scientists who must find the means of generating, storing, and accessing human records.

In Bush's vision we see an elaboration of themes appearing in the myth of the microlibrary that become essential elements of the electronic library. There is the emphasis on science and technology as a means to address the problem of the increasing abundance of the research record. Libraries and books are discounted as solutions. Instead, storage and access is provided through technological means at what some day would be called the "scholar's workstation." Bush was an engineer who took a pragmatic approach to the problem, focusing on what technology was available that might be applied to the problem rather than defining the problem as the initial step in developing a technology.[12] This faith in technology as the solution to any problem became a central element of the myth of the electronic library. If the myth of the library as place was anchored in the solidity of the image of the public library, the image of the electronic library would be as firmly anchored in technology. Librarians were increasingly faulted for not making this shift in view.

Among the many themes touched on by Bush one was reiterated over and over by later myth-makers: Librarians were slow to respond to the mounting information crisis, and especially slow in their response to the potential of technological developments. However, if we turn to a series of lectures given in 1950 at the University of Illinois Library School, we are impressed by the school's forward-looking selection of speakers. The speeches also illustrate how quickly the motif of the electronic library was coming together.

The three speeches of the school's 1950 Windsor Lectures were on the theme of "Bibliographical Controls in an Age of Science."[13] According to the moderator of the sessions, this theme was chosen because researchers and librarians were aware of the accelerating rate of the amount of research being published, of the inadequacy of existing bibliographical methods, and of the need to provide improved access to scientific literature, particularly through the use of technological means. One of the three speakers, Louis N. Ridenour, was a nuclear physicist and dean of the University's Graduate College. Albert G. Hill was an electrical engineer, director of the MIT Research Laboratory of Electronics, and chairman of the Center for Scientific Aid to Learning, which supported research on methods of collecting, organizing, and communicating knowledge. Ralph R. Shaw, director of libraries, U.S. Department of Agriculture, was a leader in the application of mechanical methods to library operations and information retrieval who was receiving considerable attention as developer of his own Rapid Selector.

Ridenour's discussion of "Bibliography in an Age of Science" illustrates how quickly the elements of the myth of the electronic library were coalescing. Ridenour stressed it was a time of change. He illustrated how Rider's rate of exponential growth in library collections was characteristic of other indicators of social and technological change. The source of this change?

"We live in a technological society, and the most prominent aspect of that society is change." This change "is wrought entirely by technological advance. It is irresistible."[14] As if to emphasize the inevitability of technological change, he proposed a mathematical law of social change.

Ridenour acknowledged that librarians were well aware of the increasing number of research publications. However, union catalogs and other cooperative initiatives to address the problem were too modest; thus, it was time to question the fundamental assumptions on which library methods were based. Libraries were operating on principles and techniques established at the turn of the century. Because any change in library procedure can have substantial cost implications due to the number of individual items and records involved, Ridenour forgave librarians for being "over conservative." Nevertheless, he called for the adoption of more radical methods. These radical methods would have to be found with the assistance of scientists and engineers. He felt it was quite appropriate that a physicist and an electrical engineer were among the lecture series speakers because technology created the problem and only technology could offer solutions. Any problem could be solved, he declared; indeed, "one should never ask whether a particular technical goal is possible of achievement; for it always is."[15] As library methodology was rapidly decreasing in effectiveness and near collapse, the only hope was the ever-greater application of more technology to each of the functions of the library.

How could each of these functions be improved by more technology? Based on experience gained during the war, Ridenour believed the first step was to bring in outside experts in operations research to evaluate all library procedures. The use of people accustomed to applying analytical modes of thought but unfamiliar with the normal operations of libraries would produce startling new ideas and positive results. For example, to tackle the acquisition problem he suggested reducing the collection of duplicate material through the cooperative development of a "communications network" that would permit the speedy transmission of material from one location to another. He also advocated looking for alternatives to the book. Drawing on the mathematical theory of communication developed by Claude Shannon, Ridenour saw the possibility of storing bits of information more economically using "computing machines" and magnetic tape.

The cataloging of material was a difficult problem because of the traditional reliance on analyzing each title. Would it be possible to simplify this process? "It can, of course, be done," Ridenour believed. With technology, "anything can be done."[16] It was only a matter of time before there would be an "electronic cataloger" to read a text, recognize key symbols for which it was programmed, and construct the appropriate catalog record. The reference (and circulation) functions would provide material on demand. The researcher would send a request to the library, where the material would be reproduced and sent directly to the requester.

Ridenour admitted that his ideas might seem outlandish and costly to some, but he drew attention to the current high costs of acquisitions, cataloging, and other library operations. The increasing magnitude of these costs would justify the expenditures required for the development of innovative and more cost-effective methods. In the end, efficiency and cost must be the primary criteria for evaluating library operations. Ridenour called for the "re-evaluation of the whole fabric of the Library, . . . where nothing should be taken for granted." For example, a library should no longer necessarily be regarded as a place where books are stored. Perhaps it could be a "first-rate communication center."[17]

When Hill gave his remarks on the "Storage, Processing and Communication of Information," he reinforced points raised by Ridenour.[18] He also believed that to achieve an "automatic library," it was first necessary to subject library methods to a thorough-going operational analysis by qualified engineers. Current technology was close to providing a library system based on the storage of information on microform or some other type of mechanical medium accessible through a binary code system. The "brain" of the system would require the appropriate programming to carry out its functions. Its "nervous system" would allow for both internal and external communication. Finally, material would be delivered to the researcher through a duplication process. What Hill was describing was, indeed, close to realization in Ralph Shaw's Rapid Selector.

Shaw described his Rapid Selector in his presentation on "Machines and the Bibliographical Problems of the Twentieth Century." The Rapid Selector used microform storage with a retrieval capability that reproduced the desired document after it was located through a photocell light mechanism based on a binary search process. Shaw acknowledged, "The basic principles of organization of knowledge applied in the present machine were developed by Dr. Vannevar Bush . . . more than ten years ago." He noted that the "basic electronic system should be credited to Dr. Bush."[19]

In the 1950s many more of those involved in computing and information processing became aware that the machine's potential extended far beyond its number-crunching capabilities. Speculation turned to its wider application, including its potential use in libraries. In 1961, in celebration of the Massachusetts Institute of Technology's centennial year, the School of Industrial Management sponsored a series of lectures on "Management and the Computer of the Future," subsequently published as *Computers and the World of the Future*. This publication further signaled MIT as a major institutional home for several of the individuals who serve as early sources of the myth of the electronic library, including Bush, J.C.R. Licklider, and Claude Shannon. Of particular interest is the presentation on "A Library for 2000 A.D.," by John G. Kemeny, chairman of the Department of Mathematics and Astronomy at Dartmouth College.[20] Kemeny's remarks illustrate again how soon the form and rhetoric of the myth of the electronic library began to solidify. In the following years, Kemeny became one of the major gurus in the use of information technology in higher education.

Kemeny began with the dramatic prediction that university libraries will be obsolete by the year 2000. The rapid growth in knowledge, the clumsy procedures required to use libraries, and the difficulties in retrieving information from the mass of published material created problems so acute that university libraries were on the verge of being obsolete. To put into effect the necessary reorganization of libraries, several basic principles had to be followed. Foremost would be the necessity to rely on technology as a solution; the library of the future must rely heavily on automation. Furthermore, it must be recognized that books are not amenable to machine processing, despite their convenience. A process of miniaturization was required, probably using some type of tape. Finally, access should be provided through a network, its pinnacle being a National Research Library. Libraries would remain, but would consist primarily of several hundred thousand volumes of heavily used (once a week) research titles, student reserve collections, and leisure reading. Access would be provided to the National Research Library by calling up the required item and receiving a copy. Specific items would be identified by searching computer-based collections of abstracts. Kemeny expected such an arrangement would change the scholarly publication process. Research articles could be submitted directly to the National Research Library, thereby eliminating the need for so many journals, which were a slow process for disseminating information.

Such ideas became increasingly commonplace and discussed. One of the active participants in the MIT series was J.C.R. Licklider, an individual who must be given a prominent place in the pantheon of myth-makers of the electronic library. With the financial assistance of the Ford Foundation, the Council on Library Resources was incorporated in 1956 to promote the investigation of solutions based on the use of modern technology to the problems arising out of the information explosion. By the early 1960s, the council wished to have a study done on "the library of the future." Licklider was selected to do the study. A psychologist with a background in acoustics and information theory, Licklider was the supervisory engineering psychologist at the consulting firm of Bolt Beranek and Newman Inc. He had previously held appointments at Harvard University and MIT and had written on the human/machine interface. For a two-year period, 1961–63, psychologists and engineers at Bolt Beranek and Newman carried out a series of studies under Licklider's direction. A summary of their report was published as *Libraries of the Future* in 1965.[21] *Libraries of the Future* became a benchmark work, along with Bush's "As We May Think," in the canon of the electronic library. Licklider acknowledged his debt to Bush by dedicating his book to him.

Looking to the year 2000, Licklider identified books as inadequate depositories of information. Books are heavy, bulky, contain more information than the reader can understand at any given time, and do not readily reveal the information they contain. Furthermore, they are expensive and their circulation is slow, limiting rapid availability to information. As books are unsatisfactory for the storage, organization, and display of information, libraries of books are equally unacceptable. Emphasizing, as did Bush, the need for dynamic interaction between the searcher for information and the body of information, Licklider asserted that "any concept of a library that begins with books on shelves is sure to encounter trouble."[22] More explicitly than anyone else at the time, Licklider foresaw the possibility of the dematerialization of the library. The physical characteristics of the book account for fundamental aspects of the physical library itself. Once we reject the physical book as an efficient transmitter of information, we reject the library. He proposed a melding of the library and the computer and called for a substitution for the word "library."

Licklider conceived of a hierarchy of "precognitive systems" forming a "neolibrary network." A user would gain access through a machine called a "Symbiont," the name implying the desired symbiotic relationship between user and information. This keyboard and display unit would allow the user to examine documents, compose notes, graphs, and bibliographic citations, and carry out bibliographic searches and other functions. To develop precognitive systems required attracting leaders from the scientific disciplines into these pioneering efforts. It would also be necessary to overcome traditional interdisciplinary barriers by bringing together individuals from library science, computer science, system science, and the behavioral and social sciences. The development of precognitive systems would be driven by the forces of the market economy. With the economic value of information increasing and the costs of technology declining, society would recognize that it would be more productive with precognitive systems than without them. Licklider also made it clear elsewhere that it is information and not knowledge that is the problem: "Although science and technology are concerned respectively, with augmentation and application of knowledge, it is not knowledge but information that is the commodity they store, retrieve, and communicate."[23]

When *Libraries of the Future* was reviewed by the library community, the application of its ideas seemed remote. Neither was there recognition that the book was a significant contribution to assembling themes critical to a coherent alternative to the traditional concepts of the library and librarianship. By focusing on the technical aspects of the book, its broader implications were missed by most. However, one review did consider *Libraries of the Future* "the best and most lucid statement of what the library may look like by the end of the century."[24] Robert S. Taylor admired the book for its imaginative attempt to extrapolate current technology into the future.

Taylor believed Licklider challenged the library profession to address questions it was not prepared even to consider. When Taylor left his position as director of the Centre for Information Science at Lehigh University in 1965 to go to Hampshire College in Amherst, Massachusetts, as director of the library, he would, through a planning report of his own, *The Making of a Library*, join Licklider in the ranks of the seminal myth-makers of the electronic library.

In 1958, a committee of faculty members from the colleges of Amherst, Mount Holyoke, Smith, and the University of Massachusetts proposed a plan for a fifth college in the Connecticut River Valley. By the early 1960s, a fuller plan, "Hampshire College Working Paper Number One," was ready and subsequently published as *The Making of a College*.[25] The objective of the plan was to establish an innovative, technologically orientated liberal arts college under the sponsorship of the four older institutions. It was claimed that formation of the college was needed because of the accelerating growth of knowledge along with the increased availability of new machines for the transfer of information. It was not expected that any of these technological developments would undermine the book. And, the document noted, "Libraries, as they are now known and loved, will still be needed and actively used in the age of electronic information transfer."[26] Nevertheless, quoting from Licklider's *Libraries of the Future*, libraries would experience immense change and Hampshire College wanted to be a leader in that change. An appendix, "The Future of Library Automation," prepared by Steven E. Firth of IBM, outlined how libraries would soon be able to operate in a cooperative network environment through on-line catalogs providing access to offsite information over the telephone line.

In the context of this college plan and with support from the U.S. Office of Education, Taylor undertook a study to formulate a concept of an "experimenting library." The result was the *Making of a Library: The Academic Library in Transition*, published in 1972 by MIT Press as "Hampshire College Working Paper Number Two.[27] In *Making of a Library*, which was selected by the American Society for Information Science in 1972 for its outstanding book award, and in other writings, Taylor added powerful elaboration to earlier themes flowing into the myth of the electronic library and launched a direct assault on the myth of the library as place. Referring to futurists and others such as Marshall McLuhan, Daniel Bell, Alvin Toffler, Peter Drucker, and Licklider, Taylor advocated the need to look beyond the traditional warehouse concept of the library toward a new concept of communication, a concept transcending the physical structure of the library. Because of their concern for books as physical entities, libraries had become static institutions. He questioned whether the word "library" should even be used; "The word carries too many connotations which, partially true and partially myth, may not let the library get to tomorrow, may inhibit its adaptability."[28] The needs of users required librarians to reject the ideal of the library "as a place surrounded by four walls where printed materials . . . are stored, organized, and lent." Instead, it was necessary to pursue "a notion that the library is not a place, but a process, . . . a process that permeates the campus."[29]

Taylor turned to the idea of the "university without walls," an idea popular at that time in extension programs in higher education. Taylor proposed an "extended library," extended in terms of the resources it would provide—traditional library collections, an art gallery, a bookstore, educational technology, computer facilities—and in its open-ended and experimental orientation to the user. It would also be extended through participation in cooperative electronic networks, a situation requiring the relinquishing of some local autonomy. As for librarians, they had concentrated too much on the "how" rather than the "why" of librarianship. They had to face the inevitable change driven by technological developments. If they did not, there was the danger they would become victims of Toffler's "future shock." Recognizing the possibility of competitive services emerging outside of the library, the extended library must be able to "merchandise itself and its 'wares.' "[30] A new institution would emerge, creating a new profession. Responding to the "electronic revolution" would require an interdisciplinary strategy involving computer specialists, librarians, microform specialists, and scientists coming together to form a communications profession. According to Taylor, this might very well require the break-up of the library profession.

There is one more individual requiring attention in our pantheon of myth makers—Edwin B. Parker, professor of communications at Stanford University. His research on communications media and technology and on the distribution and socioeconomic implications of information would be increasingly drawn on by librarians and information scientists. Additionally, Parker was instrumental in the development at Stanford of one of the earlier attempts to enhance computer-based access to information. Parker, writing in the late 1960s and early 1970s, especially emphasized the growing economic importance of information and the significant role of technology in social change. According to Parker, our human-made environment consists of matter, energy, and information. Only of information was there an infinite supply; therefore, it was the key to any long-term improvement in economic productivity and the quality of life. The efficient generation and use of information as a means of increasing productivity was a problem not just for libraries and educational institutions but for the United States if it hoped to meet the challenge of foreign competitors. Technology could provide the efficient utilization of information through national information networks. Parker called for the formulation of national policies on science, education, information technology, and libraries to ensure that the increased investment in information would pay off for society.[31]

He was able to explain more explicitly how this might be implemented when, in 1968, Stanford University held a series of lectures on "Human Values in a Technological Society." In his essay on "New Communications Media," Parker asserted that the new media of the twenty-first century would be available before then due to the potential of time-sharing on computers. By this time, Parker's description of the new media sounded familiar to anyone familiar with the works of Bush, Rider or Licklider. Physically, it would "look like a cross between a television set and a typewriter, function more like a cross between a library and a newspaper, have a network capability of a telephone, and yet be radically different from existing mass media in one major respect: namely, the extent to which communication through the channel would be controlled by the receiver instead of by the sender."[32] He predicted that within five years, on-line library catalogs would be available and that within fifteen years all library material would be stored in computers.

We have reviewed the speculations of a number of individuals whom I have categorized as early myth-breakers and makers. Their ideas were a source of inspiration for those who came later. Their individual backgrounds quickly reveal the range of sources feeding into the myth of the electronic library. We have Bush coming from electrical engineering, Rider the librarian, Ridenour from science, Licklider from psychology, Taylor from information science, and Parker from communications theory. While this is not a statistically valid sample of any sort, we are nevertheless struck by the dominant representation from outside librarianship, many of whom either contributed to or became active members of the emerging field of information science. But were they ignored by the library field? Were librarians as conservative as was so often asserted by the myth-makers?

If we turn to library planning reports and conference proceedings of the time, we see constant reference to, and in many cases, the active participation of these myth-makers. There certainly was interest and planning among librarians regarding the development of new technologies and their potential use in libraries. The examples already noted of the University of Illinois Library School Windsor Lectures, the creation of the Council on Library Resources, and the work of Rider and Shaw illustrate that librarians were pursuing the possibilities of incorporating the most recent technological marvels into library operations. During the 1960s these efforts accelerated and became more widespread. Prominent librarians speculated in prestigious library journals on the implications of the growth of scientific and technical literature and of technological developments. Librarians were encouraged to be open-minded and flexible, to be neither Luddite nor technocrat.[33] On a more practical level, the University of Illinois Graduate School of Library Science continued to show leadership in this area with the launching in 1963 of an annual Clinic on Library Applications of Data Processing. Librarians were becoming more involved in the use of computers and reporting on their experience. The myth-makers were not absent from these activities; they were active participants and there was implicit or explicit reference to their ideas. The investigations initiated at the University of Illinois at Congress Circle in Chicago are an early example.

During the late 1950s librarians at the UIC library began exploring with staff from the General Electric Company the possibilities of library automation and the need to formulate "a machine age library philosophy."[34] Their study, supported by the Council on Library Resources, considered the feasibility of machines based on the concepts of Bush, including Shaw's Rapid Selector. They found developments in this area encouraging but concluded that the current status of development prohibited their application to library operations. It was not long before other reports and planning documents were delivered by other libraries.

The Library of Congress, for one, sponsored an important study supported by the Council on Library Resources to provide a ten-year plan for the total automation of large research libraries.[35] Pointing to the information explosion in science and technology, the changes in the production and use of information, and the inadequacy of current subject analysis of the many forms in which research is published, the survey team stressed the need to extend library services through automation. Emphasis was placed on creating a dynamic catalog allowing users to establish Bush-like "search trails" through catalogs, files, and indexes. Similar ideas were propounded at a conference sponsored by the Library of Congress in 1963 on library automation. The conference brought together a distinguished group of participants (including Robert S. Taylor) to provide an overview of the current status of the technology of library automation. Sessions were devoted to the library of the future, file organization and conversion, storage and access, output printing, and communications networks.[36] Presentations at these sessions reflected earlier concepts developed by the myth-makers such as dynamic files and information networks.

The presence of the myth-makers was evident as libraries pushed ahead with automation. For example, in the fall of 1965, MIT convened a planning conference on "Information Transfer Experiments," or Project INTREX. Among those who participated were Bush and Licklider, the latter contributing as many as four working papers to the conference. Of particular interest is his paper on "An On-Line Information Network."[37] Licklider proposed the formation of an experimental time-sharing information network accessible via telecommunications lines to individuals at remote locations. He described with impressive foresight a network that would provide access to bibliographic data, databases of text, and electronic journals.

The Intrex planning conference also gave Bush a chance to return to a consideration of Memex. While he considered Memex a dream in 1945, he believed by the mid-1960s that its creation was definitely attainable. The need for a revolution in the way we create, store, and gain access to the research record was not a problem for librarians alone. Recent developments with transistors, magnetic tape, and videotape persuaded him that the possibility of building Memex was increasingly feasible. In his view, the key factor was cost. The Memex would be developed when it became profitable to do so. Businesses were making considerable use of data-processing equipment with a positive impact on efficiency and profits. Unfortunately, he observed, libraries continued to "operate by horse-and-buggy methods for there is no profit in libraries."[38] Government, he complained, spent billions on glamorous space programs while the library, lacking such glamour, received little support. He predicted that it would be some time before automation would come to libraries. By identifying market pressures as a determining factor in library development, Bush had hit on another theme that increasingly became part of the myth of the electronic library.

Edwin Parker was another myth-maker actively involved in the planning and implementation of library automation and information retrieval efforts in the 1960s. When he described the new communications media, including on-line access to catalogs and full text, in his 1968 lecture at Stanford, he was extrapolating from work arising from his own efforts there. It was his Department of Communication Research that initiated the development of the Stanford Physics Information Retrieval System (SPIRES), later changed when it became a collaborative effort with the Stanford University Library to Stanford Public Information Retrieval System.[39] We also find the active participation of both Licklider and Parker at a major conference sponsored by the American Library Association in 1970 on communications and library information networks. Licklider's presentation is especially interesting for the thoroughness with which he outlines seventeen functions of a library information network. Elaborating on his earlier thoughts, he includes among the network's functions the distribution of research papers prior to publication, the submission of papers and databases to journal editors, the provision of abstracts and indexes, retrospective search services, library acquisition and circulation functions, and the delivery of full text data.[40]

Material expression was given to many of these ideas that would become part of the myth of the electronic library when the American Library Association sponsored a major exhibit, Library 21, at the World's Fair held in Seattle in 1962. With funds exceeding $2 million provided by the Council on Library Resources, the U.S. Air Force, the U.S. Office of Education, and private industrial firms, the exhibit included a ready reference display of print material. The star attraction was the computer UNIVAC. Visitors to the exhibit were given a personalized bibliography generated by the machine. As well, they could converse with the great minds of the world by extracting quotes supplied from the *Great Books of the Western World* series.

The National Cash Register Company demonstrated how it could reduce a 400-page book to one square inch through its latest technology. Librarians staffing the exhibit were trained for their duties by Dr. Robert M. Hayes, president-elect of the American Documentation Institute and president of the Advanced Systems Information Company. The exhibit reflected several elements of the emerging electronic library myth: There was the emphasis on technology, the involvement of private firms and government defense agencies (costs of the training sessions were covered by a grant made under the National Defense Education Act), the reliance on expertise outside of traditional librarianship, and the provision of bits of information. The exhibit was considered a great success in demonstrating an innovative librarianship.[41]

While the ideas of the myth-makers were making their way into library thinking and planning, there was an additional body of material feeding into the myth of the electronic library. By the middle of the 1950s, federal government agencies, congressional committees, foundations, professional associations, and national scientific societies were generating substantial reports on what was declared a national crisis. Spurred on by the Soviet Union's success in launching the Sputnik satellite, a national effort was embarked upon to enhance scientific and technical research capabilities, including the information communications process.

Various bodies of scientists and science research administrators issued a profusion of reports and plans. The earliest noteworthy report was from the President's Science Advisory Committee, *Improving the Availability of Scientific and Technical Information in the United States*, published in 1958 and known as the Baker Report.[42] Within a decade, over twenty plans for a national science and technology information strategy were published. By 1964 it was found that federal agencies were carrying out or funding externally over 220 science and technology information studies. Often harking back to Bush's 1945 article, most of these reports shared a number of convictions contributing to the myth of the electronic library. The scientific and technical research community faced a major problem in the growth of published research essential to national security and prosperity. (The phrase "information explosion" began to make its appearance.) The problem was one of information transfer and retrieval, as opposed to the generation and diffusion of knowledge. Information was a discrete element separate from its form. The crisis was of such complexity and magnitude that its resolution could not be left to traditional agencies such as libraries; scientists and technologists must find solutions. Librarians were slow, if not reluctant, to address the crisis and hesitant to apply new technological methods. Solutions proposed typically included a national, centralized, hierarchical strategy involving new types of information agencies. These proposed agencies were to have a wider range of functions than those found in the usual library and were given various names: bureau of information, technical information center, regional center, information bank, information clearing house, and so forth. As these proposals envisioned central coordination and decentralized distribution of information, they expounded a network concept. As usual, the one factor seen as providing some hope of addressing the information explosion was the wider application of automated technology.[43]

One of the more widely read reports was the President's Science Advisory Committee 1963 publication, *Science, Government, and Information*, commonly known as the Weinberg Report. Weinberg, director of the Oakridge National Laboratory, chaired a panel of distinguished scientists and administrators. He and his colleagues asserted that it would be possible to cope with the "information explosion" only when scientists and engineers recognized that they must commit themselves to the tasks of reviewing and synthesizing information. Researchers had to discard their casual attitude toward the "information transfer chain"; this process should not "be viewed merely as a librarian's work; that is, as not part of science."[44] More human and financial resources from the sciences themselves would have to be devoted to the handling of information created by science. The essence of an effective technical information center would be the efficient operation by highly competent scientists and engineers whose stature would equal that of the theoretical physicist. The growth in the number of information centers would require many such "information scientists." Admonishing the library profession for its "token nod" to the challenge presented by the radically new mechanical systems for organizing, storing, and retrieving technical information, the report hoped this shortcoming would be overcome by encouraging more talented scientists and engineers into librarianship. The report advocated "mechanized information processing" as the means of storing and retrieving information. It was necessary to shift the focus away from the form of information to information as a thing in itself. The report emphasized that the "fundamental task is switching *information*, not documents."[45]

The Council on Library Resources also continued to turn to experts outside of librarianship to explore the implications of emerging technologies. An Information Systems Panel of the Computer Science and Engineering Board, National Academy of Science, issued a report commissioned by the council, *Libraries and Information Technology: a National System Challenge* (1972). Reinforcing earlier themes, and once again citing Bush, this report reiterated the need for a national strategy to meet the informational needs of the "technological society." The panel observed that "the hoary ways of libraries are breaking down," burdened by "ancient technologies." The solution was computers and telecommunications systems, and the scientific and engineering community would have to find the tools and methods to accomplish the tasks required. Libraries must be transformed through an extension of services that contributes to the nation's "recorded-information system." If they did not do this, the report threatened, they would become obsolete.[46]

In addition to government and association reports, there was an increasing number of scholarly and popular books dealing with technological and social change, information as an economic resource, and information processing in a technological environment. The growing recognition of the importance of information as an economic commodity owed much to Princeton economist Fritz Machlup, whose 1962 book, *The Production and Distribution of Knowledge in the United States*, was a pioneering work in the economic analysis of information.[47] Machlup identified the "knowledge industries" as the most rapidly expanding part of the economy. Management theorist Peter Drucker outlined the emergence of a knowledge society in which the efficient organization and application of information is the foundation for most work and increased productivity. The knowledge society would require a new class of professional knowledge workers.[48] The formation in 1968 of the Information Industry Association in Washington, D.C., served for many as a concrete expression of the phenomenon identified by Machlup, Drucker, and others. The association was formed to serve the interests of private, for-profit organizations concerned with the production and sale of information.

By the 1970s, these ideas achieved wide recognition as expressed in Daniel Bell's concept of the "post-industrial society."[49] He defined the post-industrial society along five dimensions. First was the shift in the majority of work from agriculture and manufacturing to services. The second key element was the increase in the number of workers engaged in professional and technical employment. The third was the importance of theoretical knowledge, in contrast to the empirically based knowledge characteristic of the Industrial Revolution. The fourth element was the need to be future-oriented, which thereby increased the necessity for deliberate planning and assessment of technological growth. Finally, the post-industrial society would experience the rise of a new intellectual technology including systems analysis, information theory, cybernetics, and decision theories.

Marshall McLuhan, a professor of English at the University of Toronto, was another author whose ideas received much attention. McLuhan gave preeminence to communications technology as the determinant of social change. He identified three historical phases, each characterized by its dominant technological mode of communication. The first phase was oral-aural, the second was print, and the third electronic. In this third stage we are experiencing the emergence of a "global village" as the network of electrical circuitry envelopes the planet. McLuhan conjoined technological determinism, the role of information in the communications process, and a sense that we are experiencing a profound historical change.[50] He and his disciples, such as Joshua Meyrowitz, explored more explicitly the role of technology and electronic media in social change. Meyrowitz offered as a common theme connecting the diverse phenomenon of social change "a change in Americans' 'sense of place.' " Our world, according to Meyrowitz, "may suddenly seem senseless to many people because, for the first time in modern history, it is relatively placeless."[51] McLuhan's ideas appealed to those librarians who believed the rapid change in communications technologies would "help to remove the stereotyped connotation of a library containing nothing else but books."[52]

These and many other works seemed to confirm that we were experiencing the rapid emergence of a technologically driven information society where the possession of information was a prerequisite to economic and national development, a critical component of high occupational status, and a determining factor in economic, social, and political decision-making processes. Many of these ideas were given more popular widespread exposure when futurist Alvin Toffler promoted the idea that industrial nations, and the United States in particular, had embarked on a third wave of development. [53] According to Toffler, the first wave was the agricultural revolution, which lasted until the 17th century, when the Industrial Revolution, the second wave, began. The second wave crested about 1955, when white-collar and service workers outnumbered blue-collar workers in the United States. As well, there was the rapid acceleration in the application of computers. Consequently, society was now riding a third wave of revolutionary change in which information constituted a critical element of the "infosphere." These ideas received official recognition when the U.S. Department of Commerce published in 1977 a nine-volume report, *The Information Economy*, by Stanford University economist Marc Uri Porat. This report supported the assertion that information-based activities were becoming the prevailing characteristic of modern economic systems. Porat's work, which received widespread attention, reaffirmed for many that information must be accepted as a legitimate economic commodity.[54]

It was not long before "Information is Power" became a cliche among librarians and many others. In making such assertions, there was often little or no distinction made between the concepts of "knowledge" and "information," although most researchers and commentators favored "information" as a unit that could be treated as an objective, measurable phenomenon suitable for scientific analysis. However, it was not the social scientists and futurists that provided the most complete objectification of information. In conjunction with accelerating developments in computing and communications technologies, mathematicians, scientists, and engineers focused on information as a statistical unit divorced from any particular format of transmission and from its content. Following up on research done as a graduate student at MIT, Claude E. Shannon, Bell Laboratories, along with Warren Weaver, developed a mathematical model to deal with the problem of noise in electronic communication.[55] To translate information into a measurable unit, they identified the smallest unit of information as the "bit," a word derived through the contraction of "binary digit." Shannon and Weaver's work achieved status as a classic in the development of communication and information retrieval theory. Their components of the communication process—source, transmitter, signal, receiver, destination—were originally related to the physical properties of telecommunications but were soon adopted by other disciplines.

About the same time, another MIT colleague, Norbert Wiener, had a profound impact on many disciplines including computing, information theory, and communications with the publication of *Cybernetics: Or Control and Communication in the Animal and the Machine*, in 1948.[56] Wiener developed a body of ideas around the concept of self-regulation, both human and mechanical, and the importance of information feedback in that process. His interest extended to communications engineering and the quantification of information. Like Shannon, he contributed to the objectification of information and its mechanical manipulation. The book was of such wide interest because Wiener explored the implications of automation and cybernetics on human affairs, including the critical role of information to the individual and society. Not only was information now perceived as an economic unit subject to analysis, but also as an objective, neutral phenomenon that could be subjected to mathematical equations. Communications, information, and cybernetic theory all provided further rationale for treating information as a discrete, measurable unit.

Meanwhile, much was happening in the library field in the use of computers. The Library of Congress was laying the foundation for significant advances in library automation with its MARC (Machine Readable Cataloging) project, an initiative arising out of the King Report. The Ohio College Library Center (OCLC) was established in 1967 as a computer-based library network that encouraged the introduction of automation in library cataloging operations across the country. Experiments were proceeding at numerous libraries in the use of computers for circulation, acquisitions, and other functions. An increasing number of remote databases of bibliographic information, beginning with the conversion of the National Library of Medicine's MEDLARS service in 1970, were making possible computer-based reference services. Developments in library automation and information retrieval were so rapid during the 1960s and early 1970s that those constructing the myth of the electronic library soon felt compelled to consolidate the electronic revolution in two ways characteristic of revolutionaries: provision of a history of the revolution as a means of justification, and the issuing of a manifesto as a declaration of intent.

According to Donald Hammer, executive secretary of the Information Science and Automation Division of the American Library Association and editor of the historically oriented *The Information Age: Its Development and Impact* (1976), the most significant aspect of these developments during the decade 1965–75 was the recognition that information was a commodity "that can be sold, given away, copied, created, stored, misinterpreted, distorted and stolen, among other things."[57] Information must be perceived as a utility whose essence needs to be defined and provided with a philosophical base. Along with this new perception of information, librarians found themselves confronted with the computer, backed by a phalanx of operations researchers and mathematicians, all of whom were leading to developments that were, according to Hammer, for many librarians, "not very far from abhorrent only a few short years ago." Another significant development noted by Hammer was the fortunate demise of the concept that any library could be self-sufficient. The creation of the MARC format would permit greater library cooperation through electronic networks. Also significant was the "commercialization" of the library field and the development of large databases provided by private-sector vendors. The movement of major corporations into what was increasingly referred to as the "information industry" heralded "the dawn of a new age for the information field."[58] The injection of the profit motive into librarianship provided libraries the opportunity to promote the sale of their own services and systems. In short, according to Hammer, the information age had arrived, bringing with it a whole new conception of libraries and librarianship.

For those who had not participated in this revolutionary decade, a call to arms was provided by Vincent Giuliano's "A Manifesto for Librarians," published in the September 15, 1979, issue of *Library Journal*.[59] Giuliano, a consultant with Arthur D. Little Inc., was moved to alleviate an "immense pain being experienced in the working lives of librarians today." This pain derived from the decline in the use of and support for libraries, a lack of jobs and low salaries for librarians, and the low professional status granted to librarians. But this situation could be changed, he declared, if only librarians recognized they were now in an information age. It was time for librarians to shift their context away from libraries as institutions to one of providing information to their constituents by whatever means, format, and structures were necessary. The traditional concept of the library, an outmoded institution of the industrial age, had to be discarded. The library, "housed in impressive buildings with stone facades and immense pillars," can no longer be a "temple of knowledge"; instead, it must bow to the recognition that information is a commodity that can be transmitted through the use of modern technology. The static library of the past has to give way to the dynamic "information access center."

What are the barriers to this revolutionary transformation? Librarians, of course! Giuliano identified two aspects of their resistance: fear of losing their jobs and their institutional base, and fear that their service ethic of providing "free" access to information will succumb to the forces of the marketplace. He admonished librarians to free themselves from the limitations imposed by their attachment to a specific institution and to recognize that if a service is free, it is of little value.

How did librarians respond to such admonitions? Here was a professional group of over 100,000 members who had an institutional base of over 30,000 libraries in towns and cities, in public and private organizations, throughout the country; who were responsible for the expenditure of millions of dollars annually; who had in the American Library Association (ALA) a powerful professional association of over 30,000 members that was among the most effective national lobbying bodies in the country; who, in 1976, had succeeded in getting more public libraries built than in any of the previous five years despite a recession and reduced federal funding; who could look back on 100 years of successful American library development. However, in 1977, as they turned to contemplate the year 2000, they were anxious about their role in the information society, fearful about the impact of technology, and apprehensive about their shaky professional status. When 1,500 members participated in an all-day session of the president's program at the 1977 ALA annual conference devoted to "The Information Society: Issues and Answers," the most crucial issue that emerged was the "identity crisis of professional librarians." More specifically, the members' concerns were:

- a serious uncertainty about the role of the librarian and, thus, the library in our modern society

- a continued malaise about library education and what is perceived as its basic inability to produce graduates equipped to deal with today's library world

- a deep-seated fear of the uncertainty of the future, brought on by changing economic conditions, rapid technological advances, and ongoing social upheaval

- exasperation with the lack of planning and coordination which they feel takes place in the library world and the feeling that libraries have little say in charting their own course.[60]

The papers presented and the subsequent discussions at the meeting were evidence that librarians were eager for a new, reassuring myth to launch them into their second century. The idea of the program arose out of the writings of Daniel Bell and Edwin Parker. With few exceptions, the underlying assumptions of the program were based on the acceptance that there was a "post-industrial," "technological," and "information" society (all three descriptors were variously used), that there will be a continued growth in published research and the increased use of electronic and other media for the dissemination of information, that information was an economic commodity, that information—not knowledge—is the appropriate focus of librarianship, that librarians should become "information transfer agents," and that technology was the driving force for change.

By now we easily recognize in Hammer's history, Giuliano's manifesto, and the ALA program, as well as the many articles, books, and reports preceding them, the emerging rhetoric underlying the myth of the electronic library. A rapid increase in scientific and technical information was identified as a national crisis in the research communication process. New methods of information handling were required, with the focus on the scientific and technical researcher. The scientific and technical community itself would have to develop the tools and methods, raising the possibility of the emergence of new information sciences and professions. Technology was considered both a source of inevitable change and the key component of any solutions to the "information problem." Information, in contrast to knowledge, was identified as an important economic commodity, indeed, to such an extent that its generation and use was an indicator of revolutionary social change, giving rise to such descriptors as "information society" or "information age." Information was also identified as an objective, discrete phenomenon separate from its content and the form in which it was embedded. As such, it could be subjected to scientific investigation and quantification. The traditional library and its methods were characterized as outmoded and threatened with obsolescence. The optimistic view was that they would likely be transformed into some type of center serving as a node in an information electronic network, although it was also anticipated that seekers of information would have onsite terminals of some kind providing direct access to a wide range of sources of information. The library should become less a place and more of a process. Librarians, overly attached to the physical book and the library, were also threatened with obsolescence. They were seen as reluctant to adopt new technology, a failure accelerating their disappearance as a profession. However, if librarians aggressively rose to the challenge, they then had the opportunity to enhance their professional status.

These themes form a common link in the creation of the myth of the electronic library, constituting the backbone of the myth and the thrust of the assault on the myth of the library as place.

3

Creating the Myth of the Electronic Library

There will be less on the shelves and more on the wires.

Pat Molholt

The library is an institution whose history is traced over thousands of years. Its role in the preservation and perpetuation of culture is an acknowledged part of the history of Western civilization. American librarians take pride in the United States' contribution to this tradition through its development of the free public library. There are many other types of libraries —academic, school, special—but for most people, "library" means the public library. Even to the many who do not use it, the public library remains, like the public school and a free press, part of what makes American democracy work, a unique creation arising out of the American democratic ethos. The foreword to the general report of the Public Library Inquiry, a major study of the American public library undertaken at the end of the 1940s, captures this perspective:

Predominantly local in character, both in support and management, it is deeply rooted in our national heritage. The community's library stands for much that is cherished in our tradition of equal educational opportunity and freedom of thought and communication. It takes its place along with the courthouse, the school, the church, and the town hall as an integral part of the American scene.[1]

Such a statement embodies much that constitutes the myth of the library as place. But, as we have seen, the library as place is increasingly challenged by a more abstract image and a new myth: the electronic library. By the

1970s the form of the myth of the electronic library is sufficiently evident to allow for comparison with the myth of the library as place.

Early myth-breakers foretold the transformation of the library, if not its disappearance altogether. They put forward a far more abstract concept of the library, one having little of that "thereness" admired by Archibald MacLeish. Among them, Robert Taylor moved most explicitly toward this idea when formulating his plan for Hampshire College. Attacking the library as place, he wrote: "Traditionally the library is looked on as a place surrounded by four walls where printed materials—sometimes non-print materials—are stored, organized, and lent." He advocated "the notion that the library is not a place, but a process, and that mere warehousing and servicing is only the first step in the process. The library should be a process that permeates the campus."[2] Technology, he claimed, permitted the development of a new type of institution, one reaching beyond four walls. Drawing on the "university without walls" concept, Taylor predicted that libraries would become switching centers in information networks providing access to information "both inside and outside the building called a 'library' "; it will become a "library without walls."[3]

More recently, James Govan echoes this abstract concept of the library: "The notion that the library is a place will give way to the recognition that it is a network of information, more a concept than a building, an abstraction."[4] The New England town public library provided an iconography vividly capturing for many people the spirit and values embodied in the myth of the library as place. What image does the myth of the electronic library offer as an alternative? The myth-makers of the electronic library reject the solidity of the library as place by advocating a more abstract concept of the library. Patricia Battin even asserts that "it is important not to seek a visual image, since we are dealing with a process, not an entity."[5] This greater abstraction takes different forms. The library becomes less a physical location and more like a "ubiquitous utility."[6] It ceases to be "*places*," and becomes "organizations of people."[7]

Mark Kibby and Nancy Evans maintain that "the library is not just a local collection of hardware and software with information stored electronically or optically, but a network of information tools and services."[8]

Perhaps one way to grasp the meaning of "electronic library" is to examine what those attempting to implement one have to say. By the 1970s, there was more explicit evidence of the myth of the electronic library as the rhetoric of the myth began to enter that of library planning. A vision of the electronic library from the public library field was presented by Kenneth E. Dowlin, while director of the Pikes Peak Library District in Colorado Springs, Colorado. Dowlin's ideas are presented in his *The Electronic Library: The Promise and the Process*, published in 1984.[9]

Quoting Alvin Toffler and others, Dowlin claims that the emergence of an information industry and the availability of powerful information technology present challenges and opportunities to libraries and librarianship. To meet these challenges there must be a change in the paradigm of librarianship. For Dowlin, the electronic library is not an institution but a concept. Picking up on McLuhan's rhetoric, it will become "a global village library." The library has traditionally been identified with the book as the most appropriate vehicle for the transmission of information. In our high-technology information society, books are increasingly less relevant for the rapid distribution of information. Dowlin's new paradigm emphasizes the provision of rapid access to information through electronic communication systems. Granted, the library will continue to collect published material, but it needs to become the community's information center, collecting information in unpublished forms and, where appropriate, publishing it itself. Furthermore, the library will need to provide locally maintained databases of community information, social services, and resources; to serve as a node in library and information networks; to facilitate teleconferencing and electronic mail messaging; and to provide on-line access to the library's holdings. Librarians can achieve a higher status and more political leverage if they aggressively adopt the paradigm of the electronic library. If they do not, Dowlin predicts like many before him, libraries and librarians will become irrelevant.

Academic libraries are also attempting to implement the electronic library, most prominently that of the Carnegie-Mellon University (CMU) in Pittsburgh. Its staff conscientiously produces reports, papers in library journals, and conference presentations on their institution's efforts to achieve the electronic library.[10] CMU has a long history of experience with computing, acquiring its first mainframe in 1954. The university had not, however, developed a library that would allow it to achieve the national status it desired in the 1980s. It was decided to turn to technology to overcome the library's limited collection and resources. In 1986, the library and university computing were brought closer together administratively with the formation of an Academic Services Division. In 1987, a proposal was adopted "to build a large-scale electronic library," to be called "Mercury."[11] In partnership with OCLC, Digital Equipment Corporation, and the American Association for Artificial Intelligence, Project Mercury was initiated in 1988 with the objective of developing an electronic library in five years. The emphasis was to be on providing access rather than on collection building.

The rationale for the electronic library at CMU draws on the earlier formulations of electronic library myth-makers. It is asserted that the need for an electronic library rests on the problems arising from current methods in information storage and retrieval: the requirement that the scholar go to the library; the frustrations of current diverse automated and manual library methods; the growing volume of research material; rising storage and preservation costs; inadequate access to unpublished information; and the emergence of multimedia electronic documents not easily integrated into libraries. There is the usual implication of technological inevitability: The "evolution, in terms of computer technology, human psychology, and the economics of publishing, is moving in this direction."[12] The Project Mercury vision of the electronic library acknowledged Bush's concept of Memex and earlier automation efforts such as Project Intrex at MIT. What, specifically, will the electronic library at CMU be like? It is not a place, "a simple entity where everything is stored." Rather, it is a "range of services and collections made accessible through networks that reach beyond individual campuses and laboratories." A fundamental characteristic of Project Mercury's vision is "independence of location." The scholar, regardless of her or his location, will have access to information regardless of its location. In short, "the Network is the Library."[13]

These two examples—Pikes Peak and CMU—illustrate how the electronic library concept is far more abstract than the library as place. However, no one has pursued the idea of the increasing abstraction of the library as logically as Frederick Wilfred Lancaster. While he does not refer to the electronic library, he foresees the emergence of the "electronic librarian," and it is rare that his extensive writings are not referred to in discussions of the future of libraries in an information age. He must be considered among the major myth-makers of the electronic library. Lancaster's contribution to the myth is his forceful argument for a paperless society and the "disembodiment" of the library.

Born and educated in England, Lancaster came to the United States in 1959. He has been associated since the 1960s with private firms and major libraries in the development and evaluation of information-retrieval systems, including MEDLARS. Since 1970 he has been a professor in the Graduate School of Library and Information Science at the University of Illinois. He has published numerous papers and books, a number of which have received awards from the American Library Association and the American Society for Information Science. His "Whither Libraries? Or Wither Libraries," published in *College and Research Libraries* in 1978, was reprinted in that journal in 1989, having already achieved the status of a "classic."[14] Lancaster's ideas on the paperless society are most fully spelled out in two books, *Toward Paperless Information Systems* (1978) and *Libraries and Librarians in an Age of Electronics* (1982).[15] (It has not gone unnoticed that probably no one has generated more paper about the paperless society than Lancaster.) Central to his argument is the proposition that the library as place will disappear.

In the early 1970s, Lancaster became aware of efforts in defense and intelligence agencies to develop various paperless information systems. Citing the ideas of Bush, Licklider, Taylor, Giuliano, Toffler, Parker, Bell, Drucker, and many others, and drawing on his own experience in developing computer-based information-retrieval systems, Lancaster could see the potential of applying the concepts of paperless information systems to the scientific and technical communication process. He became convinced that such a development was inevitable and that the replacement of paper by electronic dissemination of information would be complete by the year 2000. For Lancaster, the key factor making possible the prospect of a paperless society is the generation of machine-readable text by publishers. Initially produced as part of the process of printing on paper, publishers began to make these computer-based databases directly available on-line. This development, along with the widespread use of personal computers and improved communication technologies, creates the possibility of an entirely electronically based publication system, starting with the generation of the original "document" at the researcher's work station, its transmission to the "electronic journal," and distribution on demand to users. This technology must be welcomed by librarians because the current communication system, as so many before Lancaster have stated, is breaking down due to the growth in the number of scientific and technical publications and rising costs. Librarians, according to Lancaster, must get over the idea that books are sacred. Their existence in history is relatively short—about 500 years—and there is no reason or evidence to make one believe they should continue to exist, except perhaps for recreational reading.

If books are not sacred, neither are libraries. While libraries as collections of materials have existed for centuries, there is no more reason that they should continue to exist than that print on paper should. According to Lancaster, the public, when it thinks about libraries at all, "looks upon the library as a *place*, a kind of warehouse."[16] We have reached the point that it is no longer necessary to think of libraries as buildings housing extensive print collections. There should be, Lancaster insists, no boundaries around the library's collection. The objective is to make information accessible wherever it exists. In time, as more sophisticated electronic networks are established to link library catalogs, reference sources, cooperatively maintained files of reference question answers, and full text sources, and when most people have access to terminals in their "electronic cottages," there will be no need for the library. In short, the library undergoes a process Lancaster calls "disembodiment."[17] By 1984, the disembodiment of the library had progressed to the extent that for Lancaster, "the library without walls exists."[18] While the library will have a role to play during the transition to total electronics, he predicts the library as place will disappear by the end of the century. Only a few libraries will remain as archives of the printed resources of the past.

As we have seen, although the concept of the electronic library has had various interpretations, underlying all of them is the tendency toward abstraction, the total disembodiment or dematerialization of the library, and hence, the disappearance altogether of the library as place.

What do these myth-makers have in store for librarians as the walls of the library evaporate around them? The message is clear: Get out of the library! The myth-makers of the electronic library accuse librarians of being myopic, of having their heads in the sand, of not being dynamically oriented, of being "the most institutionalized of all professions," of being attached to a "Ptolemaic" universe of which the library is the center rather than to a "Copernican" view in which information is the center, of having as much of a future as the brontosaurus.[19] As early as 1969, Giuliano found it unfortunate that librarianship's name derived from an institution rather than the application of professional skills. What is critical, according to Robert Taylor, is for librarianship to "separate itself from the institution of the library."[20] Others soon echoed this theme. They pointed out that because of its attachment to the library, librarianship is narrowly defined by the needs and role of a specific type of institution.

According to Giuliano, "the entire purpose of being a librarian is thus thought to be to facilitate the operation of an institution called a library." Consequently, librarians concentrate too much on the tasks required to operate the institution instead of focusing on the social function of librarianship. Due to an excessive identification with the library, librarians are only concerned with the preservation of libraries as an institution. According to Giuliano, librarians are like captains of a sinking ship, making every effort to keep it afloat and prepared to go down with it if necessary. To change their identity may mean "that librarians should walk out of their institutions."[21]

The myth-makers find other problems with the institutional bases of librarianship. Those activities in the library observed most often by the public are clerical activities; therefore, the job of librarian is perceived as clerical, rather than as a specialist in the organization and retrieval of information. In the past, librarians benefited from their association with the "romantic aura of books." However, with the emergence of electronic means of transmitting information, the attachment to books will become a liability. It is time to "deinstitutionalize" the keepers of books.[22] There is the usual somber inevitable prediction that libraries "cannot continue as they are. In evolutionary terms the obvious analogy is with the spectacularly sudden extinction of the dinosaurs."[23]

The myth-makers maintain that there are advantages to librarians in moving out of the library. The proliferation of information sources will require the specialist skills of the professional librarian. This in turn will lead to enhanced professional status, comparable to that of the doctor. Librarians will benefit with higher status and salaries, as society recognizes that "information is power." However, as their deinstitutionalization progresses, it will be necessary to discard the name "librarian" for "information broker," "information manager," or some similar designation. Thus, we will see the emergence of the electronic librarian.

As we explore further the implications of the dematerialization of the library and the deinstitutionalization of librarianship, we encounter a picture of librarianship radically different from that embodied in the myth of the library as place. The public library serves as the institutional base of the library as place. The institutional base of the myth of the electronic library is the special library. The background of the myth-makers is found in the academic and special library fields and in the scientific research community. It is expected that the shift to paperless systems will occur first in special and academic libraries, followed by public and then school libraries. All types of libraries drew on the myth of the library as place, despite the myth's origin in the public library. Now we see the public library drawing on the myth of the electronic library whose fount is the research/special library environment. By the 1980s, the idea of the electronic library was actively promoted in the public library field. In 1981, the Public Library of Columbus and Franklin County (Ohio) and OCLC Inc. sponsored a meeting of public library representatives in an attempt to launch an Electronic Library Association. Participants saw the possibility of "libraries without walls" serving users in their "electronic cottages" with "tools of the online age."[24] The participants at the meeting felt an urgency to bring public libraries into the information arena. The adoption of the myth of the electronic library by the public library is further evident in a report based on a major national public opinion survey on consumers in the information age published in 1991 by the American Library Association, *Using the Public Library in the Computer Age*. The use of public libraries increased by 15 percent since 1978 and the service most often used by 91 percent of those surveyed was the borrowing of books. Still, the report maintains that the "placement of books on shelves" is no longer adequate to meet the needs of library users in "the electronic era."[25] Although the taking out of books as a service increased from 75 percent in 1978 to 91 percent in 1989, the authors of the report believed the clear message delivered by the survey was the finding that 68 percent of the respondents believe it would be "very valuable" or "somewhat valuable" to have on-line access to information from the public library. The report concluded that "in the evolving electronic era, the public library is becoming less a place than a service."[26]

The research orientation of the electronic library is further evident in its clientele orientation: the researcher in science and technology. The background of most of the myth-makers themselves is the scientific research environment. As well, of course, it has been the research community that developed and used earliest and most pervasively information technology. The myth of the library as place always stressed the library's obligation to serve the entire community. When the electronic library is discussed, it is almost exclusively considered with reference to serving the researcher or scholar. The concept of the electronic library is often joined with the notion of the electronic scholar, the scholar's work station, or a scholarly communication system. Furthermore, it is the information-seeking habits of researchers in science and technology that serve as the model user of the electronic library.

By focusing on the needs of the scientific or technological researcher, the electronic library myth also shifted the focus from collections to rapid access. Over and over again, the relevance of local collections is deemphasized while the importance of providing access to information regardless of its location is promoted. The scientists' need for up-to-date information requires the immediate availability promised by the electronic library network. To improve the quality of national life and to ensure the existence of an informed citizenry in a rapidly changing information society, public libraries are also urged to take the fullest advantage of electronic technology to provide speedy access to information regardless of its location. It is anticipated that in time all relevant literature, except perhaps some recreational material, will be available electronically.

This emphasis on the use of the electronic network contrasts with the autonomy characteristic of the local library as place. The electronic library on the electronic highway holds the promise of the cooperation so longed for by generations of librarians. The development of such a network will be a collaborative effort requiring the relinquishing of local autonomy. As the network creates the possibility of both libraries and scholars becoming publishers themselves, it is advocated that all players in the scholarly communication process become involved in the development of the electronic library. The library becomes an abstract node in a collaborative electronic network as the local autonomous physical library houses an ever-declining proportion of available information. Indeed, an advantage of the electronic library, according to its planners, is to "keep the faculty out of the library."[27] Could there be an any more explicit rejection of the library as place? Recent efforts to establish the National Research and Education Network (NREN) reinforce the desire to achieve the electronic library. Librarians are urged to become information managers and leaders in this effort, to show that libraries are exciting information centers, to acknowledge that information is not free and will have to be charged for, to stop arguing over fee versus free information, and to strive to achieve the "virtual library."[28]

The role of the public library has been a matter of debate since its inception. A 1984 analysis of articles concluded that "in spite of admonitions to the contrary, confusion, not consensus, seems to characterize the public library's attempts to establish satisfactory role concepts."[29] In contrast, the electronic library, with its narrower focus on the utilitarian role of providing information rapidly to the user for instrumental purposes, appears to offer a "hard," explicit alternative to the ambiguous and contentious role of the library as place. At last, librarians will be free from the ambiguity surrounding the role of the library in order to pursue a clearly defined path in the information society. Such clarity of purpose in a time of change is reassuring to an occupation unsure of itself even in the most stable of times.

What will be available on the electronic highway? Again we find a dramatic change in perspective from that of the library. The library as place is projected as a depository of an organized body of coherent knowledge, a proposition expressed eloquently by Ernestine Rose of the New York Public Library and the Columbia University School of Library Service. In her 1954 book, *The Public Library in American Life*, she states emphatically what constitutes the inner core of the library: "It is the same yesterday, today and tomorrow, and it is one of the most precious things in the world. This inner core is knowledge; the knowledge of the world, preserved, cherished, and made available, more and more, in useful and pleasurable forms for the people, all the people who need it and have the capacity to use it."[30] This inner core serves as the basis for the objectives of the library: "Knowledge is the first item on the agenda of the library's business." All other items on its agenda "are transmission of that knowledge."[31]

More recently, R. Kathleen Molz also makes the case for the public library as a "knowledge institution" in the information age.[32] The myth-makers of the electronic library have a different view. The electronic library is directed at the delivery of information, a term they prefer to "knowledge." According to Dowlin, the library as place, based as it is on a collection of published resources, "is a knowledge organization, and not a vehicle for information."[33] The library must be replaced by an information center run by an information manager, specialist, officer, consultant, broker, or agent.

"Information" is also appealing to the myth-makers because it moves librarianship closer to the market-economy model in recognizing information as an economic commodity. The electronic myth-makers question the allegiance to free library service associated with the library as place. Giuliano sees this commitment to serving the "information poor" resulting in the library taking on "the form of some sort of welfare institution, one that is not very effective at that." For Giuliano, the profit motive operating in the marketplace is the best means of achieving a service objective.[34] He considers it unfortunate when librarians oppose fees for service.

Lancaster also expects that the paperless communication system is "likely to be a much more 'pay as you go' one. "[35] This phenomenon will be forced on libraries by the emergence of a society in which private vendors will provide for a fee on-line access to electronic data in a market-driven economy where information is a commodity.

According to Tom Suprenant, this dynamic will require "a major philosophical shift in thinking from the concept of the library as a 'free good' to a 'fee based' structure."[36] The economics of Carnegie-Mellon's Project Mercury are marketplace oriented. It is a critical assumption of the project, that information is a commodity. According to the director of the project, it is essential information is recognized as a "public utility—which no more means 'free' than telephones, water, lights, and gas are free to our businesses and homes today." When this is recognized, "the pressures of the marketplace will then force a fair solution to the tiresome problems of property rights."[37]

The attention given to information coincides with the increasing desire to incorporate librarianship into "information science." Early librarianship was closely associated with the cultural literary tradition. With increased professionalization, there were strenuous efforts to promote a library science as a social science, most notably at the University of Chicago Graduate Library School. The Public Library Inquiry by the Social Science Research Council, completed at the end of the 1940s at the request of the American Library Association, was an important representation of this movement. However, after World War II, librarians, confronted with the emergence of the competing discipline of information science, increasingly focused on information as a discrete phenomenon that could be studied through the use of scientific methods of research. Library schools quickly incorporated "information" into their names. Thus, the electronic library is further identified with a scientific milieu.

There is a further contrast between the two myths: the nature of change. Because the library as place and the librarianship bound to it is rooted in the social sciences and humanities, the emergence of modern librarianship and the growth of libraries have been presented as an outgrowth of social, economic, and cultural forces, a perspective reinforced by most published library history. There is an appreciation of the importance of technological change in publishing, especially the importance of the book and the development of libraries, but this is placed within the context of other historical factors. Being subject to the vagaries of dynamic change and subtle historical forces, the future of libraries is thus exceedingly difficult to predict. However, the electronic library myth-makers, coming from a scientific-technical environment, see technology as the overriding source of change. Just as the book presumably accounted for the possibility of the modern library, so technological innovations in computing, communications, and storage devices make possible the electronic library. What historical analysis is given to the electronic library is usually confined to this narrow interpretation.

Technological change is not only the motivating force for change in libraries and librarianship; the electronic library myth-makers see this change as inevitable. James Thompson foresees the end of libraries due to the "pre-emptive" nature of the computer. The possibilities offered by the computer are such that there "can be no option but to embrace them."[38]

We are reminded of Ridenour's mathematical law of social change when Lancaster declares that rapid technological change should not surprise librarians, "for it is merely the manifestation of the law of acceleration of progress, a law illustrated clearly by Henry Adams almost 100 years ago and demonstrated even more pervasively by Toffler in his book *The Third Wave.*"[39] Although confronted with such inevitability, librarians are accused of being conservative and resistant to change. Reviewing in 1975 the emergence of computer-based bibliographic services, Roger Christian accused librarians of not being in the forefront of developments.[40] Hugh Cline and Loraine Sennett a few years later doubted that librarians recognized the need to adapt to technological change.[41] Lancaster accuses the library profession of having its head in the sand.[42]

By now we know what consequences the myth-makers foresee if librarians do not change. As in the past, librarians are warned that if they do not become immersed in this electronic technological revolution, they will not survive. However, librarians who grasp the opportunities offered by the electronic library will enhance their position. At Carnegie-Mellon University, an improvement in the image of librarians was one of the declared incentives for establishing the electronic library. Lancaster believes the deinstitutionalization of librarians could greatly improve their "image, status, and rate of compensation."[43] For Dowlin, the electronic library is the key to "elevating the status of libraries and librarians" and increasing their power.[44]

We can now summarize the development of the myth of the electronic library. The rapid increase in scientific and technical information underlies the inadequacy of traditional library methodologies. This expansion in information and its use is so pervasive that it characterizes our time, the information age or society. However, myth-makers claim that technology provides a solution for coping with this deluge of information. Not only is technology the solution, it is also the force for change, a force so strong that its consequences are inevitable, including the transformation if not elimination of the library as place. The organizational base for the myth of the electronic library is not the public library but an abstract concept arising out of the special or research library environment: the electronic library without walls serving as a node in an electronic network.

The profession of librarianship must free itself from its traditional institutional base, adopting a free-lance, autonomous, professional model and a new name. This move will enhance the status of and bring greater material rewards to the profession. While the objectives of the library as place tend to be ambiguous with an inclusive clientele, the objectives of the electronic library and clientele are narrow: the provision of information to the researcher. The core resource of the library as place has been the local collection, primarily of print materials, maintained with a considerable amount of local institutional autonomy. The electronic library operates within an electronic collaborative environment with an emphasis on access to information regardless of its location. The library as place adheres to the welfare liberalism concept of making knowledge available at no direct cost to the user. The electronic library focuses on the provision of information on a fee-for-service basis and celebrates the free-market economy. Information is not a public good but an economic commodity. The library as place is associated with a humanistic/social science culture; the electronic library identifies with a scientific environment, including the hope for an "information science."

The differences in these two myths have profound consequences for libraries and librarianship. The issues raised by the new myth confront librarians in their day-to-day work life as exemplified, for example, by recent debates over the desirability of constructing new urban central libraries. In the June 1, 1990, issue of *Library Journal*, we see the clash of the library as place confronting the electronic library. *Library Journal's* editor, Nora Rawlinson, faces off against editor-in-chief John N. Berry III over the issue of whether cities should continue building large central public libraries. Rawlinson asserts that the new central libraries being built are an illogical "fatal attraction," while Berry sees them as "the reaffirmation of the tradition that says that, in America, every citizen has a right to know."[45] Rawlinson decries the continued practice of major urban centers to build large, expensive central libraries. New technologies in information storage and retrieval make possible the "library without walls." She is vexed by the reluctance of librarians to resist the pressure from city politicians who exploit an old-fashioned rhetoric that equates great cities with great libraries. Instead, librarians should draw on market research results to show that "convenience" libraries, distributed like convenience stores, will more readily meet the information needs of a city's populace.

Such views greatly disturb Berry. Invoking the images of the great edifices of the Boston Public Library and the New York Public Library, Berry claims that their central locations and physical grandeur go beyond "mere symbolism." These bulwarks of democracy are concrete (both literally and metaphorically) commitments to every American's right to knowledge. This commitment, which must be upheld regardless of the cost, refutes, according to Berry, any marketing research, management theories, and quantifiable measures lodged against the central library.

In Rawlinson's attack on the central library we see the elements of the myth of the electronic library: the dematerialization of the library as place in favor of the library without walls; the dismissal of history; the survival of the library dependent on technology; the stress on efficiency, quantifiable measurement, and market economy pressures; the reference to "information" as opposed to "knowledge." In contrast, Berry praises the library as place, claiming that the corner of 5th Avenue and 42nd Street, possibly the main intersection of not only New York City but of the nation, if not the world, could only be occupied by one of the greatest and most imposing research libraries in the world, the New York Public Library. Berry calls upon history and tradition. He evokes nostalgia as he takes us into the Waterloo, Iowa, central library, a renovated WPA building, with its grand murals painted by a student of Grant Wood. (It cannot be an accident that he uses this example, with its reference to Grant Wood, the artist whose painting "American Gothic" is an icon of traditional American values.) Easily casting aside any benefits deriving from market analysis, Berry insists upon the citizen's right to a more substantive good than mere "information." The only acknowledgement of technology is a subordinate reference to the sharing of resources through networks.

The Rawlinson-Berry debate cannot be dismissed as a provocative editorial gimmick of interest to librarians alone. The debate is moving into the streets. The clash of the traditional and new is found on the pages of daily newspapers as communities debate the need for new library facilities. Shortly after the appearance of the Rawlinson-Berry confrontation, two citizens of Denver addressed the question, in an August issue of the *Denver Post*, "Should the Denver Public Library be Expanded?" Yes, says Dottie Lamm, wife of a former Colorado governor and honorary co-chair of Library 1990 campaign. No, says Marj Mickum, a Denver home owner and first vice president of the Colorado Union of Tax Payers.[46] The debate was engendered by a bond issue that would provide funds for a new central library and the renovation of several branches.

Lamm, like Berry, draws on history and tradition to support the building of a new library in the center of the city and the renovation of five branch buildings, all of which had been designated Denver historic landmarks. Referring to the "quiet corners of our public libraries" as the most suitable place to promote the "honored traditions" of free "inquiry and self development," she emphasizes the library as place. Mickum is more hardheaded in her nay-saying. She calls for more efficient management, reliance on the free market (to provide parking), and less waste of taxpayers' funds. She argues that in "the information age," less space is needed as we rely more and more on computers, laser disks, tapes, and other new technologies. In short, there is no need for the library as place.

There is much in the myth of the electronic library to appeal to librarians and others concerned with libraries. It appears to be in tune with the social and technological changes identified by social scientists and futurists. It is identified with a powerful, awe-inspiring technology—the computer. It offers concise goals for the "library" and precise roles for librarians. It promises enhanced professional prestige and the possibility of greater material compensation. And there is an inevitability about it all. But does it represent a new epoch in librarianship, the chance at last to attain the high professional status (and its material rewards) so longed for by librarians for over a century? Before we rush onto the electronic highway, do we need to stop and look in all directions before we put the pedal to the floor? Some think not.

The electronic library myth-makers are alert to any "counter-revolution-ary" attitudes that could jeopardize the transition to the information age. James Kusack, an assistant professor at the Southern Connecticut State University School of Library Science and Instructional Technology, launched an attack on such attitudes in the *Bulletin of the American Society for Information Science* in early 1988.[47] Kusack warned his fellow information scientists that the "old battle" so many thought over remained: "We see signs that the computer, engine of the Information Age, is once again an object of distrust and suspicion for many librarians and others in the information business." The signs, according to Kusack, are truly ominous. When the keynote speaker at the American Library Association 1987 annual conference urged librarians to defend the book against the unhealthy influence of the computer on society, the "gleeful reaction" of support expressed by the audience was disturbing evidence of the depth of antago-nism librarians felt toward computers. Kenneth Dowlin's defeat for the ALA presidency by a library educator is seen by Kusack as a clear signal of backsliding to traditional views. How else can one explain that a library educator, little known and from a group for which there is no great love among practitioners, beat a well-known public librarian? Kusack con-cluded that Dowlin, the "electronic *wunderkind*," was defeated because of his reputation as the "apostle of the Electronic Library."

Kusack is concerned as well because he senses that librarians are giving the "traditional role of the librarian greater value than we did a couple of years ago." This is happening to such an alarming extent that the term "librarian," until recently an "anathema" carrying "a cart-load of negative stereotypes and a wage scale many find intolerable," was regaining popu-larity at the expense of "Information Specialist." Perhaps even worse, the term "library" is threatening to replace "Information Center." Furthermore, the fad to spend vast amounts of money to develop programs for the preservation of "second- and third-rate books no one will ever look at" confirms that librarians are dangerously drifting back toward old ways. Despite "impressive victories," the struggle against traditional values in librarianship obviously has to go on. The battle is made difficult, laments Kusack, by the constant entry into librarianship of students with humanis-tic backgrounds, attracted to librarianship by a love for books and the profession's conservatism. Kusack tries to inspire a greater love for infor-mation technology in his own students by threatening them; if they do not seize control of these "deadly weapons" as a strategy to protect libraries from the "mad scientists," the bad guys will take libraries away from librarians. Only by becoming a computer expert will the "good guys" prevent the bad from destroying the social value of libraries.

The vehemence with which Kusack takes up arms in defense of the myth of the electronic library displays an insecurity as great as any number of librarians holding "traditional values" might display. However, I am encouraged by his rush to the barricades. It is for me a sign that all questions have not been resolved, that all aspects of the myth of the electronic library are not inevitable. Thus encouraged, let's examine further elements of the myth of the electronic library.

Myth of the Electronic Library in the Information Society

We are in an Information Age; information is the key resource for maintaining a healthy economy, for improvement of quality of life, and for operation of an effective participative democracy.

Vincent E. Giuliano

The electronic library is projected as a logical technological consequence of the arrival of an information society. Librarians are urged to ride this wave to a future bright with material and professional rewards. Being concerned always about collecting, organizing, and providing knowledge, librarians are understandably enthusiastic about any proposition that implies an enhanced role for their profession. Their enthusiasm for the idea of an information society is so extensive that there is little questioning of this proposition among them. It is an accepted fact with little concern about how it is defined, where it is headed, how long it will last, or what its social, political, economic, and cultural implications are beyond the benefits that it is hoped will accrue. Because librarians so eagerly accept the information society as a defining social context, we should take a closer look at the concept before we become much more enamored with it and the myth of which it is such an integral part.

Much of the foundation of the concept of the information society is spelled out in the writings by sociologist Daniel Bell and others on the post-industrial society, which give great importance to information and knowledge in society. As this theme was taken up by social planners, forecasters, and futurists, there was increasing reference to an information society. Increasingly, the phrases "post-industrial society" and "information society" were used synonymously. Bell states: "The post-industrial society is an information society, as industrial society is a goods-producing society."[1] When Bell, Machlup, Porat, and others assert that we are an information society, their conclusions are based on the categorization of statistics relating to the workforce, expenditures as a proportion of the gross national product (GNP), and other types of economic and occupational indicators. There is often a great compiling—or piling up—of statistics whose change in magnitude over time is in itself taken as conclusive evidence of social change. There is little probing beyond the statistics themselves. Toffler and others cite the vast number of scientists now living as compared with the number in the past, the growth in the number of research journals and papers, or the great number of Ph.D.'s in society. But, as sociologist Krishan Kumar observes: "No doubt we are living in the middle of a dizzying and unprecedented explosion of scientific knowledge; but this kind of evidence tells us nothing about the uses to which it is put, or whether indeed it has any use at all, or has had any profound effect on the life of society." The large number of college graduates is undeniable, but again, "it is naive simply to equate an increase in formal education with an increase in the contribution of knowledge to social life."[2] As Kumar and others have shown, much of the impetus for more schooling has been to keep young people off the streets. These compilations of statistics and trends are amassed as if, once brought together, they define the post-industrial information society. Thus, as one political scientist has pointed out, "They in essence allege that some new whole must be coming into existence because there are all these parts around which *must* somehow add up to something."[3]

Of course, how one interprets such statistics often depends on the statistics used and on definition, and not everyone agrees on the same definitions and how categories should be linked. Machlup was the pioneer leading us into this definitional swamp in the early 1960s. Few wished to follow until Marc Porat and Michael Rubin completed a nine-volume study, *The Information Economy*, in the 1970s. This work is often cited by librarians and futurists, although public librarian Thomas Ballard is probably correct when he asserts that few of these people, including himself (and this author), have read Porat's study.[4] One quickly grasps the problem of definition and classification by referring to later work by Michael Rubin, an economist who was the co-author of the Porat study. More recently, he wrote a volume updating the work of Machlup. Therefore, he is thoroughly familiar with both the Machlup and Porat studies. In *The Knowledge Industry in the United States, 1960–1980*, (1986) Rubin compares the Machlup and Porat studies. A few examples of how they differ illustrate the need to appreciate the complexity of what is being measured and the rationale underlying such analysis. For example, Machlup's study broke the "knowledge industry" into fifty groups, while Porat-Rubin had 115 "information industry" groups that were, in turn, categorized as "primary" and "secondary." The classification systems differed in other ways as well. In the education category Porat included only formal education, whereas Machlup took a much broader approach by including "education" in the church and armed forces and the rental of educational buildings among other costs. Due to these and other differences in measuring education costs, Machlup arrived at a 1972 figure of $188.6 billion and Porat-Rubin at $82.3 billion—a considerable difference.[5]

In undertaking such a complex statistical analysis, it becomes necessary to make further assumptions and somewhat arbitrary decisions, most of which are open to debate. For example, in looking at the classification of knowledge workers Machlup concluded that when a physician examines and treats a patient, the treatment is not considered "knowledge" but the diagnosis is. Therefore, Machlup considered the work of physicians to be half knowledge-producing and half not.[6] How do we know it shouldn't be a 65/35 split? Porat also had to make such distinctions when measuring the "secondary" information sector. But as Rubin indicates, "the secondary information sector is difficult to measure, since that measurement requires dividing 'noninformation' firms and industries into two parts: one part involved in 'pure' noninformation activities and the other engaged in 'pure' information activities." Each firm is divided into two "quasi-firms," one part of which carries out information activities. Thus, to continue Rubin's example, each ball bearing–producing firm must be divided between its noninformation component and its information component, for example, management, legal, and accounting functions. This split was made according to the type of workforce in each industry—an approach opposed by Machlup.[7]

The inclusion of expenditures is also questionable. Both Machlup and Porat include the cost of schools and libraries (although they placed them in different categories). But Porat-Rubin also includes the cost of office buildings. Should such costs really be considered part of the information sector? (In another context, Robert M. Hayes, dean of the Graduate School of Library and Information Science at the University of California, Los Angeles, identifies the "entertainment industry," including motion pictures, as an important part of California's information industry.[8] I had never thought of movie stars as "knowledge workers" before but I am pleased to include them among my colleagues.)

We soon see that the inclusion of certain jobs in the knowledge industry and the resulting statistics are in many cases based on arbitrary definitions, personal judgment, and a chain of assumptions, any one link of which can often be questioned to the detriment of the whole. For example, Stephen S. Cohen and John Zysman attack the "myth of the post-industrial economy," which they believe is based "on data that although overwhelming in their seeming consistency and scope to a large extent reflect a statistical muddle," due to the way economic data are organized.[9] They question the usual economic development scenario so widely accepted, that is, the supposed transition from agriculture to an industrial to a post-industrial knowledge-based service economy. It is their assertion that manufacturing still very much matters in the economy of the United States and that many sectors and jobs often identified with the knowledge-based service society have "tight linkages" to manufacturing. Without strong manufacturing capabilities there would not be, according to their thesis, active service components in the economy. For that matter, they point out that although a relatively small proportion of employment is in agriculture, there remain numerous tight linkages between agriculture and other areas of the economy, including "tractor repairing, veterinary medicine, ketchup making, and grape crushing."[10] There are workers in all of these areas that could be categorized as either agriculture, manufacture, or information workers. What Cohen and Zysman do is reverse the perspective by having us look at knowledge workers' reliance on manufacturing processes. Machlup may include the accounting department of a large manufacturing company as knowledge workers, but, as Cohen and Zysman would point out, the department's raison d'être is not that there is an information economy but, rather, that the manufacturing process requires it.

The significance of the growth of the number of knowledge workers is also an open question. As Cohen and Zysman and others indicate, many of the jobs created in the information society are not knowledge-based; indeed, many are low-paying service jobs filled by women and teenagers. When this view is put forward, those defending the information society "point to mushrooming employment in information-related services, the defining genie of post-industrialism."[11] Yet Cohen and Zysman show that the growth in such jobs as computer programmers, analysts and operators, economists, travel agents, and many others combined is less than the growth in fast-food workers alone.

Whatever the categorization of statistics, the point is continually made that the trend is to an information society. But how strong a trend? When Machlup analyzed his data using 1958 as his end benchmark year, he was able to show, according to his classification, a high rate of growth in knowledge production. Rubin's follow-up study for the years 1960–80 used Machlup's categories as closely as possible. What Rubin found was that the proportion of knowledge production of the GNP increased from 28.6 percent to only 34.3 percent between 1958 and 1980. Expenditures for knowledge production as a proportion of the GNP were 31.0 percent in 1963, 33.3 percent in 1967, 33.9 percent in 1972, 34.2 percent in 1977, and 34.3 percent in 1980.[12] He acknowledges this modest increase—3.3 percentage points in seventeen years—probably surprises readers familiar with Machlup's earlier statistics and observes that "compared to some extravagant predictions that began to appear after publication of *The Production and Distribution of Knowledge in the United States*, this represents an extremely modest rate of growth relative to the average rate of growth of other components of total GNP."[13]

Employment figures of "knowledge workers" show the same modest growth. Between 1960 and 1970, the number of "all knowledge-producing workers" did increase substantially, from 31.19 percent of the "economically active populations" to 39.21 percent in 1970. However, between 1970 and 1980 there was an increase of only 2.02 percentage points to 41.23 percent. As Rubin observes, just at the time, (the 1970s), that "the idea of a dynamic information sector in this country became commonplace, the relative growth of the information sector in the United States has slowed to a crawl and, finally, stopped."[14] Rubin's observation only confirms what Porat foresaw. Citing in 1978 U.S. Bureau of Labor Statistics projections for the period 1970 to 1980, it appeared that "the growth of the information work force has slowed dramatically." He concluded that "our bureaucracies are glutted and can absorb no more information workers."[15]

It is important to see where the growth in knowledge workers is occurring, especially if librarians hope for an enlarged role in an information society. According to Rubin, the number of knowledge workers among "professional, technical, and kindred workers," the category in which we would include librarians, increased substantially between 1960 to 1970, growing from 7.72 percent of the labor force in 1960 to 11.22 percent in 1970. It continued to increase in actual numbers between 1970 and 1980 but declined to 9.54 percent of the total labor force in 1980.[16] It is difficult to follow up on this type of analysis because more recent studies use different statistical categories. The U.S. Bureau of Labor provides elaborate studies and projections that do address the issue of service versus manufacturing but not information versus noninformation. Indeed, despite the continual reference to an information society, standard official statistical compilations follow more traditional occupational categorizations. However, we might note that a recent Labor Bureau projection of employment to the year 2000 by low, medium, and high scenarios sees a modest 5 percent, 10 percent, and 15 percent increase, respectively, in the number of librarians between 1988 and 2000.[17] (The projections for all occupations is 8, 15, and 22 percent.) As for other information workers, Porat warned that those in the secondary information sector contributing information input to such noninformation firms as auto, steel, and petroleum, are "the first economic luxury to hit the street" in the event of a resource-related recession, an observation that seems to confirm the tight linkages of many information workers to manufacturing pointed out by Cohen and Zysman.[18]

But can't we point to the widely acclaimed information explosion as evidence of an information society? Is this, however, a growth in information or in publications? And what kind of information is it? For example, the enormous annual increases in the costs of scholarly journals have generated closer scrutiny of the "publish or perish" syndrome and its weaknesses. Such weaknesses include redundant publication of research in several journals and pressure to publish ever-smaller bits of the results of ongoing research projects. Papers by an author published in a wide range of journals are collected and reissued as a book, introducing more redundancy into the system. Patricia Glass Schuman, ALA president, points out that statistics indicate that "there is more data than ever before; not that there is better data, more relevant information, or even a more knowledgeable society."[19] Langdon Winner echoes this theme when, in his examination of what he calls the "mythinformation," he asks what kind of information we are usually talking about:

We have seen enough to appreciate that the kind of information upheld is not knowledge in the ordinary sense of the term; nor is it understanding, enlightenment, critical thought, timeless wisdom, or the content of a well-educated mind. If one looks carefully at the writings of computer enthusiasts, one finds that information in a particular form and context is offered as a paradigm to inspire emulation. Enormous quantities of data, manipulated within various kinds of electronic media and used to facilitate the transactions of today's large, complex organizations is the model we are urged to embrace.[20]

Much of this kind of data, he points out, is of benefit primarily to large international business corporations, public bureaucracies, military organizations, and intelligence agencies, an observation that reminds us that Lancaster was first inspired with the idea of a paperless society by his own familiarity with developments in U.S. military intelligence units. Kumar also makes the point that the references often made to increased expenditures for research and development as an indicator of a growing information society is attributed to a great extent to specific defense-related needs and little to broader social or economic issues.[21]

In their enthusiasm to be key players in the emerging information society, librarians have ignored these qualifications and have given "information" a status beyond its merit. Without getting into an in-depth discussion of the differences between data, information, knowledge, and wisdom, most readers accept information as more than data but less than knowledge—and nowhere near wisdom. Still, information is more appealing to librarians than knowledge because it has the feel of "hardness," preciseness, and the manipulative quality of data in contrast to the "softness," ambiguity, and amorphous quality of knowledge. However, it is preferred to data because information, especially in the status it has achieved as the basis of the information society, has acquired some of the aura and respectability of knowledge.

Further, we confuse information with electronic signals. As computer pioneer Heinz von Foerster indicates:

What is travelling on that wire, however, is not information, but signals. Nevertheless, since we think we know what information is, we believe we can compress it, process it, chop it up. We believe information can even be stored and then, later on, retrieved: witness the library, which is commonly regarded as an information storage and retrieval system. In this, however, we are mistaken. A library may store books, microfiches, documents, films, slides, and catalogues, but it cannot store information. One can turn a library upside down: no information will come out. The only way one can obtain information from a library is to look at those books, microfiches, documents, slides, etc.[22]

This type of misconception confuses our considerations of communication and information. It is a misconception, according to Foerster, that arises out of the historical context of the development of the concepts of "signal" and "information." As we know from our own examination of the sources of the myth of the electronic library, these concepts, along with the development of computers, emerged out of the experience of World War II. That experience was dominated, quite naturally, by what Foerster calls a "command mode of language"—fairly straightforward commands or signals followed by an unquestioned obedient response. He writes, "Thus by analogy with unfailing obedience to commands (signals), it appeared to these thinkers as if 'signal' and 'information' were identical, for all the interpretive processes (understanding, meaning, etc.) were invisible."[23] However, the distinction between signal and information becomes clearer if the command or signal is not followed. According to Foerster, when a deliberate choice is consciously made, only then is "information" created. A system in the command mode, one where output is predetermined by input, can be characterized as relatively simple or unsophisticated; it is a system in which there is little difference between signal and information. This is the simplistic type of system the myth-makers of the electronic library wish librarians to adhere to. They accept information as an all-inclusive entity devoid of content. They concentrate on the signal, but by doing so they attach librarianship to a narrow role in society.

If data and information have achieved a greater importance in society and economy, much of it is part of data systems and use that need not concern librarians. If large private and public bureaucracies are dealing with masses of data, is it critical that such systems rely on librarians by another name? Is it really a threat to librarianship if "information managers" emerge to handle systems whose information may be extremely important today but largely irrelevant tomorrow? Such a narrow focus on information cannot be the only road down which the future of librarianship lies. Ambiguous as the library's role may be, ill-defined as knowledge is, and ineffective as the library's methods often are, the library has been identified traditionally as a "knowledge" institution. It is upon this basis that it carved out an institutional role in society. It has emphasized through collection development and classification its responsibility to organize knowledge in some kind of coherent way for the service of all types of knowledge seekers. Focusing on knowledge, rather than on information, permits librarians to formulate a broader and more profound range of objectives for librarianship. By joining the cult of information we risk not making that "vital distinction between what machines do when they process information and what minds do when they think."[24] Libraries are concerned about thinking minds, not machine processing.

Why is the information society such a popular idea? For some the idea of the information society is an ideology to serve particular political ends, a theme we will return to in a later chapter. However, there are cultural and economic sources for its appeal. British sociologist David Lyon claims that its popularity does not rest on empirical evidence but because its appeal as a slogan is "irresistible to certain policy-makers and pundits." He asserts, correctly I believe, that "as a slogan . . . the idea of the information sector emerges from a typically Western faith in the transformative power of technology. At a time of recalcitrant recession and fragile international relations, IT [information technology] is sought as a saviour. Hence the enthusiasm—and lack of critical inquiry—which too often surrounds the term."[25] Information technology is perceived as the driving force giving birth to the electronic revolution, as the steam engine did for the Industrial Revolution. From information technology will flow the plenitude of the information society. The utopian appeal of technology has had an especial appeal in American culture. We can place the myth of the electronic library within this utopian meta-myth of the electronic revolution.

The myth-makers of the electronic library assert that the basis of social change is technology and that the change and its direction are inevitable. Consequently, the emergence of the electronic library, based as it is on dominant technological innovations with revolutionary social implications, is inevitable. Lancaster asserts: "Economic, social, and industrial progress are all dependent on scientific discovery and technological invention."[26]

Going back to the earliest sources of the myth of the electronic library, librarians are consistently accused of being too conservative in incorporating new technologies into library operations. More current electronic library myth-makers have continued this time-honored tradition of librarian bashing. In fact, librarians love technology and all manner of techniques. They were actively experimenting with data-processing equipment in the early 1930s and were among the earliest clients of newly created university computer centers. Librarians not only eagerly adopt the use of various machine technologies but also enthusiastically attend workshops, seminars, and conferences to learn various techniques to improve their management skills, interpersonal skills, and many other job-related techniques. Thus, technology continues to be for librarians a means of improving both library operations and professional status. The combination of the popular interest in technology and librarianship's long-term interest in it makes librarians especially sympathetic to the view that in our "technological" society, technology must be accepted as the determining variable underlying social, cultural, and economic change. It is a happy conjunction reinforcing librarians' affection for technology.

In his study of the idea of technological autonomy, Langdon Winner identifies a paradox often found in popular and scholarly discussions of technology:

On the one hand we encounter the idea that technological development goes forward virtually of its own inertia, resists any limitation, and has the character of a self-propelling, self-sustaining, ineluctable flow. On the other hand are arguments to the effect that human beings have full, conscious choice in the matter and that they are responsible for choices made at each step in the sequence of change. The irony is that both points of view are entertained simultaneously with little awareness of the contradiction such beliefs contain. There is even a certain pride taken in embracing both positions within a single ideology of technological change.[27]

We find this paradox in much of the discussion revolving around the electronic library. Among the myth-makers there is a common theme that the development of information technology is following a biological type of evolution emerging from the innovation of writing material, to the discovery of the printing press, to the introduction of computing. New technology is cast as a natural evolutionary process, a process that takes on a Darwinian slant of the survival of the fittest. The myth-makers extend this biological metaphor to librarians with their consistent threat of extinction, even making analogous references to the disappearance of various prehistoric mammals to emphasize their point. It is a fatalistic view. This position easily slides beyond fatalism into pessimism. When questioned about the morality of his position, Lancaster states that he does not believe that what he considers to "be an inevitable evolutionary process is necessarily desirable." Nevertheless, he says, "My message, if there is a message, is that this is going to happen whether you like it or not, and we as information professionals had better be willing to say what it is going to mean to us; otherwise, not only is the library going to be obsolete, but librarians are going to be obsolete."[28]

This fatalism of the myth-makers is countered by their optimism over the benefits deriving from the electronic library. In addition to the increased status, material rewards, and power that will accrue to librarians, there is a strong strain of utopianism in the myth of the electronic library. Promoters of the electronic library maintain that the "global village library" will contribute to the information society's return to a preindustrial cottage industry, to an informed citizenry in a decentralized democracy practiced through electronic plebiscites, and to international peace and understanding. As the use of communications technologies increases in business, education, shopping, and other spheres of social and economic activity, there will be a renewal of community, a re-emergence of the neighborhood as the force of human interaction.

This technological utopianism displayed in the myth of the electronic library—indeed, the myth itself—is not a result of technological developments alone, but represents a prevailing rhetoric in American culture, a rhetoric of the electronic revolution that can be characterized as one of the meta-myths of American culture. Just as the library as place took its position among the meta-myth of nineteenth-century democratic institution-building, so the electronic library assumes a place within what James Carey and John Quirk call "the mythos of the electronic revolution."[29]

For over a century, electricity has served as a source of imagery, metaphor, and rhetoric in American thought and utopianism. Eighteenth- and nineteenth-century Americans had an abiding faith in their ability to ensure the march of progress on a new continent. This progress was perceived to be based on technological progress to such an extent that American utopianism became one and the same with technological utopianism. Critical to technological progress was energy, the physical generation of power through wind, water, and steam. Increasingly, in the nineteenth century, this energy paradigm revolved around electrical power so that "connecting all sectors of utopia are superbly efficient transportation and communication systems powered almost exclusively by electricity."[30] Electrical metaphors became pervasive in American culture. A striking early example, Nathaniel Hawthorne's reference in *The House of Seven Gables* (1851) to the world as a great nerve, a simile arising from the spread of electricity, inspired one of the greatest twentieth-century contributors to the rhetoric of the electronic revolution, Marshall McLuhan, to coin his famous phrase, "the global village."[31] The rhetoric of the electronic revolution "attributes intrinsically benign and progressive properties to electricity and its applications" and "displays a faith that electricity will exorcise social disorder and environmental disruption, eliminate political conflict and personal alienation, and restore ecological balance and a communion of man with nature."[32]

As the rate of industrialization and electrification rapidly accelerated after the Civil War, those directly involved in the production of electricity were quick to reinforce the electronic metaphor. In 1897, the General Electric Corporation established a publicity department to promote an image of social progress based on technological progress. This effort was so effective that it is claimed Thomas Edison should be recognized as the inventor of public relations. By its very nature, the spread of electrical power to American homes established a "continuous and instantaneous link . . . between the family and a corporation." As the use of electricity increased in the home, this bond began to seem part of the natural order of things, "until full electrification appeared to be the equivalent of full civilization."[33] General Electric worked to reinforce this bond through carefully calculated advertising campaigns. In 1925 it targeted eight specific groups with the theme of "Developing an Electrical Consciousness," followed a few years later by a lecture tour promoting the "Romance of Power." Much of this effort to forge a strong link between electrification and American culture on the part of private corporations was to preserve the commercial value of electricity as opposed to having it distributed as a public good through public utilities.[34] Is it any surprise then that the perception of information as both electronic impulses and as a commodity are embodied in the myth of the electronic library?

By the 1930s, the social critic Lewis Mumford was proposing the electric grid as a metaphor to be applied to a whole range of social institutions, including the library: "The principle of the electric grid must be applied to our schools, libraries, art galleries, theaters, medical services; each lone station though producing power in its own right must be able to draw on power, on demand, from the whole system."[35]

Electricity as a metaphor for progress in the myth of the electronic revolution was given an added dimension when it was incorporated into public policy and national planning. New Dealers in the 1930s promoted social and economic revolution through electrical energy. The Tennessee Valley Authority (TVA) and the Rural Electrification Administration (REA) were two conspicuous manifestations of this utopian impulse. On November 23, 1936, the first issue of the immediately and immensely popular *Life* magazine was published. Its cover was a dramatic photograph of massive concrete buttresses of a New Deal hydroelectro dam project in Montana. This picture and others taken by the outstanding photographer of America in the 1930s, Margaret Bourke-White, was for the *Life* editors a vivid indication that frontier life had returned to the West. This conjunction of imagery derived from electrical power, the Western American frontier, and New Deal enthusiasm to create a "new power age" is representative of an enduring tract of American culture.

The rhetoric of the electronic revolution would expand from the political to the theological with the writings of Marshall McLuhan in the early 1960s. The invisible hand of technology will lead to universal harmony and well-being. Confronted by the inevitable unfolding of technological evolution, there is little alternative but to submit to the fatalistic quietism later also found in Lancaster. In *Understanding Media*, McLuhan states:

Electromagnetic technology requires utter human docility and quiescence of meditation such as befits an organism who now wears its brain outside its skull and its nerves outside its hide. Man must serve his electric technology with the same servomechanistic fidelity with which he served his oracle, his canoe, his typography and other extensions of his physical organs.[36]

With McLuhan the general enthusiasm for the electronic revolution begins to concentrate more narrowly on communications technologies. With the wedding of computers and communications in the succeeding decades, information technology becomes a central component of the rhetoric of the electrical sublime. It takes on the aura of an "almost religious conviction that a widespread adoption of computers and communications systems along with easy access to electronic information will automatically produce a better world for human living."[37] Finally, the myth of the electronic revolution transcends information technology as the power associated with electrical energy is transmuted to information itself. "Information is power!" Information and the electronic signal become one and the same thing.

The meta-myth of the electronic revolution, then, embodies the proposition that science and technology have brought great power and rewards to humankind. The power attributed to information and information technology as part of the myth of electronic library, along with the myth itself, are manifestations of the mythos of the electronic revolution. Recent concerns about medical ethics, the environment, and other "quality of life" movements have raised serious questions about this faith in science and technology. However, there remains the general belief that the solution to many of the problems arising out of technological "progress" can and will be resolved through even more sophisticated technologies. For most people, the benefits they experience in their daily lives from technology are so pervasive that there is little questioning of technology. There is also the feeling that a technological momentum exists over which no one has control.

The myth-makers of the electronic library advance the proposition that technological developments preordain the triumph of the electronic library over the library as place. As in the wider culture, there is considerable compulsion for librarians to adopt a technologically deterministic stance. But we should not be taken in by the view that we are confronted with a technological juggernaut sweeping us along either to oblivion or to unsurpassed power. Any number of social scientists have attacked technological determinism, showing that technology is not the only cause or agent of change but that it is as much an effect arising out of an array of social, cultural, and economic factors. In a groundbreaking study, *Networks of Power: Electrification in Western Society, 1880–1930*, historian Thomas Hughes indicates that of all the significant technological projects of the nineteenth century, "none has been more impressive in its technical, economic, and scientific aspects, none has been more influential in its social effects, and none has engaged more thoroughly our constructive instincts and capabilities than the electric power system."[38] The virtue of Hughes' study, which looks at the different early electrical systems emerging in the United States, Germany, and England, is his concept of "technological systems." Technological systems consist not only of hardware, but organizations (e.g., corporations), formal and informal knowledge, and legislative elements (e.g., regulatory acts). Consequently, electric power systems made in different countries have similar basic technological components but also "reveal variations in resources, traditions, political arrangements, and economic practices from one society to another and from one time to another." He concludes from this that "in a sense, electric power systems, like so much other technology, are both causes and effects for social change."[39]

Others take a similar view. Raymond Williams looks at television and asserts that "technology, including communication technology, and specifically television, is at once an intention and an effect of a particular social order."[40]

David Lyon also rejects any technological determinism in his review of the development of information technology. For Lyon "the worst forms of hype present 'information society' as a *fait accompli*, . . . a result of the social diffusion of IT." Lyon shows how military, commercial, and political factors promote the development and diffusion of information technology. He asserts that "far from witnessing some ineluctable juggernaut of change whose motor is a microelectronic techno-logic, the evidence presented reveals no single historical tendency, no unique or overwhelming contribution from one factor." He agrees with Winner that " 'autonomous technology' is indeed a mistaken notion."[41]

This chapter has examined the social context envisioned in the myth of the electronic library, and calls into question the idea of the information society and the technological determinisms of the myth-makers. The myth of the electronic library is a component of the American meta-myth of the electronic revolution. As such, it is a construct arising out of various cultural factors. Rejecting the technological determinism of the myth-makers provides an opportunity to consider as well other elements of the myth of the electronic library and possible alternatives.

The Sensuous Library

A real electronic library is no library anymore.

Wilhelm K. Neubauer

Let's explore further the abstract quality of the electronic library by looking specifically at the idea of the dematerialization or disembodiment of the library as place. As in the discussion in Chapter 4, we are drawn to the wider cultural context of the library. The idea of the dematerialization of the library reflects a more general sense of dematerialization in modernist culture, closely allied with the mythos of the electronic revolution.

In analyzing the development of technology during the Industrial Revolution, philosopher Hans Jonas makes a distinction between the mechanical, the electrical, and the electronic. In the initial mechanical phase of technological development, "its products were machines made of rigid parts and powered by the mechanics of volume expansion under heat—thus operating with the familiar solids and forces and on the familiar dynamical principles of classical mechanics."[1] To Jonas there was a naturalness to this phase in that the technology was directed toward meeting basic human needs. Technology also resembled familiar forces, which contributed to its "natural" quality. (Think of Benjamin Franklin, his kite and key, and electrical storm.) While originally electrical technology was developed, like the mechanical, to provide power for machines, it had an abstract quality quite different from the mechanical. As Jonas observes, "whereas heat and steam are familiar objects of sensuous experience, and their force is bodily displayed in nature, electricity is an abstract entity, disembodied, immaterial, unseen; and to all practical intents, viz., as a manipulable force, it is entirely an artificial creation of man."

However, for Jonas, "the height of abstraction is reached in the passage from electric to *electronic* technology."[2] Although we may attempt to relate the computer chip to nature—the brain—there is really nothing "natural" about it physically or conceptually. It is a physical representation of an instrumental abstract concept.

Drawing on Jonas's observations, Kathleen Woodward notes that "just as the technology of electronics transfigures the material world, so the metaphor of the invisible transforms our way of interpreting the world."[3] The myth-makers of the electronic library absorbed this "metaphor of the invisible."

Lewis Mumford grasped this metaphor, including the library's place in it, long before Lancaster propounded the disembodiment of the library. In his *The City in History* (1961) Mumford discusses the "de-materialization, or etherealization" of urban institutions, resulting in the "invisible city." Mumford was commenting on the fact that many functions once confined within the boundaries of a specific city had been transformed through the availability of worldwide electronic transmission. The "visible city" is confined to those functions and encounters available on a personal basis. This visible city is surrounded by the vast impersonal network of the invisible city. He points to the power grid and communication systems as perfect technological examples of this dematerialization. But he also uses, as a parallel example in the cultural realm, the national interlibrary loan system in England. Mumford hoped for greater cooperation in many areas of social life extending from the remotest village to the largest city. In such "a well ordered world, there would be no limits, physical, cultural, or political, to such a system of cooperation; it would pass through geographic obstacles and national barriers as readily as x-rays pass through solid objects."[4] Today, of course, the power grid and communication systems and the interlibrary network are joined, making possible not only Mumford's Invisible City but, according to our myth-makers, the Invisible Library as well. What could be more appropriate than that the name of a widely used electronic networking system is Ethernet?

Futurist Hazel Henderson maintains that new lightware technology such as fiber optics, lasers, optical scanning and computing, and other light conversion technologies allow us to move "into the sunshine of the Age of Light."[5] The image becomes ever more effervescent!

Lancaster's disembodiment of the library reflects the impulse toward dematerialization as a metaphor for cultural change evident elsewhere. Writers and artists are often among the first to be sensitive to and explore the implications of social, economic, and technological change. The experiments of early modernists such as the cubists or James Joyce in dealing with time and space and the manipulation of text and language continue through the potential current use of hypertext poetry whereby words or phrases are linked through multiple layers or paths as a means of extending "our experience as process rather than experience."[6] This dematerialization is seen by political theorist Marshall Berman as the very essence of our modernist culture. For Berman, "to be modern is to be part of a universe in which, as Marx said 'all that is solid melts into air.' "[7] The dematerialization of the library can be seen, then, to be part of a more general modernist metaphor, the dematerialization of culture itself. The library becomes a series of electronic impulses that can be grasped only as measurable "bits." All that is solid about the library melts into air.

However, before embracing the dematerialization metaphor and the complete dissolving of the library, we should ask what we may lose by doing so. The electronic library myth-makers ignore an important aspect of the library as place: its appeal to the senses. A sense of place serves to elicit an emotional attachment to the library that, in addition to being a positive experience in itself, is also an effective means of ensuring support for the library as an institution. Let's start looking at the sensuous library by going inside.

When a teenager in St. Paul, Minnesota, with a compelling need to get out of the house I, like many other teenagers, would head downtown. One of the places where I hung out was the St. Paul Public Library. I remember various large reading rooms where you could sit at large wooden tables with shelves all around the walls and large windows overhead. The library had a pleasant feel to it. Others have had the experience and caught the feeling.

Annie Dillard evokes the library as place in her book, *An American Childhood*, when she describes the importance to her of the Homewood branch of the Pittsburgh Carnegie Library. It had engraved across "its enormous stone facade: FREE TO THE PEOPLE." In "an enormous silent room with marble floors" she discovered the nonfiction collection.

Beside the farthest wall, and under leaded windows set ten feet from the floor, so that no human being could ever see anything from them—next to the wall, and at the farthest remove from the idle librarians at their curved wooden counter, and from the oak bench where my mother waited in her camel's-hair coat chatting with the librarians or reading—stood the last and darkest and most obscure of the tall nonfiction stacks: NEGRO HISTORY and NATURAL HISTORY. It was in Natural History, in the cool darkness of a bottom shelf, that I found *The Field Book of Ponds and Streams*.[8]

For Dillard "this was the most private and obscure part of life, this Homewood Library: a vaulted marble edifice in a mostly decent Negro neighborhood, the silent stacks of which I plundered in deep concentration for many years."[9]

A *New Yorker* editor writes of the St. Agnes branch of the New York Public Library at Amsterdam Avenue and Eighty-first Street:

The people of the Upper West Side of Manhattan congregate here, at the end of the twentieth century. People of every age and race, mostly not too rich, cram together in a smallish room in order to read. Getting a seat at one of the venerable and sturdy oak tables is never easy. Elderly men look up from their newspapers to watch small children carefully climb the fine old staircase to the picture books. Frail old ladies move down aisles of mysteries and romance, pulling shopping carts behind them.[10]

Across the continent, on a hot California afternoon, poet Timothy Steele contemplates "The Library" where "Still, tracking books by way of data bases, I feel I'm playing Faustian video games." Intuiting the possibility of a paradigm shift to an electronic library, Steele asserts:

> I could construct a weighty paradigm:
> The Library as Mind. It's somehow truer
> To recollect details of closing time.
> Someone, at slotted folders on a viewer,
> Tucks microfiche squares in their resting places;
> Felt cloth's drawn over the exhibit cases;
> The jumbled New Book Shelves are set in shape;
> The day's last check-outs are thumped quickly through a
> Device which neutralizes tattle-tape.[11]

Two lovers of libraries, Susan Allen Toth and John Coughlan, compiled an extensive volume of passionate writings about libraries in their collection *Reading Rooms*. They state that "Many writers have noted the sensuous pleasure they felt then, and often still do, upon entering the library."[12] Such accounts should not be assigned to the realm of quaint nostalgia.

The impact of the spaces in which we live, work, and play is increasingly studied by social scientists. As a result of the work by such researchers as anthropologist Edward Hall and sociologist William H. Whyte we are far more aware that our "spatial experience is not just visual, but *multisensory*."[13] People enjoy variety, archaic design, congestion, noise, and "the sensory street."[14]

Although Carnegie libraries are often criticized as inadequate for modern library operations and seen as embarrassing relics of an earlier era in librarianship by those yearning for the electronic library, they have become, according to their historian, "part of Americana. Built largely in small towns across the nation, they are often loved and idolized by their communities."[15] Despite problems caused by high ceilings, grand entrances, and steep stairs leading to the entrance of these "temples of learning," efforts are being made from Seattle to Braddock, Pennsylvania (the first Carnegie library in the United States) to preserve and restore Carnegie libraries. This allegiance to the older library is not confined to the small town. The Carnegie Library of Pittsburgh was renovated to produce a functional library but in a way that maintains its "classical ambience" and "that doesn't allow staff or public to forget they are in a historic library."[16] The architects restored original color schemes to highlight arches, columns, and marble facings. Such sensory images and places have a texture that evokes memories and elicits emotion declaiming the library as place. The importance of a sense of place and the library's contribution to the preservation of that sense, and hence the preservation of the library as place, is deserving of careful consideration. In a fast-changing world lacking any coherence, there remains among people an abiding need for a sense of place.

A sense of place is existential. It is a combination of sacred and profane, perceptual and geographical, natural and built, cognitive and emotional. As Edward Relph notes:

Places are fusions of human and natural order and are the significant centres of our immediate experiences of the world. They are defined less by unique locations, landscape, and communities than by the focusing of experiences and intentions onto particular settings. Places are not abstractions or concepts, but are directly experienced phenomena of the lived-world and hence are full with meanings, with real objects, and with ongoing activities. They are important sources of individual and communal identity, and are often profound centres of human existence to which people have deep emotional and psychological ties.[17]

Tony Hiss, in his widely read book, *The Experience of Place*, has helped to popularize what Relph, Hall, and other social scientists have discovered and what most people experience in their daily lives. Hiss calls the full use of our senses to experience place "simultaneous perception," a consciousness that serves like a sixth sense.

With the help of this extra sense, the familiar hard-and-fast boundary between ourselves and our surroundings seems softened, expanding our sense of the space occupied by "here" and the time taken up by "now," and uncovering normally ignored patterns of relationships that make us part of larger groups and events. It's simultaneous perception that allows any of us a direct sense of continuing membership in our communities, and our regions, and the fellowship of all living creatures.[18]

Simultaneous perception connects us with places, allows us to feel a sense of place. Hiss suggests two criteria to apply to the experience of place: "Whether it provides richness of information reaching all the senses, and whether there is an absence of alarm signals."[19] The accounts cited above testify that libraries meet these two criteria without question. Both the physical attributes of the library and its contents stimulate the senses and the intellect while also providing a place apart.

> The sculpture garden has a recessed seat.
> I take it, thinking of the afternoon
> and of the library. Cultural oasis?[20]

The library as place has nurtured generations of users through an appeal to sentient feelings of loyalty, affection, safety, excitement, and awe. Librarians should not lose sight of the fact that places are important as loci for the exercise of simultaneous perception and social interaction. After spending sixteen years studying the social life of urban public places Whyte writes of the city:

More than ever, the center [of the city] is the place for news and gossip, for the creation of ideas, for marketing them and swapping them, for hatching deals, for starting parades. This is the stuff of the public life of the city—by no means wholly admirable, often abrasive, noisy, contentious, without apparent purpose.[21]

While some within librarianship decry the continual practice of cities to build large public libraries in central locations, isn't this where the library should be, where it can serve as both part of "the stuff of public life" and as an oasis within it? It is the tactile, the sensory, and the solidity of the library as place that makes it for so many people a special place. Hiss asserts we are only beginning to really understand "that particular places around us, if we're wide open to perceive them, can sometimes give us a mental lift," that there are places that "welcome experiencing."[22] For years librarians deplored the limitations of the thousands of extravagantly designed Carnegie libraries that were spread throughout the English-speaking world as a result of the philanthropy of Andrew Carnegie for a period of about thirty years, beginning in 1886. But people, the users of libraries, want them restored so they can again experience them as sensuous places. This experience of the library as place, combined with its external image, are critical elements of the ideology that propels the library as an important American institution. So let's move outside and give some consideration to the external image of the library.

Images reflect how a profession sees itself and how it wants others to see it. Librarians are obsessed with their image; therefore, the popular image of the library is also of great concern to librarians. They are aware that the image of the library influences the public's image of the librarian. Librarians become disturbed over the popular affection for the Peterborough and Boston public library images. For many librarians these images represent an almost ignoble, outdated nineteenth-century image of the library and librarianship. They want an image for the electronic age. This is not the first effort of librarians to promote a new image of librarianship through a new image of the library.

Many of us are probably unaware of the extent to which federal, state, and municipal governments have had an impact on the rural and urban landscape through the construction of canals, dams, highways, courthouses, capitals, military camps, signage, and many other projects. This process goes back to the founding of the country but was greatly accelerated during the New Deal of the 1930s. The design of public facilities was done with specific messages in mind, for example, to project an image of a "wise and caring government."[23] Many official buildings, including public libraries, followed a neo-classical design reflecting the Republic's roots in classical democracy. The greatest concentration of this imagery is, of course, in Washington, D.C., which draws many visitors seeking "the opportunity to gaze upon the sacred places and objects of Americanism, to join in a kind of nationalistic communion."[24] The image of the "wise and caring government" was spread throughout the nation perhaps most effectively with the ubiquitous federal post office building. The post office became a critical part of the identity of any community. After 1920, many post offices were built in a simplified neo-classical style that reflected the rational administrative efficiency favored by Progressive and, later, New Deal reformers.

When, in the 1930s, librarians became disenchanted with the Carnegie designs, they turned to the public architecture of the post office as an example to follow. In their landmark book on library planning, *The American Public Library Building*, published in 1941, Joseph Wheeler and Alfred Githens include an illustration of a 1902 design for a Carnegie Library showing the "pretentious display" of complicated rooflines, domes, elaborate ornamentation, classic columns, and a high flight of stairs. This style is contrasted with an illustration of an austere post office and accompanied by the question, "Why should a post office be more attractive than a library?" These library planners were convinced that "few public libraries are more inviting than the post office at Salem, Ore., with its simplicity and beautiful proportions."[25] Wheeler and Githens back up their argument with photographs of the Concord (New Hampshire) Public Library and the Toledo Public Library, both of which look like the Salem post office. (The influence of Wheeler and Githens extended beyond the U.S. border. I only need to go to the Halifax (Nova Scotia) City Regional Library to see a replica of a U.S. post office.)

We see in Wheeler's and Githens's admiration for public architecture a desire to project a more efficient and professional image of the library. They called for a "total departure from the buildings of the past," that gave the impression libraries "are aloof, unaware of what is going on in the world, unresponsive to current problems and demands." Wheeler and Githens accused these libraries of being "palaces for the learned, pretentious, withdrawn, dull, self-sufficient, making no appeal to the average passerby to come in." When compared to banks, post offices, and contemporary stores, they believed most libraries were "totally eclipsed in their architectural appeal to the people."[26] Trustees, civic leaders, and public officials had to realize that the library should not serve as a "refuge for the idle nor civic monument." Rather, it should be a center of activity adjacent to the banks, stores, and office buildings in the mainstream of traffic, an argument used fifty years later by Rawlinson in her *Library Journal* editorial advancing the virtues of the electronic library.[27] Quoting the utilitarian ALA motto, "The best books, for the greatest number, at the least cost," Wheeler and Githens wanted the new library to be as efficient and professional as any business or government bureaucratic operation. (Remember that people held the post office in much higher esteem in the 1930s and 1940s than they do today!)

I have suggested that the image of the library can reflect the desire for professional status of those responsible for its operation. However, this purpose may clash with the popular perception of the library. There were indications of this conflict with the planning of the new Chicago Public Library, the largest municipal library in the United States. After an intense international design competition, a post-modernist neo-classical design was selected. Librarians were upset by a design they saw as a return to the intimidating "cathedral of learning" stereotype characteristic of the monumental libraries of the nineteenth century. One prominent library consultant was disappointed "in how libraries and librarians were viewed" in the public debate. She felt the architectural design unfortunately favored the "romanticized versions of a sacred, silent place."[28] We discern here the voices of Wheeler and Githens; yet we are witnessing the renaissance of the Carnegie library and the building of a large urban library in the neo-classical style. Why is this so? People are rejecting the professional facade (and values) in favor of a return to a more emotive and flamboyant image. The Chicago Public Library and the restored Carnegie libraries have a sensuality that generates an emotional response not derived from professional, bureaucratic, rational instrumentalism. These buildings have what Kevin Lynch calls *"imageability*: that quality in a physical object which gives it a high probability of evoking a strong image in any given observer."[29] Lynch identifies Copley Square, Boston, as an area that is not especially "functional" but is "very sharply imaged," due to "its unique individual buildings: *the Public Library*, Trinity Church, the Copley Plaza Hotel, the sight of the John Hancock Building."[30] And so we are back to one of our initial images of the myth of the library as place, the Boston Public Library in Copley Square.

Some librarians do recognize the power of such images as a means of generating support for libraries. The image of a library that is most fixed in people's minds is that of the New York Public Library. Hiss recounts how many people have vivid experiences of place, such as "walking up Fifth Avenue in New York at Christmas time, dodging past roast-chestnut and hot-pretzel vendors, and catching a glimpse of the two stone lions in front of the Public Library, with fresh snow on their grey manes and big green wreaths around their necks."[31] A director of the New York Public Library, Richard de Gennaro, acknowledged the power of that image when stating:

We have a symbolic location in mid-town Manhattan with a landmark building. The marble building with the two lions out in front. That says "library" to millions of people when they see that image, and we use that image a lot, our lions and the facade of our building.

Symbolically, it's a very important thing. Of course, that same building gives us problems. It's not a flexible building, but as a symbol it's absolutely fantastic.[32]

The myth-makers of the electronic library are not unaware of the potency of the imagery surrounding the traditional library. A 1990 publication on *Campus Strategies for Libraries* includes chapters about the efforts of ten university libraries moving toward the electronic library.[33] Each chapter is preceded by a photograph. Seven out of ten photographs are of the interior or exterior of a library; only three photographs include any electronic equipment. The most intriguing is the photograph accompanying the chapter about the Carnegie-Mellon University Libraries, the institution most actively pursuing the goal of an electronic library. Yet its photograph is an interior shot of a pleasant library reading room with a student sitting at a carrel surrounded by plants and book stacks. Here there is no electronic imagery, only a marvelous picture of the library as place! Another example of the electronic library drawing on the myth of the library as place is the Pikes Peak Library District. This library system is often claimed to be a prototype of the electronic library. Still, its developers named its computer system "Maggie's Place," after the longtime head of their Technical Services, perhaps attempting to project an image of endearing humanism and geographic specificity, that is to say, a projection of the library as place.[34]

Myth-makers of the electronic library claim the physical library as place must go; nonetheless, they recognize the power of its imagery. But librarianship will lose much of its power if it abandons the substance and the image of the library as place, a point we will pursue in the succeeding chapters.

The Therapeutic Librarian

I hope we are not forced to disembody the library . . . either architec-
turally or intellectually merely for the sake of cost control or to aggran-
dize an information power base.

Dennis Trombatore

The social context of the myth of the electronic library is the Information
Society, a world view endorsed by the majority of librarians. This chapter
will pursue the idea that even if we accept as valid some of the elements
usually associated with the Information Society, it is enlightening to examine the role of the librarian in the context of an alternative depiction of
society: the therapeutic society. By looking at society as saturated with an
ethos promoting the objective of personal self-fulfillment founded on
secular therapeutic values, we get a radically different perspective of the
development and objectives of librarianship than that promoted by the
myth of the electronic library.

The dramatic social change of the nineteenth century called forth the
emergence of the personal service professions, including librarianship, that
adhered to the therapeutic idea of client self-sufficiency. In this role the
librarian is one among a number of "helping professions." This role can be
contrasted with another tendency within librarianship, one extended in the
myth of the electronic library: the desire to follow the model of the traditional professions, in particular, medicine. This latter model casts the
librarian in the role of an "information intermediary" who provides the
client the information he or she needs on a fee-for-service basis.

The myth-makers of the electronic library impress on us the rapidity and depth of change with which we must cope as if this were a new phenomenon. Perhaps every generation flatters itself by assuming that it, more than any other, is burdened with an ever-accelerating rate of change. However legitimate the claim that "future shock" is unique to the last half of the twentieth century, the trajectory, depth, and speed of change began well into the nineteenth century. Many of the technologies, social and cultural institutions, economic structures, and political values familiar to us are the product of dramatic change during the period between the Civil War and World War I, including the emergence of modern librarianship. Historian Samuel P. Hays has documented how, by 1914, "seldom, if ever, in American history had so much been altered within the lifetime of a single man."[1]

Sociologist Robert N. Bellah and his associates assert in their widely cited study of American life, *Habits of the Heart*, that "if all generations of Americans have had to confront 'future shock,' surely the turn-of-the-century generation faced the most severe challenge."[2]

This was the period in which there was the final break from a world view and social structure built on an intricate hierarchy and connectedness among humans, nature, and God. Each individual and class knew its place in a chain linking the lowest creature through a hierarchy reaching to God. This chain was broken, beginning in the eighteenth century, by an increasing individualism sparked by the American and French revolutions in conjunction with the Industrial Revolution. There was a general consciousness of a collapse of those ties or connections forged by family, religion, and communal association. The acute consciousness of this change is manifested in the emergence in the nineteenth century and early twentieth century of modern sociology.[3] Our conception and imagery of the Industrial Society, supposedly superseded by the Information Society, arise out of the work of sociologists who were attempting to grasp the nature and implications of the very change they were experiencing around them. Karl Marx, Ferdinand Tonnies, Emile Durkheim, Max Weber, and many others formulated most of the concepts—bureaucratization, secularization, industrialization, urbanization, professionalization, rationalization—that form the understanding of change in our own time. These social and economic changes were accompanied by severe religious and psychological adjustments. It was a time of profound moral change involving "a shift from a Protestant ethos of salvation through self-denial toward a therapeutic ethos stressing self-realization in the world—an ethos characterized by an almost obsessive concern with psychic and physical health defined in sweeping terms."[4]

As secularism replaced religion, the authority of the minister waned while that of the doctor increased. Thus, nowhere else was psychoanalysis so quickly and enthusiastically embraced than in the United States after Sigmund Freud's visit and lectures at Clark University in 1909. His lectures were an instant success that made him famous overnight.[5] After all, it was in America that the "pursuit of happiness" had been established as a natural right. Wrenching social change created a climate ripe for a psychological response providing relief for the anxieties generated by this change. People craved something to help them make sense of the rapidly changing world around them. Psychoanalysis provided a specific response scientifically based and, thus, serving as a primary element of the emerging therapeutic ethos. As one study of the role of psychoanalysis in America observes: "Because religious leaders had fewer answers and fewer followers, psychoanalysis, with its belief in personal autonomy and in the possibility of 'salvation' through individual initiative, was particularly suited to modern living."[6]

By the turn of the century, medicine became the professionalizing model for a host of psychologically and social science-based disciplines intent on providing advice and support for those seeking greater self-awareness and fulfillment. The rage for psychoanalysis reached its peak in the 1950s, but there were many alternative psychotherapies available and therapeutic strategies were embedded in many other professions. By the 1980s the prominent therapist Rollo May observed, "We live in an age of therapy. There is a kind of therapy to meet every kind of problem—over 300 kinds at the last count. There is not only psychological therapy; there are marriage therapists, sex therapists, voice therapists, and even therapists for your pets at home."[7]

There is no need to touch on these therapies except to note briefly the work of Carl R. Rogers (1902–1987). After Freud, Rogers has had a more profound impact on American culture than any other therapist. His formulation of non-directive client-centered therapy represented a fundamental shift from the medical model of patient/therapist relationship to a non-authoritarian client/therapist relationship. After Rogers, psychotherapy was no longer concerned alone with healing the sick. Indeed, its greatest area of interest became the analysis and fostering of the personal growth of the "normal" individual, which Rogers called "self-actualization." Rogers established the idea that the therapist must acknowledge the client as a peer; hence, the individual coming to the therapist is a client rather than a patient. He stressed that the potential for growth and better health resided in the client. It is the counselor's responsibility to provide a facilitative environment enabling the self-fulfillment of the client.[8] Rogers himself was awed by the extent to which his ideas became so pervasive in so many fields. Librarians joined those professionals who responded to the therapeutic ethos, especially as represented in the client-centered humanistic psychology of Carl Rogers.

The displacement beginning in the closing decades of the nineteenth century of religion by the new secular ministers of self-actualization is captured by Sarah Fine, library educator and practicing psychologist, when

she identified for librarians one of the characteristics of an effective counselor: "An understanding of some of the universal themes in human
existence, a recognition of the existential loneliness of the human condition
and the need to find some meaning in life. Counselling responds not only
to the intellectual and the emotional, but the spiritual existence of the
client."[9] As psychotherapy became the preeminent mode for initiating
personal change, it had for those concerned about maintaining the status
quo and social control the further attraction that it placed the problem
inside the individual. Thus, it also placed the responsibility for solving the
problem with the individual—with the assistance of a therapist. Reference
to economic or social causes as grounds for personal distress were not
recognized by most therapists. As individualism became a dominant cultural characteristic over the older religious communal configuration of
social life, the question of "How are we to be saved?" became a social
psychological question rather than a religious one.

This psychological saturation of American society has been noted by
numerous social scientists. In her comparative study of psychoanalysis in
several Western countries, sociologist Edith Kurzweil finds America, with
its vast array of therapies, the most prominent therapeutic society: "Even
though the classical Freudians have been reduced to an even smaller caste,
psychoanalytical ideas—if not directly then indirectly—have penetrated
every American hamlet and intellectual endeavor. And like Coca-Cola,
Ivory soap, and blue jeans, they have been marketed and accepted throughout the rest of the world."[10]

A major study of the inner life of Americans between 1957 and 1976 states
that the "shift toward a psychological orientation in our culture" represented the "dawning of a therapeutic age."[11] This shift stressing individual
self-fulfillment is further confirmed by Daniel Yankelovich in his study,
New Rules: Searching for Self-Fulfilment in a World Turned Upside Down.
According to Yankelovich we are witnessing a "search for a new American
philosophy of life" whose emphasis on self-fulfillment "is the leading edge
of a genuine cultural revolution."[12] His firm's studies over the years found
the vast majority of Americans spending much of their time dwelling on
their inner life. Consequently, "the rage for self-fulfilment . . . had now
spread to virtually the entire U.S. population."[13]

Bellah's *Habits of the Heart* devotes a chapter to examining how the
therapist has become a cultural mode of American life. He argues: "Today
we are likely to see not only our marriages but also our families, work,
community, and society in therapeutic terms. Now the 'interpersonal'
seems to be the key to much of life."[14]

The pervasiveness of the therapeutic ethos is manifest in a "community
of therapy consumers," that growing proportion of the population committed to therapy. While some are prepared to commit to the long-term
requirements of classical psychoanalysis, most prefer varying degrees of

brief therapy to cope with crises as they arise in life. These individuals possess a commitment to therapy as a means of personal growth. Further-more, they transfer their experience and knowledge of therapy to other spheres of their life.[15] Sociologist Philip Rieff has identified "psychological man" as the dominant character type of this therapeutic culture.[16] The moral philosopher, Alasdair MacIntyre, follows a similar line of thought in his proposal that the therapist and the manager are central twentieth-cen-tury social character types.[17]

Bellah builds on these ideas with his concept of "representative charac-ters." He defines a representative character as "a kind of symbol, . . . a way by which we can bring together in one concentrated image the way people in a given social environment organize and give meaning and direction to their lives."[18] A representative character serves as a model or image of the type of personality traits encouraged by a particular society. In the dynamic, rapidly expanding capitalistic industrialization of the nineteenth century, the entrepreneur or self-made man was such a representative character. In the twentieth century of bureaucratic rationalization, Bellah identifies the professional manager as a representative character. But in addition to the manager, Bellah identifies another character type: the therapist. The thera-pist, "Like the manager, . . . is a specialist in mobilizing resources for effective action, only here the resources are largely internal to the individual and the measure of effectiveness is the elusive criterion of personal satis-faction." It is Bellah's view " that "the manager and the therapist largely define the outlines of twentieth-century American culture."[19]

British sociologist Paul Halmos has also explored the social psychological implications of social change. In his view, which complements those of Rieff, MacIntyre, Bellah, and others, there has emerged a group of therapeutic or personal service professions that share a set of assumptions about human nature, as well as beliefs and moral precepts that underlie their theoretical and methodological propositions. He concludes that this set of beliefs and assumptions constitutes a "faith of the counsellors," an ideology that is client-oriented. Because of the central role of the professions in society, the counseling ideology is a pervasive social value.[20] Now, it strikes me that Bellah's concept of representative characters as expressed in the professional manager and the therapist, along with the concept of the personal service professionals, is very apt for considering the social context and role of the librarian. The librarian is both the professional bureaucratic manager and the therapist. Furthermore, librarians represent a new type of professional, representative of the twentieth-century therapeutic society. In contrast to the traditional professions of medicine and law, it is one of the personal service professions embodying a counseling ideology. How is this so?

A common, although increasingly discredited, approach to analyzing the professional status of a specific occupation is to compare it with attrib-utes derived from such traditionally acknowledged professions as medicine and law. With this approach occupations such as nursing, social work, teaching, and librarianship are relegated to the categories of either non-, semi-, or emerging professions. I contend that librarians need to recognize as personal service professionals that their occupational development, objectives, and methods differ from those of the older professions. These differences are not the result of professional immaturity but are inherent in librarianship as it has evolved (along with other personal service professions) to meet the cultural needs of a therapeutic society. Halmos makes a distinction between personal and impersonal service professionals. Personal service professionals attempt to change the body or personality of the client; physicians are personal service professionals. In contrast, engineers are impersonal professionals because they are concerned with the manipulation or creation of things. Other personal service professionals, according to Halmos, are nurses, clergy, teachers, and social workers.

The sociologists William S. Bennett, Jr. and Merl C. Hokenstad, Jr. make a further helpful distinction among the groups Halmos includes in his personal service category. They identify "people working professions" as those workers whose primary focus is the personalities of their clients.[21] People working professions include teachers, social workers, and mental health workers because their objective is to achieve a change in the behavior or development of the client. Those medical practitioners, such as surgeons, who concentrate primarily on parts of the body as objects or intellectual problems are outside of this category and more akin to the impersonal service professionals dealing with things. Librarians belong among those professions Bennett and Hokenstad identify as "people working professions" and, consequently, are fundamentally different from the more traditionally acknowledged impersonal professions.

We see more specifically what makes the personal service professions distinct, following Bennett and Hokenstad's criteria of people working professions, by considering further the client-professional relationship. In the older professions there is an authority relationship of the professional over the client based on the professional's monopoly of a specific body of knowledge and techniques. The doctor prescribes a solution to a client's problem to be accepted without question. (How many of us feel guilty about asking for a second opinion?) In contrast, personal service professionals "function as catalysts who, through the communication of information and sharing of insights, attempt to help the client help himself."[22] The personal service professional helps the client grow or change through their encounter so the client can handle the problem independently if encountered again; the client is expected to become self-sufficient. The work of these professionals

involves the transference of knowledge, not just the use of it. . . . In short, they can be said to idealize growth or change in the client, so that, if he does not become a carbon copy of the worker, he at least grows in some capacity, and most importantly is able to handle functionally similar situations (a family crisis, a need for information, a future economic problem) *on his own* without the help of the worker the second time around.[23]

This relationship is in marked contrast to impersonal service professionals who expect the client to return for further consultation for any recurring problem; the lawyer or engineer typically does not expect the client to become self-sufficient. (We recognize much of Carl Rogers' ideas embodied in the conceptualization of the personal service professionals.) It is in this respect—the sharing of knowledge with the client—that the therapist becomes the model for the personal service professional as well as for the client. Following the therapeutic model, other personal service professionals also serve as models for their clients. They are most interested in the transference of knowledge and skills to clients, thereby allowing the client to use this professional knowledge independent of the professional.

Librarianship is usually given a low score on professionalism because, critics assert, librarians do not prescribe solutions for the client in the way doctors or lawyers are perceived as doing. Librarians may guide clients but, critics note, it is the clients who determine their informational needs. Librarians are described as unassertive in dealing with clients, unwilling to strongly recommend specific sources or directions to library users, and incapable of taking the initiative by providing clients the information they need. Instead, the client is directed to a range of sources from which the client, based on his or her own judgment, extracts the required information.[24] Unfortunately, critics arrive at these assertions by using models based on the traditional professions and by failing to recognize that librarianship belongs with those occupations committed to client self-sufficiency.

This professional-client relationship relates closely to the concept of professional knowledge. The traditional models of professions recognize only one type of knowledge: scientific knowledge. The exclusive right to apply this knowledge is claimed as the basis for the profession's autonomy and for the practitioner's authority in prescribing solutions to the client's problems. Failure to develop a substantive body of scientific knowledge on which to base their practice is ascribed to many of the personal service professions, including librarianship. However, this is a narrow view of what constitutes knowledge; it excludes "intuitive knowledge, rule making knowledge (as in making rules, devising games, etc., not just knowing the rules), techniques of helping, and perhaps several other types."[25] Much of this type of professional knowledge can only be generated and learned through training and experience. Hence, one finds in the therapeutic literature much relating of case studies. Librarians have often been critical of their own body of literature as containing too much "how-we-do-it-good" material. Yet this type of experiential reporting is a legitimate characteristic of a personal service profession.

The skills of the practitioner are not as instrumental as those of the traditional professional. The methodology is to assist the professional by serving as a catalyst, aiming for a change in the client, rather than being directed toward the achievement of a specific goal external to the personal make-up of the individual. Consequently, the personal service professions achieve their authority not through the monopoly of a body of scientific knowledge but through their interpersonal skills and skills relevant to the transference of knowledge. Librarianship is a personal service profession reflecting a therapeutic ethos because it embodies the value of fostering client self-sufficiency and it has striven to develop a body of experientially based techniques formulated to promote that aim. However, the power of attraction of the traditional impersonal professions has been a countervailing, almost overwhelming tendency to construct librarianship as an impersonal profession, that is to say, through the objectification of the client and the effort to develop a body of scientifically based professional theory. Because of these contending concepts, we find throughout the history of modern librarianship an ambivalence about the role of the librarian. As the reference interview is the most explicit professional-client encounter, it is around that function that we identify traits of the personal service profession and of the contending impersonal service profession.

The idea of promoting user self-sufficiency is as old as modern librarianship itself. As with so much in this field, we go back to that historic year, 1876. Among other well-known noteworthy events, it was in that year that Samuel S. Green, librarian at the Worcester Free Public Library, published his pioneering article, "Personal Relations Between Librarians and Readers" in the *Library Journal*.[26] Green's article illustrates a personal-service orientation toward client self-sufficiency and is one of the earliest attempts to formulate guidelines and techniques revolving around the professional-client relationship. He does so, as would much later commentators, by focusing on the reference encounter.

Green urged librarians to teach library users to be independent. He also provided illustrations on how the librarian can be a sympathizing friend. Like the case studies so often reported in the early therapeutic literature, Green was attempting to muster empirical knowledge to assist the practitioner. Green describes the necessary qualifications of the librarian—courteous, sympathetic, cheerful, patient—and the way librarians should deal with the seeker of information, by showing a respect for reticence, by suppressing their own views on religion, philosophy, and other potentially controversial topics. As well, while in some instances the librarian may provide the information sought, she should strive to teach the user to be independent. Drawing on Rogerian therapeutic concepts, later librarians would look back to Green as one of the earliest, if not the earliest, advocate of "client-centered" professional service.[27]

The implementation of reference service provided an institutional framework for the client-professional relationship. However, there was the consistent problem commented on over the years: the difficulty of extracting from the seeker precisely what information he or she was seeking. It was soon recognized by everyone engaged in reference work that librarians often had to assist users in clearly delineating what information they really required. Although it was not until the 1940s that librarians began to speak about the "reference interview," increasing attention was given to the techniques needed to elicit from library users their real needs. This problem, of course, is common to other personal service professions, therapists in particular.

Like other personal service professionals, librarians were attempting to formulate a methodology focusing on the helping relationship between client and professional. They were beginning the process of developing a body of professional knowledge that includes those qualities identified by Bennett and Hokenstad: "intuitive knowledge, rule making knowledge, . . . techniques of helping."

James Wyer, in his 1930 classic text, *Reference Work: A Textbook for Students of Library Work and Librarians*, discusses library "mind reading," the ability "to know how to give people what they do not know they want."[28] The "inquirer" must be approached, according to Wyer, by a librarian displaying evidence of a "reassuring psychology" and "a sympathetic manner."[29] Wyer disclaims any intention to outline a "contact technique," but does acknowledge that it would be possible to do so with "psychologic minuteness as similar contacts in salesmanship or welfare work." Despite this disclaimer, he does go on to discuss "a distinct process of interrogation or elucidation" that he calls, admittedly too forbiddingly, "cross-examination."[30]

While librarians were formulating a body of knowledge out of their direct experience, in the 1930s they also began to draw on other personal service professions such as psychology and counseling. In doing so they began to give more attention to the interpersonal objectives of the reference interview. The development of readers advisory services further encouraged this tendency. Alice I. Bryan, a consulting psychologist, taught a course at the Columbia University School of Library Service in 1939 on the psychology of the reader. She stressed the importance of having an understanding of the motivations, emotional needs, and background of individual library users before the librarian could provide effective readers guidance. Bryan was writing at a time—after ten years of economic depression and the threat of worldwide war—when many were advocating social and economic change through political action as opposed to individual adjustment or initiative. However, she argued that individual guidance of all types was needed more than ever to assist people in understanding the problems facing the world, to counter destructive propaganda, and "to help the individual to retain his emotional and intellectual balance while values and standards shift, change, and disappear." In this environment it was crucial for librarians to "approach the individual from a psychological point of view."[31] Bryan presented several of her own case studies of ways that individuals could be helped and concluded that the ideal person to be a readers adviser was someone who combined the abilities of both librarian and psychologist. She urged library schools to include a course on psychological adjustment, public libraries to have consulting psychologists on their staff, and greater cooperation between the library and psychology professions.

Bryan actively pursued this latter goal as co-chair of a joint committee, established in 1939, by the American Library Association and the Association for Applied Psychology. The other co-chair, prominent librarian Ernestine Rose of the New York Public Library, later advocated more training and experience for librarians in the fields of psychology and sociology in her book, *The Public Library in American Life*.[32] The outbreak of the war impeded any substantial accomplishments by the committee and it ceased to exist in 1945. Nevertheless, it was indicative of the empathy between librarianship and other counseling professions.

It was in the midst of World War II that the American Library Association, the publisher of Wyer's text, published another important work on reference service. In 1944, Margaret Hutchins' *Introduction to Reference Work* appeared.[33] Hutchins' book is noteworthy for the entire chapter she devoted to the "reference interview," a phrase she established firmly in library jargon through the long-standing popularity of her text. Hutchins insisted on the importance of the interpersonal relationship in the process of assisting the library user. Success in this process depends, she said, on maintaining a balanced relationship between two personal factors (the inquirer and the reference librarian) and two impersonal factors (the reference materials and the question). The relationships among librarian, question, and materials, or inquirer, question, and materials consist of both personal and impersonal factors. If any one of these factors does not get sufficient attention, the interview process will be flawed.

According to Hutchins, too much emphasis was often given to the impersonal factors by librarians. Reference courses, for example, gave students the incorrect idea that reference work was primarily a technical process unconnected to the social objectives of the library. Focusing on the many largely impersonal "ready-reference" questions typically encountered in the library leaves librarians with little feeling for the need to establish a rapport with the individual being assisted. For Hutchins, the personal relationship between the inquirer and the librarian was basic. The librarian must not only be physically accessible but provide easy intellectual and spiritual access by showing a personal interest in the individual. Drawing on interviewing techniques of psychologists, Hutchins pointed out the need to devote sufficient time to the inquirer. This could often be difficult because, unlike the conditions that are available to the psychologist, the librarian had little opportunity to find anything out about the inquirer, limited time to assist, little or no privacy, and constraints imposed by the physical arrangement of the reference room or collections. Hutchins provided a number of case studies followed by the advice that librarians maintain a friendly interest in the inquirer, talk the language of the inquirer, listen carefully, and put themselves in the inquirer's place.

It was apparent to others that librarianship could learn from the experience of other personal service professions. Perhaps the most explicit practical effort at the time to link librarianship with other personal service professions was David Maxfield's initiative at the University of Illinois, Chicago Undergraduate Division, where he established in the library in 1951 a Department of Instruction and Advisement staffed by "counselor librarians."[34] It is instructive to examine this initiative as an illustration of the therapeutic or counseling ethos in library service.

The Chicago Undergraduate Division of the University of Illinois (UIC) was established in 1946. By 1949, the library decided to improve the effectiveness of its services by replacing its Reference Department with a new entity called the Department of Library Instruction and Advisement. This change, according to Maxfield, the head of the library, was based on four factors: the adoption at UIC of the philosophy of the general education movement; the need for the library to respond to this movement through a more active library instruction program; an awareness of the activities of the UIC Student Counseling Bureau and the potential of a library-bureau collaboration; a critical questioning of the limitations of the library's traditional approach to the provision of reference service. Maxfield and his staff concluded that by drawing on the resources of the Student Counseling Bureau, it was possible to combine specialized counseling skills with library skills. The objective was to aid the student in "understanding and developing . . . personal and social responsibilities, along with his intellectual aptitudes" to allow the student to formulate for himself appropriate standards and values, to solve his own problems, and to contribute to a democratic way of life. The specific objective derived from the counseling factor was the now-familiar one of getting the individual "to do *for himself* in relation to his personal goals, values, plans, beliefs, feelings, and the objective facts of his own past and present situations."[35]

Maxfield identified five levels of psychological counseling and their appropriateness to the library setting. The first level was the straightforward answering of relatively simple questions. These can often be answered by almost any library staff member. The second level was "advisement," which in the library may involve, for example, a readers adviser or reference librarian recommending certain titles or a bibliographic technique. It is at the third level that much of the work of the counselor librarian resides; there is a more sophisticated process of defining the informational needs of the user and providing assistance in problem solving. The fourth level, clinical counseling undertaken by trained psychologists, has no analogy in librarianship. Among those counseled at this level are individuals referred by third-level counselors. The fifth level also has little parallel to the counselor librarian as it consists of extensive psychiatric consultation, often in a clinical or hospital environment.

Maxfield argued that counseling, especially at the third level, was close to much of the reference and readers advisory work offered in many types of libraries. Still, due to the lack of training either in library schools or on the job, there was a need to equip librarians with the skills necessary to be an effective counselor librarian. This was done at UIC through the preparation of job descriptions, the determination of relevant qualifications, and the provision of an extensive preservice and in-service training program by the Student Counseling Bureau. A counselor librarian was defined as:

A rigorously selected, trained and experienced librarian, with special personality and job qualifications including reference, teaching, and group discussion leadership ability, who, through a carefully planned in-service counsellor training program that he undergoes, is able to:

1. Perform conventional reference, library instruction, and readers advisory work in new perspective, and with unusual effectiveness, through application of modern personnel philosophy and procedures;

2. Serve as a trained counsellor, adviser, and group guidance leader at the part-time, sub-clinical level; and

3. Give library assistance to clients of post-graduate clinical counselors, or make suitable referrals, as appropriate on occasion.[36]

As an example of the therapeutic ethos of reference work, Maxfield stressed the educational and psychological aspects of the counselor librarian. He pointed to the serious limitations of conventional college reference service and urged librarianship to "give more careful attention the student *as an individual person.*"[37] When reporting on the UIC effort, he provided considerable background material drawn from counseling, applied psychology, and the student personnel movement, all of which reinforced the therapeutic objective of promoting both the student's intellectual and personal growth. Among the first librarians (but by no means the last) to draw attention to the client-centered ideas of Carl Rogers, he advocated the Rogerian non-directive approach to counseling. As if anticipating those who would concentrate on the reference encounter as an impersonal information-seeking process alone, Maxfield countered that "the major emphasis in counseling . . . is not upon any information that is to be imparted, but upon aiding the individual toward self-motivation and self-decision: that is to say, it is developmental in character."[38]

After three years' experience, Maxfield reported that the response from students and faculty to the shift from reference to counseling was excellent. He believed the UIC experience was applicable to other libraries and claimed it was time for librarians, library administrators, library schools, and library associations to pursue the possibilities of an increased use of applied psychology in librarianship.

Maxfield's and earlier librarians' efforts illustrate the therapeutic ethos in librarianship but there was a contending perspective, one reflecting a desire to move librarianship toward the impersonal professional model. This impulse toward a science-based discipline was not concerned with client self-sufficiency or growth. Instead, it focused on providing the information the user desired rather than instilling an ability to search it out independently. By the 1930s leading librarians began to promote this idea with increasing vigor. What was emerging within librarianship has been characterized as the "information versus instruction" debate. The role of the librarian as information intermediary, a core element of the myth of the electronic library, became increasingly evident.

The Intermediary Librarian

Librarians, particularly reference librarians, must seize the initiative and boldly launch out in new directions.
                              Thomas T. Suprenant and Claudia Perry-Holmes

In the debate on information versus instruction, "the information side argues that it is the role of the reference librarian to concentrate practice on the delivery of information extracted from the source in which the information is found in as complete and digested a manner as possible—in short, 'question answering.' " Supporters of this position believe it less than true professional service to teach users to find information for themselves. However, according to Brian Nielsen, "the instruction side argues that an appropriate and desirable reference activity, though not the sole activity, is to help users by teaching them how to find answers for themselves. A key element of the instruction side of the debate is the advocacy of self-reliance."[1] As variations of these positions were elaborated over the years, at least three distinct approaches emerged. The instructional approach places a responsibility on the reference librarian to teach the user to become self-sufficient. This approach arises out of the therapeutic ethos in librarianship. The informational approach says the reference librarian's job is to get the information wanted by the user. This is the stream favored by the myth-makers of the electronic library.

A third position is described as "situational." According to this position, "as personnel and materials become increasingly expensive, the reference librarian cannot and should not provide complete service but should exercise his professional judgment in providing information to some and instruction to others."[2] In short, the service offered will depend on the situation or environment in a particular library at a particular time. This is the position that prevails in most libraries. Others have characterized these distinctions as conservative, liberal, and moderate,[3] or minimum, maximum, and middling.[4]

Advocates of the provision of information have attracted those librarians especially avid to achieve the professional status of the traditional impersonal professions. To them, the librarian as information intermediary appears most like the client-dependency role of the impersonal professional practitioner. The advent of on-line bibliographic searching gave this contention additional substance. Now, a high-profile technology veiled in mystery is available with the potential of increasing client dependency on the librarian. The ability to quantify the time spent on the task, as measured by the computer, and to relate that time to fees for service, further reinforced the analogy to the traditional impersonal professions. The contention that librarians should provide the information needed combined with the availability of on-line search technologies in the 1970s fitted nicely with the desire of the electronic library myth-makers to promote the role of the librarian as an information broker. The perpetual anxiety among librarians over their professional status and image provided fertile soil for the growth of the idea of the information professional as intermediary. Furthermore, the striving to provide a scientific foundation to the discipline, to convert librarianship into a "hard" discipline of information science, further perpetuated the model of the impersonal profession. As part of this initiative, the client was objectified as one variable in the communication process. Maxfield's account of the UIC experience with counselor librarianship is a vivid example of a methodology imbued with a therapeutic ethos promoting individual self-sufficiency and growth. However, it was not long before an equally vivid example emerged of the impersonal impulse, that is, a methodology focusing primarily on the technique of the reference interview, to be studied objectively as a communication process concerned solely with connecting information and information seeker.

Robert S. Taylor, one of our most prominent myth-makers, is also one of the earliest and most influential representatives of this impersonal approach. When Taylor turned his attention to the interview technique in an article in 1962, "The Process of Asking Questions," and, more fully, in 1968, "Question-Negotiation and Information Seeking in Libraries," we encounter a perspective and language entirely different from Maxfield's.[5] There is no discussion here of counseling, self-development, or other therapeutic concepts. We are now clearly in the domain of the impersonal professional approach to reference work, couched in the rhetoric of the emerging myth of the electronic library. In the early 1960s, we began to see a greater divergence of values and strategies emerging between the therapeutic ethos and the intermediary approach.

Maxfield attempted to bring together the reference encounter and library instruction within a theoretical framework promoting client self-sufficiency as a whole person, drawing for his ideas on counseling methodologies and ideas. Taylor shifted the focus of the reference interview away from that encounter as a helping one in a counseling sense, thereby placing it in the context of the communication process and drawing on the work of Claude Shannon and his cohorts. This shift led to a line of investigation and thought that remains active today: the analysis of the reference process as an impersonal professional encounter. This stream of investigation would, like Maxfield, draw on psychological and counseling methodology. But the focus was on the techniques of counseling in the context of the reference interview as a communication problem, rather than on the goal of counseling as a client-centered helping encounter.

Taylor's early writings were a result, like so much of the research at the time, of studies conducted for the military. As director of the Lehigh University Center for Information Sciences, he was working for the Air Force on the "ManSystem Interface in Libraries." In his ground-breaking efforts to analyze the interview process, Taylor was not concerned in the least about the personal development of the library user. He was trying to understand the communication functions of libraries because, he emphasized, *"this is what libraries are all about."*[6] Thus, Taylor turned to communications, not psychological, theory for his model. Taylor was among those who believed that "we are leaving the era of Gutenberg and entering the era of Shannon, in which information is dependent on a basic unit that offers the illusion of certainty through the probabilistic reading that is taken from the digital bit stream—the totality of digital knowledge, reduced to the dots and dashes of the computer."[7] In the communications model, the library user and information are objectified, observable variables in the communication process. There is no use by Taylor of fuzzy concepts from the therapeutic vocabulary. Instead, he discusses "noise" in the communication process, levels of questions to which he gives pseudo-scientific labels (Q1, Q2, Q3, Q4), schematic representations of the communication process, flow charts of decision points encountered by the information seeker, and filters through which questions must pass.

Taylor does not ignore the inquirer; he stresses the need to understand her motivation and background. However, this information is not required as a means to assist the librarian in helping the inquirer to help herself. It must be known to understand the context of question negotiation so as to minimize the amount of noise in the system. Taylor hoped further analysis of this process would help librarians understand their emerging role as intermediaries between inquirers and information systems. Characterizing traditional librarians as "wholesalers" of information and libraries as "warehouses (however grand the Gothic windows or beautiful the new carpet)," he wanted librarians to become "retailers" in an "urban technico-scientific culture."[8]

Since Taylor there has been over the past two decades a continuous effort to explore the issues and extend the models he posed. Much of this effort can be charted in the work appearing in the American Library Association Reference and Adult Services Division's official publication, *RQ*. Between 1968 and 1991, at least twenty-five articles dealt with the reference interview as a communication process. Over half of these cited Taylor's 1968 article on question negotiation. Responding to the desire to develop a body of objective knowledge characteristic of the impersonal professions, there emerged in this literature an expression of the need to develop a theory of reference free from the empirical personal professional approach of the early writers on reference work.

A leading exponent of the call for a reference service based on communication theory was Bernard Vavrek of the University of Pittsburgh. Like Taylor, Vavrek maintained that communication was the common denominator of librarianship. The study of reference should not be reference books, the traditional library school approach, but rather, the dynamics of interpersonal communication. He believed Taylor's comment that communication is what libraries are all about was the "quintessential" statement about libraries. In Vavrek we find clear evidence of the effort to formulate a scientific theory of reference when he offers his own formula as a model of the reference process, designating "A" as the source of an inquiry, "B" as the reference librarian, and "X" as the message.[9] Others followed with further efforts to build a theoretical foundation for reference. Challenged by Vavrek, Helen Gothberg, a specialist in speech communication, examined communication patterns in the reference process.[10]

Researchers soon attempted to break down and analyze the interview process itself. These efforts often resulted in elaborate flow charts and detailed lists enumerating each step in the encounter between librarian and inquirer. Extending Vavrek's formula to recognize the role of feedback in the process, and citing Taylor, Shannon, and many others, elaborate diagrams of the reference process were refined.[11] Others concentrated on the nature of reference questions by examining open and closed questions and the entire question-handling process.[12] Closely related to these efforts were the numerous attempts to explore the interpersonal aspects of the reference interview. These researchers called on not only communications theory, but also the findings of the behavioral sciences, counseling in particular. However, their approach differed from that of Maxfield. They were interested in counseling methodology relating specifically to the techniques of the reference interview rather than as a philosophy of helping.[13] Research in this area included such aspects of the communication process as non-verbal behavior.[14]

Every aspect of the reference interview was scrutinized as librarians continued their efforts to build a theory of reference. The cognitive style of librarians was explored as well as the need to consider the intercultural differences between librarians and library users.[15] The question of user satisfaction and the evaluation of the reference process received increased attention.[16]

The above review was based on one journal alone. Similar writings appeared in many other journals and books.[17] Perhaps likening themselves to theoretical physicists, some hoped to bring much of this research into one "unified theory." Particularly prominent in this effort was Patrick R. Penland, a professor at the University of Pittsburgh Graduate School of Library and Information Sciences. In the late 1960s and early 1970s, Penland was involved with the Program of Research in Library Communication at Pittsburgh. Under his editorship a series of publications promoted Penland's own concept of counselor librarianship, an amalgam of ideas drawn from counseling and communication theory. Penland's texts drew on the work of Claude Shannon and Carl Rogers, of Marshall McLuhan and Norbert Wiener, of Robert Taylor and David Maxfield.

Penland, a colleague of Vavrek's at Pittsburgh, was among those calling for a general theory grounded in science that could serve as a foundation for library and information science. As for others, communication theory provided that source. He attempted to further enhance communication theory by drawing on recent developments in cybernetics and systems theory in the hope of formulating his unified theory. Penland and others searched for this theory in a series of texts published in a *Communication Science and Technology Series* that explored communication and systems theory, non-verbal communication processes, interviewing techniques, group dynamics, and community psychology.

Starting with a consideration of the traditional readers advisory service, Penland's thinking moved into the concept of counseling. He was impressed by Maxfield's efforts at UIC and often used the phrase "counseling librarianship," and gave greater emphasis to the interpersonal behavioral aspects of communication, in contrast to Taylor, who represented, in Penland's view, "the flow-chart school of reference or retrieval service."[18] Nevertheless, although he acknowledged that counseling aimed at self-development had an important role to play in the communication process, the general thrust of his thinking favored an impersonal professional approach, through its elaboration of communication techniques supported by numerous esoteric tables, diagrams, and flow charts.

I wish one could say that Penland and his colleagues successfully merged the personal therapeutic ideas of Maxfield with the impersonal systems approach of Taylor. Unfortunately, Penland's efforts to meld various currents of thought in a unified theory attracting librarians and information scientists at the time were hindered by his own failure to communicate a coherent theory with any clarity. The texts are weighted with an opaque prose sometimes impossible to penetrate. It is bewildering to read, for example, that "the function of the librarian counselor is to hypothesize about the unspoken concerns of the patron and to vocalize about the intellectual content of what is said as well as the feeling tones which are conveyed."[19] The result is a hodgepodge of theory, concepts, and jargon. As one reviewer of five volumes in the *Communication Science and Technology Series* correctly observed: "While all five propose to improve communications processes, issues are often beclouded with inscrutable jargon. While all assert the primacy of self-actualization and social progress, people are often described in strictly mechanistic terms."[20]

The Pittsburgh material illustrates an almost pathetic desire to assume the scientific trappings of the impersonal professions. Unfortunately, other examples also exist. Thus we find this effort to translate a Shannon-like model to the library:

Reader, Mr. A is a communication source, he has a purpose or need in producing a message. His central nervous system orders his speech mechanism to construct a message to explain his purpose and the speech mechanism acts as an encoder producing the message; "May I see a copy of yesterday's *Times*?" The message is transmitted by sound waves (the channel) so that assistant Miss B can receive it. Miss B's hearing mechanism decodes the message into nervous impulses, sending them to the nervous system which responds with the message and complies (hopefully) with the request.[21]

This represents a further desperate attempt at "scientific" theory building in librarianship.

The search for a scientifically based unified theory continued. For example, the spring 1983 issue of the *Drexel Library Quarterly*[22] included essays dealing with the meaning and use of theory, provided another attempt to develop a model of the reference process, and examined the role of communication theory in the reference interview, all with appropriate reference to Taylor, Vavrek, Shannon, and others. This ongoing research is further incorporated and codified into the knowledge base of librarianship through successive editions of William A. Katz's widely used textbook, *Introduction to Reference Work*.[23] Katz, a professor at the School of Library and Information Science, State University of New York at Albany, has provided regular revised editions of his text since it was first published in 1969. It includes a discussion on the Information Age, formal and informal patterns of communication, and the reference interview and search process.

The intermediary role in the context of the impersonal professions is easily conjoined with the myth of the electronic library. Thomas T. Suprenant and Claudia Perry-Holmes, of the Graduate School of Library and Information Studies at Queens College, New York, and the University of Rhode Island, respectively, argue that librarianship is at a critical juncture, a point at which librarians have an opportunity to become active players in the technological information society.[24] If librarians do not seize the initiative and step into the "information stream," others will quickly fill the role of information specialists. They accuse librarians of resisting change out of a fear of becoming "technological junkies." Librarians must take advantage of the opportunities offered by information technology and change many of their long-held values. The library must be transformed into an "information-switching mechanism" in which the reference librarian will carry out a critical role and the format of the material will become less important than the "provision of information." Librarians must move to "service-point offices" outside of the library. Where they work will be "virtually irrelevant," as they will be attached electronically to a host library.

In looking at the specific role of the librarian, Suprenant and Perry-Holmes draw on the popular perception of the traditional impersonal professions. Itinerant librarians will go directly to clients, with whom they will establish the relationship one finds between client and physician. The salary of the professional will come directly from fees paid for services, a percentage of which will go to the library to support central services. The more expert the librarian and the higher the level of service, the higher will be the salary. Like doctors in family practice, more difficult cases will be referred to other appropriate information experts. As have many in the past, they warn that "if librarians do not seize this initiative, there are profit-orientated entrepreneurs who will be anxious to skim the cream off the information market and reap the rewards."[25]

By now we easily recognize in Suprenant and Perry-Holmes' scenario the rhetoric of the myth of the electronic library: the accusation that librarians are conservative, the threat of extinction or the promise of rewarding opportunities; the focus on access over collections; the emphasis on information over knowledge; the endorsement of the market economy for the allocation of services (they propose an "information stamp" for those who can't pay); the transformation of the reference librarian into a freelance entrepreneur; the abandonment of the library as place. The specific role of the electronic librarian is that of an intermediary providing access to information through the use of sophisticated technology for a fee, a role that promises greater material rewards and higher professional status.

Because the myth of the electronic library emerged out of the special or research library environment, it is there that we find the most ready acceptance of the intermediary information specialist. From the beginning of the special library movement in the early decades of the twentieth century, the view strongly held by special librarians was that they were a distinct type of reference librarian. As early as 1915, Ethel Johnson provided a distinction that hints at both the myth of the library as place and of the electronic library. Referring to the special library, she observed that "before everything else, it is an information bureau. The main function of the general library is to make books available. The function of the special library is to make information available."[26] Many academic librarians would now agree with Johnson. In contrast to public librarians, who have always favored the educative role of the library, academic librarians are moving closer to special librarians in their focus on access to information and knowledge. Academic reference librarians are urged to abandon the hopeless task of trying to teach clients the skills needed to find information on their own. Such an objective is seen as "yet another well-intentioned, but self-defeating move" that will only leave the impression with clients that libraries are easy to use and leads to the fear librarians constantly harbor that they will be held in low esteem.[27] Librarians, according to these advocates of the information intermediary, are not teachers; rather, they must recognize that they are in the information business and give up their pursuit of the windmills of bibliographic instruction.[28]

But while the desire to amass a body of objective knowledge as a foundation for a reference theory proceeds in the hope of fostering the role of the librarian as an intermediary, librarians also continue to formulate the rule making, intuitive knowledge, and techniques characteristic of the personal service professions. For example, we find in one study based on empirical evidence provided by practicing librarians the proposal of rules for identifying the subject and purpose of reference queries.[29] In another instance, Patrick Wilson, a widely read professor from the School of Library and Information Studies, University of California-Berkeley, acknowledges a need for rules regarding the reference interview. He argues that a rule is "not simply a technical matter but essentially reflects, and partially defines, the professional character of librarianship." While he warns against rules so strict that they become routine (that is, non-professional), he suggests, "A defensible rule of thumb . . . will do very nicely."[30]

While Katz draws heavily on library communications research of the past twenty years, his text also recognizes that there remains much of value derived from the cumulated experience of practitioners. He observes, "Over the years different reference librarians, through experience more than through scientific analysis or theoretical considerations, have compiled useful approaches to searching." He proceeds to provide a number of "Rules of the Game."[31]

The authors of another recent text conclude that despite the extensive amount of scholarly work accomplished, the reference interview must still be seen as a creative act. Elaine and Edward Jennerich recognize that much valuable research has been accomplished over the years on the reference interview and, inspired by Patrick Penland, have themselves applied micro-counseling skills to the analysis and teaching of the reference interview. However, it is their conclusion that "reference work in general is a creative act and that the reference interview in particular is a performing art."[32] As the Jenneriches and others illustrate, it is the nature of the personal service professions that their work will have a large creative element and that their body of knowledge is indeed more intuitive and experientially based than that of the impersonal professions.

The personal profession's impulse to promote the more general self-development of the client also has not been extinguished by the drive for an impersonal professionalism. A librarian and a psychologist, Judith Powell and Robert LeLieuvre, borrow from humanistic education and psychology in an effort to demythologize librarianship. They advocate the sharing of professional knowledge in order to promote increasing self-awareness, to develop feelings of self-worth, to enhance thinking and problem-solving abilities, to encourage creativity, and to assist in the exploration and choice of values. To emphasize the client-oriented thrust of their argument, they titled their book *Peoplework*. Like many others, they see the work of librarians as a problem in communications, but they believe that much training in this area has been too cognitively based. Referring to Carl Rogers, they suggest the need for librarians to have an understanding of a humanistic communication that allows them to be "positive forces for understanding and for learning."[33]

How can we characterize the current situation? It is one of profound ambiguity. There remain the attempts to draw on communications and general systems theory as a means of providing a theoretical framework encompassing communication, information, and library studies.[34] And at least one library school, observing the closing of other schools, declining enrollment, and the impact of electronic technology, has found a haven in joining with the disciplines of communications, journalism, information science, and mass media to form at Rutgers University a School of Communication, Information, and Library Studies.[35] However, a scientifically based body of reference theory that would reward librarianship with the status assigned to the impersonal professions has not been achieved. Meanwhile, those coming from the special library field continue to promote the concept of information intermediary over client self-sufficiency. One of the most prominent is Herbert S. White, former dean of the School of Library and Information Science of Indiana University, who has a distinguished career in special librarianship and is one of the most prolific and provocative authors in librarianship. White urges librarians to de-emphasize an outmoded narrow educational tradition of librarianship and to choose service values characteristic of the corporate information center.[36] White faults innocent librarians for their "continued abduction of our role as information intermediaries in favor of the lesser role of trainers of tricks and memoric aids." He anticipates greater professional status for librarians when they are recognized as "information empowerment specialists."[37]

And so librarianship's commitment to client self-sufficiency remains ambiguous. The instruction versus information debate remains unresolved. The bibliographic instruction movement has focused on promoting information literacy within the context of an information society rather than in the context of a helping profession. The prominent academic librarian Anita Schiller speaking strongly for the intermediary side of the debate in 1965, concluded by 1980 that there was little to debate as "instruction and information become less distinguishable from one another, as instruction takes on some of the characteristics that may be associated with maximum, rather than minimum, service."[38] Brian Nielsen, another academic librarian who has given much thought to the role of the reference librarian, foresees a new role for the librarian emerging out of the bibliographic instruction movement and technological innovation. The teacher and information provider will merge, he believes, into a consultant on information-management technologies.[39]

Mary Ellen Larson, an instructional specialist with the Penn State University Library, also seeks a middle route. She sees the need and possibility of maintaining traditional reference objectives while taking advantage of technological developments. She maintains the hope that the emergence of the electronic library will strengthen the best aspects of the traditional reference model. With the lowering of geographic barriers in the electronic environment, librarians can share to a greater extent than previously the control of the information environment. Larson believes the status of librarians will be enhanced by a model of reference service "where the librarian shares knowledge with the user, acting as a teacher and advisor (much like the first reference librarians of a century ago) rather than a purveyor of books or information."[40] In this way, librarians will "empower" library users with self-sufficiency.

Perhaps Elaine Jennerich describes the situation of most librarians. On the philosophical question of whether reference service is a helping encounter or one devoted to the provision of information, she maintains that most librarians "run down the middle. We believe ourselves to be more than mere purveyors of information, but we are uncomfortable in the role of counselor, social worker, or confessor."[41] Rather than choosing either position, she concludes that the reference interview is a professional encounter unique to librarianship. In other words, we find ourselves back to the triad identified earlier by Wyer, Rothstein, and others.

While the situation is certainly unclear, it is possible to formulate a role for librarians within the framework provided by the concept of the personal service professions. However, before doing so it is first necessary to look at the institutional context of librarianship, in the next chapter. That, in turn, leads to a consideration in Chapter 9 of the political aspects of librarianship. We will then be able to return to the question of the role of the librarian.

The Librarian and the Library

Libraries cannot exist without librarians and librarians cannot exist
without libraries.

Richard De Gennaro

The role of the librarian has been inextricably linked with the institution of
the library. The myth-makers see this link as an unfortunate heritage to be
decisively rejected. They offer the vision of an autonomous information
broker connected to an electronic network. But what are librarians giving
up if (with apologies to Gertrude Stein) there is, with the electronic library,
no there there? I believe librarians, by too eagerly promoting the image of
the dematerialization of the library, are not only treading into an area of
such abstraction that their clients will have difficulty grasping the role of
the librarian, but, as well, risk forfeiting an institutional base that is crucial
to any hope that librarians can have of maintaining or increasing their
professional status. The myth-makers' turn to communication theory and
its narrow interpretation of information has a further potentially deleteri-
ous effect in that it denigrates the role of the library vis-à-vis other "information handling" units such as the computer center. It is worth giving
consideration to the relationship between librarians and the library, specifically the library as a bureaucracy, and the relationship between libraries
and computing.

Prior to any thought of electronic libraries, there was an active anti-li-
brary as bureaucracy strain of thought within librarianship. The general
sociological literature has promulgated the idea that there is an inherent
contradiction between professionalism and bureaucracy, a view favored

among librarians eager for enhanced professional status. The rules, regulations, and hierarchy of bureaucratic authority are considered constraints
on professional autonomy and inflexible barriers separating professional
and client.[1] It is claimed that as libraries get larger and more bureaucratic,
there is increased rigidity in the application of policy, growing alienation
between the organization and those it is designed to serve, and a decline in
the commitment of those providing the service. Critics assert that librarians, constrained by organizational regulations and bureaucratic specialization, have little opportunity to plan and control their own workload, that
their direct contact with clients is limited and fragmented, and that many
of their tasks are easily routinized, if not clerical in nature.[2] Bureaucratic
values of efficiency tend, according to this analysis, to displace professional
values of service. Furthermore, it is maintained that there are few rewards
for professional competence; thus, advancement requires the librarian to
enter the administrative career ladder. The result is the de-skilling and
proletarianization of librarians.[3] In contrast, the doctor, perceived as the
heroic solo practitioner, is held up as a model of a widely recognized, fully
autonomous professional, free of any constraining institutional attach-
ments.

This anti-bureaucratic orientation of librarians makes them sympathetic
to the idea of the deinstitutionalization of librarianship promoted by the
electronic library myth-makers. Giuliano criticized librarianship as a profession defined by its institution, while pointing to medicine as an example
of an occupation that did not develop into "hospitalarianship."[4] Lancaster,
who had much contact with the medical profession through his work on
the National Library of Medicine's computer based bibliography
MEDLINE, agreed with Giuliano. Medical education, he asserted, does not
prepare "hospitalarians"; therefore, library education should not focus on
preparing librarians for what goes on in a library. Just as physicians, nurses,
pharmacists, and others can operate outside of a hospital, librarians, argues
Lancaster, should be prepared to operate outside of the library. If a physician can prescribe drugs without working in a pharmacy, why can't librarians prescribe sources of information away from the library? According to
Lancaster, the librarian should be a "recorded-knowledge consultant" just
as the physician is a "health care consultant."[5]

Unfortunately, Giuliano and Lancaster show little understanding of the
institutional situation of either the traditional impersonal professions or the
newer personal service professions. Like other personal service professionals, librarians gain much of whatever professional status and power they
do possess because of, not despite, their attachment to the library as a
bureaucracy. Let's explore further the relationship between bureaucracy
and the personal and impersonal professions.

The 1870s witnessed the emergence of a rationally oriented public
bureaucracy in conjunction with increased professionalization of those

occupations found in these bureaucracies. The growth of government bureaucracies was supported by social reformers of the time as a means of destroying corrupt political machines and of promoting the general welfare of the citizen. They received the support of business because of their bureaucratic commitment to efficiency.[6] Many of the professionalizing bureaucracy-based occupations are those we now recognize as modern personal service professionals: teachers, mental health workers, social workers, nurses, librarians. A sufficient mass of members in these occupational groups and their opportunity to professionalize were due to the creation and expansion of bureaucratic organizations: the public school, the state mental institution, the government welfare agency, the modern hospital, the public library. The expansion of these institutions in both number and size provided the institutional base for the personal service professions.

There is no doubt that bureaucracies are the dominant organizational structure in both the public and private sectors of society. They wield a tremendous amount of power and influence over many people. Consequently, the bureaucracy-based personal service professionals, by their placement in these public bureaucracies, have a significant impact on the lives of many individuals. Although librarians look to the traditional impersonal profession of medicine as their ideal, it is the personal service professions, including librarianship, that represent the twentieth-century mode of professionalization. The traditional professions' idea of the solo practitioner working outside any bureaucratic organization is in sharp contrast to those more contemporary professionals who are

from the beginning a member of a highly organized group, or even series of such groups: the professional school; . . . the occupation itself, with many thousands of colleagues, numerous subgroups and interest groups, including many different kinds of professional associations; and the organization within which the work is done: library, law firm, hospital, government agency, corporation, school, and so on.[7]

It is time for librarians to abandon as a professional model the ideal of the solo practitioner exemplified by the doctor. By 1984, the number of salaried professionals reached about 75 percent of the total number of working professionals.[8] The autonomous medical practitioner is largely a nineteenth-century ideal. They are, like other professions, being integrated into corporate organizations to such an extent that sociologist John B. McKinlay asserts that

The single feature that most distinguishes present-day medical practice from earlier forms—indeed has altered it almost beyond recognition—is its high degree of bureaucratization. The once-familiar physician with his little black bag is being replaced by a complex 'health care system,' centered in a proliferating number of large, urban-based bureaucratic settings, such as university medical centers, hospitals, community health centers, and health maintenance organizations.[9]

Rising health care costs increase the pressure from the public and govern-ment to limit the autonomy of physicians even more as they are incorpo-rated into national health care plans. There is not a professional group practicing today, including most doctors, that cannot be found in a bureau-cratic organization. Since 1950, there has been such a dramatic increase in the number of salaried professionals that the change has been designated as the bureaucratization of the professions. Neither through the electronic library nor by any other means will librarians increase their professional status by trying to become more like the autonomous medical practitioner; rather, physicians are joining the overwhelming number of professionals found in bureaucracies.

Librarians, like other personal service professionals, are "street-level bureaucrats" providing on the front line a social good and service to the public.[10] The teacher, social worker, and librarian are those government representatives most people meet directly when seeking assistance or service provided by the political system. The personal service profession-als' location in bureaucracies and the power gained through that associa-tion allows the professional to serve a gate- keeping role in the provision and allocation of social and economic benefits. The teacher in the school provides access to learning. The social worker in the welfare agency pro-vides access to public funds. The librarian in the library provides access to knowledge and information. The professional authority librarians have derives, then, not from the monopolization of a body of scientific knowl-edge and its application by a solo practitioner, but from their control of a bureaucratic organization having the power to distribute a public good. Their placement in public bureaucracies permits them considerable inde-pendence in the performance of their responsibilities and the opportunity to have a significant impact on the lives of the general citizen.

Reference librarians in particular fall within the typology of the personal service street-level bureaucrat. If there are constraints on their performance as professionals through administrative policies and procedures, these constraints are more often than not of their own devising, arising out of a mentality that is all too eager to accept the security offered by bureaucratic regulations formulated to avoid the responsibility of decision making. Librarians may question the extent of their impact on the general public, but it is considerable. Helping the library user at the reference desk can be, a personal interaction during which the librarian has considerable inde-pendence in dealing with the patron. There can also be a considerable negative impact when the service is not provided at all or only on a limited basis.[11]

Some would argue that whatever the validity of this analysis, technology is changing society to such an extent that current bureaucratic organiza-tions are increasingly irrelevant. It is claimed that technology will break down the traditional hierarchical, rule-bound structures characteristic of bureaucracy. Yet it can also be argued that the use and growing reliance on technology by many professionals are major factors drawing them into bureaucracies. Doctors must have access to the sophisticated and expensive technology found only in the hospital and large clinic. Not only must they rely on technology, but they also rely on technicians and other medical specialists, including medical librarians, to use the technology or to inter- pret the data it provides. As the use of technology and the cost of operating it increase, there remains the necessity to have bureaucracies to acquire and operate it.

There has been little attention given to the organizational context of the electronic library. Of course, for those who anticipate the dematerialization or withering away of the library, it is a non-issue. The electronic networking environment has the potential of increasing even more the amount of bureaucratic involvement of librarians. Technology may in many cases, such as libraries, allow for a greater distribution of services through elec- tronic networks, but these services will remain part of a bureaucracy. Certainly my own experience with automation in a networking environ- ment bears out this observation. The Dalhousie University Libraries are a founding member of Novanet, a consortium of Nova Scotia university libraries jointly owning and operating an on-line integrated library system. Novanet, as an electronic cooperative network, has an elaborate adminis- trative and governance structure. It is a division of Interuniversity Services Inc. (ISI), a corporation established by several Nova Scotia universities to provide a number of cooperative services. There are committees of repre- sentatives from all of the participating libraries to deal with each of the system modules: on-line catalog, circulation, acquisitions, cataloging. Each of these committees reports to a Novanet Advisory Committee, which in turn reports to a Novanet Management Committee. The Novanet Manage- ment Committee reports to an ISI Management Committee, which is re- sponsible to an ISI board of directors. In addition, there is a Novanet systems staff and office. Contracts between Novanet and the Dalhousie University Computing and Information Services, and between Novanet and the system vendor stipulate various policies, practices, and obligations. Novanet has generated the need for coordinated standards, policies, and protocols, none of which can be changed without working its way through the elaborate governance and administrative system. As a cooperative venture this structure may be more elaborate than other types of electronic networks; nevertheless, it is because of the widespread participation of so many staff members that Novanet is a success. Whatever the merits or weaknesses of the Novanet structure, it tells me bureaucracy will remain with us in the electronic era. If we can look forward to the electronic librarian and the electronic library, be prepared for the electronic bureau- cracy as well. We may need to formulate a new model of bureaucracy, but bureaucracy there will be.

There are other considerations arising out of the myth's incorporation of communication theory and a narrow focus on information: the relationship between libraries and computer centers. Again, academic libraries are the focus of this issue. As we saw earlier, in the 1960s Robert Taylor and others turned to communications theory and its objective definition of information as an alternative source for a theoretical framework within which to place the library and emerging technologies. The library is to be seen as one among various components—the mass media, instructional technology, computing, telecommunications—that constitute society's communications system. Taylor strove to translate this theory into reality at Hampshire College, where the objective became to move away from a print-oriented library to a multimedia communications-oriented institution. The "extended library" should include, physically and administratively, according to Taylor, the traditional library, a gallery, a bookstore, computing, educational technology, and duplication services.[12]

This multimedia communications perspective received powerful support with the formation of EDUCOM. In October 1964, six founding universities incorporated the Interuniversity Communications Council, called EDUCOM for short, "to bring about collaboration among institutions of higher learning in their efforts to utilize communications sciences."[13] Membership grew rapidly so that when EDUCOM sponsored a month-long study session in the summer of 1966, it already had forty-two institutional members from twenty-three states and a five-year operating grant from the Kellogg Foundation. The Summer Study on Information Networks, held in Boulder, Colorado, brought together over 180 representatives from various academic disciplines, computing, university administration, information science, and libraries to plan a strategy for the development of EDUNET, an educational communications network. Prominent among the participants were J.C.R. Licklider and Robert Taylor. It was clear that EDUCOM was going to become a powerful body promoting inter-university development of computing and network development.

From the beginning, EDUCOM adopted a multimedia communications philosophy that envisioned the scholar having access to information regardless of its location or format. A basic premise of EDUCOM was "the belief that electronic multimedia information networks ultimately must make material in many forms almost instantly available to scholars wherever on the continent they may be."[14] The possible merging of computer centers and libraries was advanced. Participants at the summer session could imagine a network as "an idealized super institution combining within it the functions of the library and the computer center, together with suitable formalizations of audio-visual departments and other instructional media," to provide an interconnection between informational resources and subscribers.[15] It was noted with surprise in the report of the conference that there had been no effort to address the relationship between libraries and computing at those universities actively pursuing networking. George W. Brown, a professor from the Graduate School of Business Administration, University of California at Los Angeles and chairman of the conference, observed in his introductory remarks to the meeting that while libraries and computer centers appeared to be contrasting institutions in the way they collected, preserved, and disseminated information, their differences were not as great as they may appear and those differences would diminish. He predicted:

> While it need not be true that the library and computing center will merge into each other and lose their separate identities, it seems likely that the subscriber will ultimately not be able to tell where one ends and the other begins. In this event, he will probably not care, so long as he is well served by the system.[16]

From the scholar's perspective there would be in time little or no apparent difference between his or her interaction with the library or the computer center. Furthermore, this blurring would not be confined to libraries and computing alone, but would, according to Brown, extend to current and future media used to disseminate information.

With EDUCOM and other advocates of information technology, the myth-makers of the electronic library could feel justified in their conviction that technological innovations would have significant implications for organizational structures within academic institutions. The emergence of computer center directors and media or learning resource center directors in many universities alongside the director of libraries provided evidence of this technological change. Focusing as they did on the narrow perspective of the library as an information-handling organization, the library was increasingly perceived to be only one among a number of disparate units in the "information package," a package that could even include duplicating and mail services. Consequently, Taylor's efforts at Hampshire College were not unique, as other universities began to adopt a "communications model" of organization.[17] In the late 1960s, for example, at Dalhousie University, my own institution, the director of communications was responsible for the library (which contains three copies of Taylor's *Making of a Library*), audio-visual systems, computing, the university press, and management information systems. When the university's new library was completed at the end of the 1960s, it contained, in addition to library services, the computer center, printing services, and learning resources. A publication celebrating the new library asserted that it had the potential of becoming a major research library

> as the complex has been built around all the design concepts necessary to insure that services and facilities keep pace with the communications revolution of today and tomorrow. With such media as closed circuit television, language laboratories, movie, tape, record equipment, and online computer facilities, the library has been equipped to translate its programmes of university, community, and regional service as it seeks to fulfil its role as communication centre.[18]

Like many other institutions that moved in this direction in the 1970s, this administrative arrangement was later abandoned. Nevertheless, for those who remain convinced that technology is the determining factor forcing organizational change, the communications model remains an attractive goal and those individuals and institutions that attempted to implement it in the 1970s are seen to have been pioneers ahead of their time.[19]

With the rapid convergence of computing and communications technologies in the 1970s and 1980s, there was renewed interest at academic institutions in how best to structure the relationship between those units involved with what was increasingly referred to as "information technology" (IT). By the mid-1980s it appeared to some the time had finally arrived when the communications model, including the merging of computing and libraries, could be implemented. EDUCOM once again was a meeting place for proponents of this communications model.[20] In preparation for the impending day when such mergers would sweep through academic institutions, librarians felt compelled to explain the library and librarianship to computing center professionals who, it was believed, had far less knowledge of libraries than librarians had of computing. The *Journal of Academic Librarianship* inaugurated in early 1987 a newsletter, *Libraries and Computing Centers: Issues of Mutual Concern*. Librarians were urged to bring this newsletter to the attention of computing personnel on their campus as a means of educating them to the ways of librarianship. Its first issue featured an article by Pat Molholt, titled "On Converging Paths: The Computing Center and the Library."[21] While it recognized that there were similarities and differences between libraries and computer centers, it asserted that both had one fundamental common denominator: information. C. Lee Jones of the Council on Library Resources declared, "It has been said many times, but it is worth repeating, that libraries and computing centers deal with the same commodity—information."[22] Thus, it was at the information nexus that libraries and computer centers would meet.

Librarian Patricia Battin of Columbia University pointed out that librarians have always made a distinction between information and knowledge and have been committed to the organization of knowledge, while computer specialists have perceived all information as data. Nevertheless, she too sees information as the link between libraries and computing; consequently, they would merge into a Scholarly Information Center.[23] Librarians are encouraged, as envisaged by the myth of the electronic library, to narrow their focus on information and to forge alliances with technologically grounded computing centers. The director of libraries becomes, along with the directors of computing and media resources, only one among an array of information managers.

However, only two years after starting its newsletter aimed at preparing computer specialists for their wedding to librarians, Pat Molholt was forced to ask, "What Happened to the Merger Debate?"[24] The merger simply did not happen. After soliciting the views of its readers, the editor of the *Journal of Academic Librarianship* discontinued the newsletter in early 1989. The problem from the start was the expectation that a common interest in such a narrow concept as information was a sufficient basis to change long-established organizational structures. Looking back, it is embarrassing to see how some librarians were so eager to immediately transform the library into a technologically based information-processing center.

However, if libraries, computing, and media centers were not to be restructured soon into a new type of information center, it was becoming apparent that they, as well as many other units and individuals on campus, should be linked through the development of electronic networks at the local, regional, national, and international level. Information was not going to be the factor linking computing and libraries. Rather, the view emerged that it would be networks and the "converging technologies." Whether a library had its own stand-alone system or relied on the computing center, it was clear that plugging into various networks for communication and access to electronic databases had tremendous potential for any library to expand its services for the benefit of its users. Individual universities began to formulate networking strategies internally and joined in such bodies as the Coalition for Networked Information (CNI), an organization established by EDUCOM, the Association of Research Libraries, and CAUSE, a nonprofit association whose objective is to promote the effective use and management of information technology in higher education.

The creation of the CNI as a coalition signaled a greater awareness of the complexity of the organizational and cultural factors enveloping the "information-handling" process. Thus, a "Vision Statement" of the CNI acknowledged, "The future academic computing environment will be technically heterogeneous, and interoperability across elements of this environment is an important objective."[25] Nevertheless, the CNI still advanced in its "Vision" the idea of a shift to a "new information delivery paradigm," including a future environment in which multimedia-based information will be available through geographically independent work stations and in which reference librarians will be transformed into an information-management professional.

Regardless of the rate of acceptance of any new paradigm, the rapid diffusion of microcomputers throughout university campuses and the potential of electronic networks encouraged the view that centralized planning of computing and communications was necessary. Consequently, some universities established the position of chief information officer (CIO). There is little consistency in the actual titles assigned to these positions or in the responsibilities of the positions, some of which are at the vice presidential level. Neither is it clear how many of them there are. Anne Woodsworth, who has devoted the most attention to exploring the role of the CIO, estimated there were about fifty CIOs in ninety-one American research universities by 1989.[26] Woodsworth, who sees the emergence of the CIO as a necessary and positive organizational development, adopts the narrow informational/technological perception of the library when she places it, along with academic computing, administrative systems, and telecommunications, among the major information areas. Furthermore, her advocacy of the communications model is based on the premise that technology is the element generating change and linking the four areas. While the communications model expects the library to be wedded to the other "information areas," thus far, the differences between computer centers and libraries in their cultures, in their history, in such policy differences as charging for services, in the training, skills, and perspectives of their staff, and in their mandates have kept these units apart. Nevertheless, the search for the appropriate model or working relationship between libraries and computing services continues, as it must.[27] Nevertheless, Woodsworth expects that in time technology will drive them together. In the meantime, the CIO is seen as a transitional campus entrepreneur who will bring these disparate units together administratively, based on a technological foundation. In short, the communications model of the myth of the electronic library is expected to prevail.

It is interesting that the myth of the electronic library foresees a disembodiment of the library due to the space-transcending ability of information technology, yet it ignores the fact that computer centers, themselves a creation of such technology, are even more susceptible to disembodiment. The development of communications technologies in conjunction with powerful distributed work stations has decreased the status and influence of central computing. We can imagine that the history of the computer center as place will be far shorter than that of the library.

We have examined the relationship of librarians to their institutional framework. Electronic library myth-makers wish to divorce librarians from the library, using the solo medical practitioner as their model. They also adopted a model derived from communication theory that envisages the multimedia provision of information and perceives the library as only one variable in the communication process. By doing so, they have diminished the status of the library relative to other units, in particular computing centers.

However, I have maintained that librarians, as personal service professionals, draw their strength and professional status from their association with a specific, largely public-supported institution or bureaucracy. It is ironic that at a time when librarians are eager to abandon their long-standing attachment to a public institution and aspire to a professional status comparable to the medical practitioner's, the latter is moving into the bureaucratic environment familiar to the librarian. Traditional institutional models of the impersonal professions are not appropriate, then, for librarianship. The challenge for librarians is not to see how fast they can abandon bureaucracy, the library as place. Their obligation is to ensure that the bureaucracies for which they are responsible are client-oriented. They should not allow their desire for increased professional status to obscure the need to develop more effective bureaucracies, ones that foster client self-sufficiency.

The Politics of Librarianship

The skill with which a group integrates its own ideology into the prevailing political values of the community is a primary determinant of its success, and particularly is this true of a profession administering a public service.

Oliver Garceau

We examined the relationship between personal service professionals and bureaucracy, between librarians and their institutional base in libraries. We recognize that these professionals serve a gate-keeping role in the allocation of a public good, usually through tax-supported bureaucracies, and in the case of librarians, through the provision of access to information and knowledge through the library. Because of this gate-keeping power to provide access to social and economic benefits, personal service professionals have a substantial political element to their work. Aside from the typical internal bureaucratic politics of their own organizations, they participate in external political actions aimed at increasing the resources of their agencies and of their clients. Furthermore, they usually work in agencies subject to the scrutiny or direction of political bodies such as school and library boards.

When Oliver Garceau conducted his study, *The Public Library in the Political Process* in the 1940s for the Public Library Inquiry, he found that librarians did not consider themselves government employees. He warned librarians that they are "inescapably a part of government and involved in 'politics' " and urged them to understand the political environment of the public library.[1] If Garceau were able to repeat his investigation today, he would find that librarians have indeed gained an appreciation of the political process surrounding libraries. They actively engage in political activity. Library associations at the local and national level vigorously lobby in the political arena. The American Library Association is one of the most effective lobbying groups in Washington, D.C. Periodic White House conferences on libraries attest to the political astuteness of librarians.

E. J. Josey's *Libraries in the Political Process* provides a collection of essays on the political activities of librarians in twenty states. Other essays are devoted to strategies for developing grass-roots support for libraries, the use of statistical data, methods of organizing legislative workshops, making effective use of the mass media, and establishing coalitions with other professional organizations. Josey observed that these accounts "do not show any kid-glove political approach; rather, they are the activity of committed professionals who are no longer afraid of 'dirty politics' and who are in an all-out effort to obtain legislative support for library service."[2] The objectives of this political manual were expanded a decade later by Josey and Kenneth Shearer in their volume, *Politics and the Support of Libraries*, in which the political environment at the local, state, and federal levels of government is examined for all types of public and private libraries.[3] Josey reiterates that "politician-librarians" must emphatically generate a case for libraries and participate actively in the political process.

Librarians also take political stands on many social issues. The American Library Association has formally adopted policies and positions on a wide range of issues having major political implications. It urges libraries to collect material on environmental issues. It supports a freeze on the development and deployment of nuclear weapons and encourages libraries to include material in their collections on nuclear arms, disarmament, and nuclear moratoria. The ALA has policies directed at combating prejudice and discrimination, and encourages libraries to provide services ensuring that the poor have access to information.[4] It is apparent that there is inherent in librarianship the political aspect characteristic of personal service professions.

Librarians readily acknowledge that their profession participates in political activities, especially with regard to generating support for library services. However, they maintain that this activity is pursued without any commitment to a specific political ideology. Hoping to attain the objective authority that the impersonal professions presumably achieve through their reliance on a body of scientific knowledge, librarians wish to project, as well, a neutral image. As early as 1889, library leader Charles Amey Cutter insisted in his presidential address to the American Library Association that the librarian must be "of no party in politics. He helps all alike, as the physician heals all alike."[5] During the highly politicized 1930s, younger librarians could not ignore the social and political challenges facing a world confronted by a terrible economic depression and the threat of world war. However, their efforts to inject political and social values into librarianship, including a proposed League for Liberal Librarians, were easily turned aside by the library establishment of the time.[6] Thus, fifty years after Cutter's declaration of neutrality, Garceau would claim in his Public Library Inquiry study that "the library has traditionally been neutral in partisan politics. Librarians have in general scrupulously maintained their neutrality."[7]

Like the 1930s, the 1960s were a time of much social and political turbulence, a turbulence sweeping through librarianship as well. In contrast to the 1930s, there was a large enough influx of youthful activists to constitute a more serious challenge to the library establishment and many of the traditional values of librarianship. However, these activists cast their movement in a social rather than political cloak. They eschewed any political agenda or ideology. The phrase "social responsibilities," coined to describe their efforts, evoked the genteel middle-class reformism characteristic of earlier eras of librarianship.[8] Part of their efforts included an attempt to bring access to information closer to those who need it, especially groups who were not traditional middle-class users of the library. Neighborhood information and referral centers were established to offer "store-front" service. But here, too, there was no acknowledgment that there could be any political or ideological impetus to this initiative. Indeed, the "I & R" centers were presented, in the tradition of middle-class reform movements, as value-free public agencies. They were represented as professionally staffed public bureaucracies consciously created as an alternative to any ideologically or class-based sources of information such as the ward heeler characteristic of more traditional community information systems.[9] The desire to display political neutrality continues when Jane Robbins-Carter suggests that "librarianship has conceived of itself as importantly apolitical."[10]

Another library educator imparted to his students the position that "no matter how precious to us any faith or philosophy or social movement might be, we have to keep our distance and maintain our impartiality as we help insure that all the people can hear all the arguments and establish for themselves what is right or true."[11]

In their desire to project a value-free professionalism, it comes as no surprise that librarians wish to remain discreet about their own political views. Studies about librarians ignore or downplay their political values. Alice Bryan studied public librarians in the 1940s for the Public Library Inquiry but gave little attention to their politics. She simply reported that their preferences ranged from Henry Wallace to Herbert Hoover.[12] However, a later analysis by sociologist Seymour Lipset of unpublished data assembled by Bryan found that 17 percent of her sample of librarians gave as their first choice for president progressive, socialist, or Communist candidates, a preference putting "librarians in the forefront among groups backing such parties."[13] More recent studies continue to present librarians as a moderate group. While it is acknowledged by one such study that the library profession has, like other occupations, a fringe of extremists, "such as authoritarians of the left," it asserts that " the great majority of librarians are of a moderate persuasion."[14]

One of the attractions of the myth of the electronic library to librarians is that it perpetuates the presumed neutrality of the impersonal professional. By attempting to embody a corpus of scientifically derived knowledge, it allies information science and communication theory with the neutrality of scientific investigation. The close correlation usually drawn between science and technology assigns a further value-free status to technology. Thus, the myth of the electronic library ascribes social change and the emergence of the electronic library to technology, a technology claimed to be inherently neutral. "Technology, like power, is neutral in its implementation," according to Kenneth Dowlin.[15] Those desiring to increase the status of librarianship as an impersonal profession hope to find in technology and the myth of the electronic library a means of projecting librarianship as a technologically based, value-free profession and the librarian as an unbiased information technician.

Thus, while librarians, as personal service professionals, readily pursue political action to generate support for library services, they have consistently maintained that they provide those services as objective, impersonal professionals. However, as the political landscape becomes ever more ambiguous, the relationship between political and professional values becomes even more problematical. Consequently, there is increasing questioning whether librarians are so neutral—indeed, whether it is even possible or appropriate for them to be so. This questioning assumes particular significance within the context of the challenge the myth of the electronic library presents to long-standing values embodied in the myth of the library as place. Let's examine further the political values of librarianship and then, in the next chapter, the implications that the myth of the electronic library holds for those values.

An understanding of the political values of librarianship requires an understanding of the political culture of the society of which it is a part. This is not as easy to grasp as one would hope it would be. The three main currents in Western political ideologies are conservatism, liberalism, and socialism. Elements of all three of these ideologies are usually found to a lesser or greater degree in most Western political cultures, including that of the United States. However, the extent to which any one of these is the prevailing tendency is open to interpretation by students of the issue. Some contend that the American political culture is fundamentally conservative, while others argue that it is liberal. While generally acknowledged as a lesser influence than conservatism or liberalism, socialism is nevertheless recognized as contributing significant concepts to the American welfare state. As we saw in the quotation at the beginning of this chapter, Garceau maintains that the success of any public service group will depend to some extent on the integration of its ideology with that of the prevailing political culture. Public library ideology and programs have reflected the ambiguity of the general American political culture, although we will see that liberal tenets constitute the strongest components of the political culture.

Efforts to delineate the essence of the American political culture demonstrate the difficulty of doing so with precision. In his classic study of race in the United States, *An American Dilemma* (1944), the noted Swedish sociologist Gunnar Myrdal found Americans "conservative in fundamental principles. . . . But *the principles concerned are liberal*, and some, indeed, are radical".[16]

Cultural historian Warren I. Susman, in his assessment of the nature of American conservatism, warns that one runs into various paradoxes in doing such an assessment. In his view, "There are, to be blunt, certain key notions that are generally associated with conservatism." However, like Myrdal, he finds that "when [these notions] appear in modern culture, they are not, by the majority of thinking Americans anyway, regarded as 'conservative.' Rather, in some strange, almost perverse, sense they seem to reflect a redefined liberalism or even radicalism."[17] Susman found paradox in his examination of conservatism; Robert Paul Wolff encountered paradox as well in his examination of American liberalism. He states

The confusion of contemporary American political thought shows itself nicely in the paradoxical fact that while liberals invoke the authority of John Stuart Mill's great libertarian tract, *On Liberty*, conservatives echo the rhetoric and deploy the arguments of Mill's other great contribution to social philosophy, *The Principles of Political Economy*. What is more paradoxical still, Mill's strongest arguments for what is today known as conservatism are set forth in *On Liberty*, a fact which liberals seem congenitally unable to notice; while in the pages of *Principles*, we can find the germs of justification of that welfare-state philosophy which modern conservatives abhor.[18]

However, Louis Hartz counters in his classic study of American liberalism that "radicalism and conservatism have been twisted entirely out of shape by the liberal flow of American history."[19]

If there is ambiguity surrounding the precise nature of American political culture, we similarly find ambiguity in the political values found in librarianship. American public library ideology contains elements drawn from the values and ideas of conservatism, socialism, and liberalism. In looking at the public library, the case can be made that there is a strong element of conservatism in the ideology surrounding this institution. Conservatism conceives the successful achievement of personal freedom and self-fulfillment within the nurturing environment of a stable, hierarchical society rich in social institutions: the church, the family, voluntary associations. To conservatives these institutions play an important role as means of ensuring social order through a strong sense of community. The primary responsibility of government is to promote public order through the strengthening of these institutions. We find conservatism's emphasis on the importance of an organic community reflected in the stress placed in library ideology on the library as a "community institution." The library serves as the social memory of the community.

From its beginnings, the public library has been promoted as a community institution. Its origins are traced back to such "communal institutions" as the eighteenth-century social library, a voluntary institution emerging when most peoples' social and economic relationships were circumscribed by the village, religious institutions, and the family. Through these ties the individual was bound to the local community and derived from it accepted norms of behavior reinforced by tradition and face-to-face relationships.[20] However, this sense of community was severely challenged by the onslaught of change. By the early decades of the eighteenth-century New England, the birthplace of the public library, was undergoing rapid change. Higher birth rates, a longer life span, and a steady stream of immigrants provided the concentration of people needed to fill the needs of an accelerating industrialization. It is within this urban industrialization that the modern public library movement began with the opening of the Boston Public Library in 1854. Although the public library is clearly an urban institution, an impetus behind its invention was the preservation of community, an objective shared with other new urban public efforts such as the emerging park and playground systems.[21]

A sense of loss of community was reinforced after the Civil War when industrialization, secularization, and urbanization assumed such a momentum that there was a prevailing feeling in all levels of society that things were getting out of control. As we already noted in Chapter 5, the period from the 1870s to the 1920s experienced the most profound change in American history. In response to this upheaval there was a tremendous outburst of creativity, resulting in the formation of political movements, private and public corporations, and associations to cope with this change. Through these efforts people hoped to preserve a sense of community that many could still vividly remember from growing up in small rural villages.[22]

Librarians were aware of the many efforts directed at maintaining a cohesive social order and successfully promoted the public library as one of the institutional bulwarks of the community, both as its social memory and as an important contributor to social order. Recognizing the public library as an urban institution committed to preserving the sense of community of the small American town reveals the need for the two images of the public library delineated earlier: the small town public library and the urban public library.

The conservative premises underlying the public library became the foundation for specific library programs. In response to the rapid social changes of the closing decades of the nineteenth century, services were developed to inculcate in the foreign-born and new urban masses a sense of community that would ensure social stability and the status quo. It was hoped that these programs would overcome the alienation and rootlessness of the emerging industrial centers by preserving the close-knit ties reminiscent of the American rural community. Reformers recognized that in an urbanized and industrialized country like the expanding United States, the informal communication of the village was no longer possible. However, it was claimed that the public library would serve as "an effective symbol of communal fraternity."[23] Commenting on the variety of programs developed by branch libraries, Rosemary DuMont states in her history of the urban public library:

All of these efforts were made in order to provide a new locus for loyalty and commitment to replace the rural community from which most individuals had formerly received their identity and definition of right and wrong. The branch library, along with local public schools and settlement houses, wanted the individual's educational and recreational experience to promote the social unity of a rural America in an urban setting.[24]

The idea of the library as an important community institution is consistently reiterated in library literature to the present day. The standard text on public library administration defines the public library as a community agency for the diffusion of knowledge, the consequences of which include the enhancement of the quality of life of the community.[25]

Socialist ideology shares with conservatism a concern for the enhancement of community. However, it places a greater emphasis on egalitarianism through an activist role for government, a role whose primary objective is to ensure equality of result for all. Public library ideology reflects these themes in its emphasis on the library as a publicly funded agency accessible to all. In addition, its programs to disadvantaged groups could be conceived as instruments of public policy designed to promote greater economic and social equality. The socialist concern for equality complements the conservative stress on community through those library programs directed at the poor, the newcomers to the city, and immigrants. Hoping to be vital community social centers, libraries opened their doors to numerous organizations, some of which were very progressive. Within one week, for example, an urban branch library at the turn of the century allowed such associations as the Committee for Social Service Among Coloured People, the Socialist Party, the International Workers of the World, the Jewish branch of the Socialist Party, and the Woman's Trade Union League to hold meetings in its quarters.[26] Over the years, the egalitarian strain of public library ideology was strengthened by those librarians advocating the library's responsibility to serve the total community. Stung by critics who accused the library of being a middle-class institution, librarians intensified their efforts through outreach programs to serve such non-traditional groups as the economically disadvantaged, older adults, illiterates, and racial minorities.

The library's ability to serve as an egalitarian gateway to the cultural and economic advantages of America is enshrined in the folklore of the public library through autobiographical accounts of the rise of "disadvantaged" individuals because of the availability of a local public library. These homages to the public library strike such a responsive chord that the library profession deliberately generates accounts of such experiences. The Public Library Association's, *The Library Connection: Essays Written in Praise of Public Libraries* includes chapters by individuals from various economic, social, and racial backgrounds, each of whom describes how libraries played an important role in their lives.[27]

It appears then that public library ideology, which in itself represents the foundation of much of the ideology of librarianship as a whole, includes elements attributed to both conservatism and socialism. It is difficult to ascertain whether these elements can be attributed directly to conservatism and socialism, or if they are more accurately reflections of American liberalism's ability to respond to social change and to incorporate ideas from competing ideologies. If we look further at American public library ideology, we find sufficient components of liberalism to assert that public library ideology draws most of its substantive values from liberalism. In doing so it is in accord with the wider political culture. Despite the various interpretations put forth by Hartz, Lowi, Susman, and others, the fundamental values of American political culture are founded in liberalism. However, when we attempt to define more concisely those liberal values, we meet again ambiguity and various interpretations.

Liberalism has had different meanings at different times and places. Part of the problem in assessing liberalism's relation to the values of American political culture is, to borrow sociologist Edward Shils' words, that "it is so ambiguous in its major concepts and so vague in its boundaries."[28] Unlike many other Western democracies, there has never been in the United States one party, institution, or intellectual tradition promulgating a clearly defined liberal ideology. Nevertheless, it is the "liberal-view," according to Anthony Arblaster, rather than conservatism or socialism, that prevails in modern Western societies.

In his useful analysis of liberalism, Arblaster states that liberalism is not "so much a set of ideas or doctrines to which people subscribe by conscious choice; it is a way of seeing the social world, and a set of assumptions about it, which are absorbed by the individual in so natural and gradual a manner that he or she is not conscious of there being assumptions at all."[29] The same may be said about librarianship's own absorption of the values of liberalism.

With its ambiguity, we find again numerous efforts to sort out the ideas of liberalism in America. Political sociologist Seymour Lipset, for example, makes a distinction between "economic liberalism (issues concerned with the distribution of wealth and power) and non-economic liberalism (issues concerned with civil liberties, race relations, and foreign affairs)."[30]

However, political philosopher Benjamin Barber identifies three "dispositions" of liberalism: the anarchist, the realist, and the minimalist. He believes that these three dispositions can be found in all democratic societies but that the American political system in particular "is a remarkable example of the co-existence—sometimes harmonious, more often uncomfortable—of all three dispositions."[31] Barber contends that American liberalism is anarchist in values, with the emphasis it places on privacy, liberty, property, and rights; realist in its means, with its use of power, law, and mediation; and minimalist in its political temper, with its promotion of tolerance, separation of power, judicial review, and pluralism. But Shils offers yet another alternative. For him there are two types of liberalism: autonomist and collectivist. In contemporary America, autonomist liberalism, which stresses individualism, is now often perceived as conservatism or libertarianism. In contrast, collectivist liberalism, with its emphasis on the use of central state authority to promote the common welfare, is perceived as becoming an increasingly social democratic ideology.

As reference to these authors suggests, the ambiguity noted earlier that is characteristic of American political culture in general applies as well to efforts to define American liberalism. Indeed, the problem of the ambiguities of liberalism is compounded because many of liberalism's values are shared by socialists and conservatives. It is the priority each gives to specific values that distinguishes one ideological bent from another. As liberalism's priorities over time have changed, certain values that were once the core of eighteenth-century classical liberalism are now often considered primarily within the domain of present-day conservatism. In America, the eighteenth-century Lockean liberalism that blossomed into the rampant economic individualism of the nineteenth century is distinct from the human rights, social welfare liberalism of the late twentieth century. Nevertheless, vital remnants of earlier values remain within the broad ideological liberal spectrum. Despite the confusions and ambiguities, certain values remain central to liberalism and thus to librarianship.

A fundamental value to liberalism is its commitment to individualism. Barber states this commitment in the starkest terms: "The liberal psychology of human nature is founded on a radical premise no less startling for its familiarity: man is alone."[32] His declaration serves to emphasize the importance individualism and personal liberty have to an understanding of liberalism in American political culture. Liberalism's stress on and respect for the individual and his rights have been among its most enduring contributions to Western political thought as well as the target of much criticism from both conservatives and socialists. It is liberalism's commitment to the individual over the group, first formulated in the eighteenth-century effort to break the constraints of a feudal social order, that is the basis for the self-reliance and freedom from external restraint that liberalism claims as a natural right for each person. One's morality or beliefs should not be based on religion, tradition, communal norms, or other social institutions, but arrived at rationally through careful, objective assessment of concrete data and facts.

It is this liberal faith in the thinking autonomous individual that is the foundation for the belief that no group, and especially not the government, has a right to say what is best for an individual. It is the liberal assumption that each individual knows what is best for himself. Based on this premise, threats to individual privacy are of great concern to liberals, while tolerance is valued as a basic prime virtue. It is from this philosophical commitment to personal liberty that the concept of intellectual freedom and opposition to censorship are founded.

A further aspect of the liberal orientation to individualism is its emphasis on self-fulfillment or development. Liberals place a special premium on intellectual development: "To the modern liberal, our liberties are instruments of development, at the heart of which is intellectual growth."[33] Consequently, liberals place great importance on education. The school serves as a means of providing individuals with the opportunity to acquire the skills contributing to self-development. Because of the liberal's concern for self-development through equality of opportunity, "education clearly emerges . . . as one of the most politically relevant institutions within a liberal democracy, second only to the institutions of representative democracy themselves."[34]

The liberal commitment to individualism is also in accord with the concept of the self-seeking economic person. Liberalism is a middle-class ideology whose economic philosophy is capitalism. Liberalism emerged with capitalism, and its values are most evident in capitalist countries. Classical liberalism of the eighteenth and early nineteenth centuries strongly endorsed the concept of *laissez-faire,* a principle that became increasingly difficult to defend as the negative results of industrialization became apparent and the criticism of liberalism by socialists became more potent. As socialists promoted the idea of equality of result, liberalism moved away from *laissez-faire* and stressed the idea of equality of opportunity, accepting that some state intervention was necessary to ensure this equality. While liberalism may have absorbed certain elements from the social democratic left to soften the harsher realities of capitalism, these revisions have not fundamentally shifted liberalism from its belief in individual initiative and responsibility, support for private property, and opposition to widespread state intervention to promote the distribution of wealth. In the United States, liberal individualism was particularly emphatic. Liberal democracy, the free enterprise system, and a highly rhetorical commitment to liberty ("Give me liberty or give me death") constituted "the American way of life."

In turning to public library ideology, we find clear representation of liberal values and the orientation to individualism. Equal, if not exceeding, the public library's commitment to community is its commitment to the individual. As a library planning guide observes, "Communities don't have information needs; individuals do."[35] Even when librarians discuss the need to work with various ethnic, racial, occupational, and other groups and organizations in their community, they emphasize these associations served as channels "to the individualized service which is perhaps the library's most unique and valuable contribution to an expanding and intelligent society."[36]

A public library leader endorsed this concept when he stressed that the public should focus on the "betterment of the individual." Thus, when working with community groups, the librarian's "responsibilities are not for the advancement of the common end of a group, which may be in competition with other groups, but for the development of the individual group members." Consequently, he concluded, "we should work not with groups but through groups to individual men and women and children."[37] The most recent text on public library administration stresses that the major objective of the public library is "to recognize and aid individuals as such, even though they are most easily reached through a group."[38]

Individualized service has not been considered contrary to serving the community because it has long been a basic liberal assumption among librarians that the community is improved through the betterment of the individual. By identifying through community studies the needs of individuals and meeting those needs, the needs of the community as a whole will also be met, according to this logic. The text noted above claims, "Facts, information, ideas, flowing into the community through the individual interests, curiosity, and intellectual inquiries of some people will have a generally beneficial effect upon decisions that are made affecting the welfare of all citizens."[39] This emphasis on an individual in librarianship is a long-standing commitment in accord with liberal principles. Liberal egalitarianism and individualism during the nineteenth century, based on the philosophical foundations established by eighteenth-century utilitarian rationalism, were reinforced when individual self-interest became a positive end of the emerging economic ideology of a national market economy, and by the steady pace of urbanization. While nineteenth-century reformers hoped to preserve community, their means often emphasized the individual over community. It was believed that the autonomous, rational individual must be given priority over those bonds of community that limit, in a time of change, the exercise of individual will and imagination. Reformers favored the liberal's faith in the individual's ability to achieve moral regeneration through his own initiative, an article of faith that could also be ascribed to by upper-class leaders such as Andrew Carnegie. Social reform would not come through the actions of groups or classes, but rather through individual reform, for society was conceived as a mass of individuals, not a collection of groups. The individual, when properly presented with the facts, would be able to adopt through the application of reason appropriate cultural norms and behavior. Such a perspective naturally encouraged the development of educational institutions such as the public library.

During the last decades of the nineteenth and early years of the twentieth centuries, the rationalist and utilitarian orientation of liberalism encouraged support for social reform movements and the increasing bureaucratic professionalism that we have already noted. The emerging social sciences provided the methodology for aspiring professionals to eagerly collect data on a variety of social issues with the objective of providing the foundation for more enlightened public policies. Armed with their statistical compilations, these aspiring professionals could promote their professional autonomy while also attempting to change society from within. This tendency toward liberal professionalism encouraged the replacement of politically based administration, such as the patronage of the local political machine, with a devotion to administrative efficiency through the use of trained experts, in short, the bureaucratic manager. The professionalization of librarianship is an example of liberal technical rationality applied to a public social agency: the library.

The liberal emphasis on individualism, self-development, and rationalism provided the ideological foundation for the establishment of public and other types of libraries, for the promotion of professionalism in librarianship, and for efforts to formulate a social science-based discipline of library science. The emergence of professional public administration, bureaucratic professionalization, and the social sciences formed the mold in which librarianship was cast. Liberalism's concern for the free flow of ideas provided the philosophical basis for librarianship's most fundamental principle: intellectual freedom. Liberalism's faith in the role of education provided an educational role for the library in a democracy and the teacher as a model for librarians.

Librarians eagerly embraced the liberal perspective in their belief that individuals, through a combination of their own initiative and the guidance of a librarian, would draw on the library's resources to better themselves as individuals. Although during much of the nineteenth century librarians felt obliged to limit their selection of library material to titles that would not threaten the equilibrium of the social, religious, and political mores of the community, they increasingly shifted to a position in support of intellectual freedom and other universal values. To promote this objective, the librarian was encouraged to emphasize quality over popularity and "keep open a broad highway of free access to the more daring, more provocative, often unpopular current ideas, proposals, and customs," recognizing that this strategy could create tension between the librarian and the lay members of the community.[40] The library became less an institution inherent to the local community and more of a link to, and a reflection of, the larger society as librarians joined other emerging professional groups in introducing cosmopolitan values at the local level. As one historian has stated, "Just as the depot and the telegraph office had, by the end of the 19th century, become outposts of national economic coordination in nearly every American town and city, so the school, the doctor's office, the lawyer's chamber, the church, and the library became recruiting stations and transmitters of national intellectual and professional life."[41] The public library promoted community but, under the control of professionalizing liberal librarians, it became as well a transmitter of trans-local or cosmopolitan values. Librarians assumed linkage roles between the social patterns of their local community and those of the larger society. This situation placed them in the ambiguous situation in which there could easily be a discrepancy between the values of the larger society, with its emphasis on individualism, and those of the community, with its reliance on more personal and group relationships.

The favoring of the individual over society and institutions is so pervasive in American political culture that one could easily believe that this is the way the world is. However, liberals and non-liberals recognize that the freedom gained for the individual has had its costs. Liberalism's intimate association with all the complex elements of evolving modernity for at least the past two centuries marks it with the virtues and vices of that evolution. As the political philosophy of modernity liberalism shares, according to Benjamin Barber, in "modernity's victories—emancipation, science, tolerance, reasons, pluralism, rights," it is also "diminished by modernity's vices—alienation, deracination, nihilism, meaninglessness, anomia."[42] Conservatives and socialists criticize liberalism's emphasis on individualism, blaming it for a prevailing lack of sense of community. Liberals usually have been suspicious of the perceived constraints represented by those institutions—family, church, local norms—that are typically considered the building blocks of community. Instead, the liberal is a cosmopolitan, open to ideas regardless of their sources. This liberal conception of the rational, uncommitted, autonomous individual clashes with the conservative's attachment to hierarchy, family, and tradition, and with the socialist's belief that people are social beings who can only achieve self-fulfillment in the context of collective action. To some, liberalism's excessive drive for individual rights has resulted in a narcissistic concern for self over others, a striving for personal gain over public needs, and a pervasive sense of alienation. The negative consequences of individualism and for the quest for community are receiving increasingly more attention in both the scholarly and popular literature. To one astute observer, "To strike the balance between 'community' and the mobile individual is liberalism's great task."[43]

While liberalism provided congenial ground for the growth of librarianship, library ideology reflected the emerging contradictions of twentieth-century liberalism. The paradoxes derived from both autonomist and collectivist liberalism are embodied within library ideology and services. These confusions are a reflection of library ideology's sources in the paradoxical tenets of American liberal political culture. In the last quarter of the twentieth century, nothing has dispelled these paradoxes. Public librarians remain concerned about the lack of clear goals for their libraries, while their programs range from outreach projects aimed at the disadvantaged to specialized services to the business community. Library ideology casts the public library as one of the institutional foundations of a stable community (a view sympathetic to conservatives) while, as well, promoting an intellectual freedom that some (especially conservatives) perceive as undermining important community norms. Because librarianship has incorporated liberal values from both autonomist liberalism and collectivist liberalism, it is, like liberalism, vulnerable to criticism from the entire political spectrum. Some attack librarianship's liberal promotion of intellectual freedom while others attack librarianship as a conservative bastion of middle-class values.

As negative results of liberalism's values—personal alienation, decline of community, mounting costs of ineffective social programs—became more acute, there has been an ascendance of conservatism. There is no indication in recent years that the American political ideological landscape will become any clearer. Shifting values and priorities generate new groupings and labels such as neo-liberalism and welfare conservatism. Issues and positions generated by such social movements as feminism and environmentalism do not always fit easily into the older political ideologies. Peter Clecak observes that "thoughtful people routinely adopt conservative positions on some matters, liberal stances on others, and socialist perspectives on still others." He continues, "Although individuals may carve out a sensible outlook in this way, the immediate public impact of such efforts seems disappointing: ideological confusion and political vacillation emerge precisely when unprecedented problems demand more concerted responses."[44]

It appears that we can also apply Clecak's observation to the professional ideology of the public library, with its various elements drawn from classical and welfare liberalism, if not directly from socialism and conservatism. Similarly, confronted with the prospect of dramatic social change, librarianship can be credited with displaying the "ideological confusion and political vacillation" cited by Clecak. Anxious that a librarianship forged in the context of the industrial age may be outmoded for the Information Society, librarians are open to the alternatives offered by the myth-makers of the electronic library. From a political perspective, what do the myth-makers offer?

The Politics of the Electronic Library

To the myth-makers, there is no political agenda for the electronic library. Based on technology, it is as politically value-free as technology itself is presumed to be. The information broker, as a free-lancer, is divorced from any values or political ideology that might adhere to a social institution such as the public library. This assumed neutrality is further reinforced by the focus on information as an objective commodity, in contrast to the traditional concern for knowledge, which embodies judgment and commitment. By focusing narrowly on information alone, by defining the role of the librarian within the parameters of the information broker in a market economy, and by cutting loose from any institutional connection, the myth of the electronic library appears to resolve many of the issues and ambiguities surrounding questions relating to the role of the librarian, the purpose of the library, and the values of librarianship. However, we need to examine the assertion that technology is neutral and, by extension, the neutrality of the myth of the electronic library. Technology is political and there is a political ideology underlining the myth of the electronic library as much as there is one underlining the myth of the library as place.

The political aspect of technology is a complex issue about which there continues to be extensive debate. Langdon Winner, in his careful examination of the issue, claims that "no idea is more provocative in controversies about technology and society than the notion that technical things have political qualities."[1] Winner advocates a theory of technological politics that takes into account the characteristics of technical objects and the implications of those characteristics. There are two ways, following Winner's argument, that technologies have political properties. In the first instance, a particular technology, by its nature, is used to resolve a political issue. Winner cites as an example the way the overpasses on the expressway to Jones Beach on Long Island, New York, were built—certainly to allow traffic on the expressway to move rapidly from the city to the park, but at such a low height as to prevent public buses from using the expressway. Preventing cheap public transportation was a means of excluding minority and other low-income groups from encroaching on what was intended to be a white, middle-class park.[2]

The second way technologies can be political is that certain technologies by their very nature are "inherently political technologies." As Winner explains: "According to this view, the adoption of a given technical system unavoidably brings with it conditions for human relationships that have a distinctive political cast—for example, centralized or decentralized, egalitarian or inegalitarian, repressive or liberating."[3] The use of a particular technology requires certain political and social arrangements. The classic analogy, going back to Plato, is the ship at sea. It is accepted that ships by their very nature and function require firm direction. Consequently, it is essential that the crew respond to the unquestioned authority of the captain. Similarly, technologies such as nuclear and solar energy systems can be classified as inherently authoritarian or democratic. Nuclear energy requires centralized authority control, while solar energy is more efficient decentralized and, hence, more participatory and democratic. The atomic bomb is cited as an example of a technology that demands a very centralized, secret, and hierarchical command structure. The technology of the bomb necessitates certain social and political arrangements, to the extent that democratic states must ensure that arrangements and attitudes required to manage nuclear weapons do not impinge on more democratic aspects of government and politics.[4]

Whether a technology is used to assert certain forms of power and authority or has characteristics that in themselves demand particular social forms, technologies can have political attributes or implications. We should ascertain the political qualities adhering to the idea of the electronic library. The electronic library is advanced as a necessary, indeed, inevitable response to revolutionary change. However, this position disguises the true nature of the myth. The general thrust of the myth of the electronic library is conservative, a conservatism rooted in the technology that is asserted to be the source of revolutionary change. Considering the central place the computer holds in the myth of the electronic library, it is useful to consider, as a start, the remarks of Joseph Weizenbaum, professor of computer science at the Massachusetts Institute of Technology.

Weizenbaum points out that as the computer becomes more ubiquitous, it is hard to imagine how we could operate without it. How would large corporations function or assembly lines operate efficiently? How would banks or airline reservation systems handle the massive number of transactions generated each day? Would not these services and others, including many library services, break down under the need to process large amounts of data? With hindsight, can we not conclude that the computer arrived "just in time" to save us all from massive system breakdowns? Yes, the computer did arrive "just in time," according to Weizenbaum. But, he asks, just in time for what? It arrived "in time to save—and save very nearly intact, indeed, to entrench and stabilize—social and political structures that otherwise might have been either radically renovated or allowed to totter under the demands that were sure to be made on them. The computer, then, was used to conserve America's social and political institutions. The adoption of the computer by large public and private organizations and bureaucracies made it possible for these entities to cope with the pressures being placed on them for increased services by a growing population while also providing a technology to perpetuate these organizations, thus entrenching systems and resisting innovation. The computer, most often perceived as a destabilizing innovation, is just as much a perpetuator of the status quo in its ability to foreclose other innovations. Admittedly, the computer can be a disruptive innovation, "but of the many paths to social innovation it opened to man, the most fateful was to make it possible for him to eschew all deliberate thought of substantive change."[5] It is in this context that the myth of the electronic library has important political implications.

What the myth-makers put forward is close to the "autonomist liberalism" defined by Shils, a liberalism now more often identified as conservatism. Autonomist "conservative" liberalism shares with Shils' collectivist liberalism several values. They both focus on the individual; are scientifically and technologically oriented; support formal education as a means toward self-improvement; believe in the desirability of the improvement of the general population along with equality of opportunity; tend toward rationalism over tradition; and favor democratic pluralism. However, autonomist liberalism, according to Shils, looks to the rationally motivated individual as opposed to the "affectively sensitive and expressive individual," the primary focus of collectivist individualism.[6] The myth-makers' concentration on the rationally motivated seeker of objective information is in accord with the autonomist perspective and in sharp contrast to the more traditional public library orientation to the broader educational, recreational, and self-fulfilling affective needs of users. Penland expresses a decidedly conservative bent about the implications of the rise of the "expressive individual" when he exclaimed, toward the end of the 1960s, "Unless the trend to micro-chauvinism and personal-amorphism can be reversed or at least objectified, it may lead to a breakdown of industrial civilization. Chaos will rapidly spread to the engineering sector. An electronic world cannot be run by a 'hippie' mentality, even if it is in the tribal village of mass media communication."[7] Penland advocates an elitism when he justifies readers advisory work as a means of developing individuals whose problem-solving abilities will allow them to become "an integrating force in the lives of others and in their society." Thus, "by force of example, others will be lead into socially integrative habits."[8]

Elitism is also found in Giuliano's attack on the ethic of free public library service. This ethic, according to Giuliano, reflects nineteenth-century values characteristic of the Industrial Age, when books were expensive for the average worker. Because information was not a significant economic commodity, equal access to it could be made available "free" to the general public through the institution of the tax-supported public library. However, with the Information Society, libraries have been dislodged from the communications process. For the affluent, the traditional users of the library, it is now more economical to purchase their information rather than spend the time to retrieve it from the public library. According to Giuliano, "The information 'poor' either tend to be nonusers or nontraditional users (e.g., users who steal records and current magazines) who create problems for the library." He claims that the ethic of the free library drives librarians to constantly attempt to attract the information-poor even though they do not want the services offered. Consequently, the library "assumes the form of some sort of welfare institution, one that is not very effective at that."[9] Meanwhile, being "free," the library is not valued by those who can afford to pay for informational services. It is not surprising that the myth-makers wish to dissociate themselves from the public library and promote the special library as their model. The myth-makers' consistent reference to the private-sector special library as a model for electronic library services, in contrast to the tax-supported public library, is in line with autonomist liberalism's sympathy for the private over the public sector. Their willingness to allow the allocation of library services through free market forces in opposition to public policy priorities further reflects autonomist liberalism's suspicion of government and its favoring of the free market economy. There are the repeated references to information as a commodity, the stress on efficiency as the criterion for measuring library services, the advocacy of fees for services, the characterization of librarians as information brokers or managers, the promotion of the idea of marketing library services, and the desire to be called chief executive officers.

When Shils made his analysis of liberalism in the 1970s, he believed that collectivist liberalism was the prevailing tendency in America. However, the inauguration of Ronald Reagan as president of the United States in 1981 confirmed that during the 1970s it was the conservatism of autonomist liberalism that was in the ascendancy. This autonomist liberalism was caught nicely in Reagan's inaugural address when he tied opportunity to productivity: "Government can and must provide opportunity, not smother it; foster productivity, not stifle it."[10] In the area of science and technology a major shift occurred to "a desire to reshape the political and administrative apparatus of the state in the interests of private corporations."[11] While this goal in itself was not new to American politics, David Dickson and David Noble describe how it was new to use science and technology policy to achieve it.

Starting under the presidency of Gerald Ford, spurred on by Carter, and accelerated by Ronald Reagan, scientific and technological policy was directed toward the objective of improving economic strength through increased productivity in the private sector. Science policy was shifted from serving social goals to that of achieving economic ends. This objective was vigorously promoted by a business community concerned about the growing suspicion of science and technology among the general public and the increasing demands for broader public participation in determining environmental policies and technological developments. The counterattack launched by business, as described by Dickson and Noble, consisted of four interrelated thrusts:

1. The rediscovery of the self-regulating market, the wonders of free enterprise, and the classical liberal attack on government regulation of the economy, all in the name of liberty.

2. The reinvention of the idea of progress, now cast in terms of "innovation" and "reindustrialization," and the limitation of expectations and social welfare in the quest for productivity.

3. The attack on democracy, in the name of "efficiency," "manageability," "governability," "rationality," and "competence."

4. The remystification of science through the promotion of formalized decision methodologies, the restoration of the authority of expertise, and the renewed use of science as legitimation for social policy through deepening industry ties to universities and other "free" institutions of policy analysis and recommendation.[12]

This strategy aligned nicely with autonomist liberal adherence to rationalism, science and technology, minimum government intervention, and efficiency. Throughout there is a prevailing utilitarianism as business fostered its greater integration into educational institutions and the research centers of the universities. As well, it sought a close integration with high-tech developments within the military establishment. Such a productivity-oriented utilitarian policy finds democratic questioning and participation troublesome and inefficient. Thus, business leaders, along with such prominent scientist and future EDUCOM gurus as educator and scientist Dr. John Kemeny and top IBM scientist Dr. Lewis Branscomb, warned that it was no longer possible to muddle through with the imperfect structures of democracy in dealing with advanced scientific and technological policy formulation and implementation.[13]

The emphasis placed on productivity fed the call for greater innovation. This argument found fuel in the social analysis provided by Bell and others who warned that we were moving out of an industrial society into a high-tech post-industrial information society. (As we observed earlier, descriptions of the "post-industrial society" and the "information society" began to meld into each other.) Thus, the demands for more information, for more sophisticated means of handling it, and the privatization of all means of its production and distribution were part and parcel of the productivity drive. In an economy dedicated to an ever-expanding supply of goods and services, more and more information, produced and sold by the private sector, was counted as a necessity. As inflation, unemployment, and economic constraints intensified, the allegiance to a high-tech information society only increased as a strategy to meet the challenge of a highly competitive international market.[14] The political ideology underlying the myth of the electronic library arises out of technical- and productivity-oriented politics and policies prevailing in the 1970s and 1980s, including its strong military component. However, the myth-makers of the electronic library prefer to avoid the political implications of the electronic library by placing it within the context of the concept of the post-industrial/information society.

Those advancing the idea of the post-industrial society anticipated the end of ideology. As political scientist Victor Ferkiss and others point out, much of Daniel Bell's early intellectual development was at a time when Marxism was a major issue of debate among American intellectuals, with Bell himself being influenced by Trotskyism.[15] One of the problems at issue was how to account for the survival of class domination and subordination within a society—Soviet society specifically—that had abolished private property, the source of class conflict. Ferkiss maintains that Bell's conception of the post-industrial society is really a response to this vexing question. Recall that in the post-industrial society, information as a commodity replaces property as the basis for social and economic power. With property no longer the basis of power, there no longer remains a revolutionary role for the proletariat and, hence, no need for ideology. (Ferkiss reminds us that it was also Bell who wrote an earlier well-known book, *The End of Ideology*, published in 1959). Because the post-industrial society will be one with an increasing abundance of information and a universal middle class of information workers, the older ideologies are deemed obsolete. Information technology, rational planning, and expanding participation in higher education will ensure the ever-expanding abundance of information and its equitable distribution. Bell looks forward to a society run by technicians in which, according to Ferkiss, "systems analysis will essentially replace politics."[16] In the Information Society pure politics will be replaced by rational calculations and decision-making based on pure knowledge.[17]

This non-ideological analysis is easily drawn on by the myth-makers and adopted by librarians favoring the myth of the electronic library. It is utopian enough in its commitment to abundance for all to meet the social conscience needs of most librarians. It appears scientifically and technologically based, therefore devoid of any troubling ideological biases, and it promises enhanced professional and personal status and reward for librarians. Until recently almost no one within librarianship examined critically the validity of this analysis. Few in librarianship would state, as two scholars in communications studies did, that:

Perhaps none of the other myths of past epochs—be it twelfth century Christianity, nineteenth century industrialism, or post-World War II consumerism—have been constructed with such deliberation and rapidity as the ideology of the information age. From public relations firms, advertising departments, and newsrooms to government agencies, think tanks, and heavily endowed researchers, a great effort is underway to focus precisely the vision of future salvation founded on new information technology.[18]

Fay M. Blake, a professor at the School of Library and Information Studies, University of California at Berkeley, was one of the few to raise a cry against the "arrant nonsense" of the post-industrial society at the 1977 ALA President's Program. She pointed out that more service workers did not necessarily mean more professional workers and that political power and science policy would not issue forth from the university or research library but would remain where it had always been, with the corporations. Meanwhile, the library establishment, in her view, proceeded to be most concerned about the development of a profitable information network, the information industry was pushing for greater privatization, and academic and public libraries were becoming more sympathetic to fees for services. Blake warned that librarians' desire to serve the information needs of the decision-makers of the post-industrial society would widen the gap between the information haves and the have-nots.[19] Perhaps Blake's call was too impassioned for the cool rationality called for by a profession about to take its rightful place among the elite of the Information Society. Her comments were largely ignored. After all, not only in the United States, but in France, Canada, England, and Japan, government reports, committee studies, and the research of social scientists all proclaimed an international economic realignment transcending national borders and differences in political cultures based on technological developments in communications and information processing (both of which were often seen as one and the same thing). However, as much as librarians might like to believe that the electronic library in a post-industrial information society is free of any ideological implications, this is not the case. The concept of the post-industrial information society has numerous flaws as social analysis; nevertheless, it has been widely adopted because of its functionality as an ideology. It serves this function in several ways. While most advocates of the post-industrial society would not consider themselves conservatives, they accept the status quo: a capitalist, free market society whose economic growth is to be extended through the use of science and technology. The post-industrial information society does not represent a radical break from the traditional industrial economic and political culture but actually projects its dominant characteristics. The ideology of the post-industrial society justifies an elite class of scientists and technical managers in government, university, and corporate bureaucracies. It is here that the myth-makers and their librarian adherents would like to find themselves, among the elite decision-makers of the information society. Would they go unchallenged?

We noted that within government and the private sector there have been since the early 1970s growing efforts to promote productivity in the national economy through the use of federal science and technology policy, a policy reflecting autonomous liberal tenets incorporated into the myth of the electronic library. Part of this trend includes the privatization of information; the shifting of responsibility for the distribution of information initially collected by the federal government to private-sector distributors. The Information Industry Association (IIA), not surprisingly, was an eager advocate of this policy. The privatization of government information proceeded apace under the Carter administration to such an extent that the American Library Association was roused to express concern. These concerns were further explicated at the first White House Conference on Library and Information Services, held in November 1979. Several resolutions adopted at the conference reaffirmed librarianship's commitment to free public access to information. These resolutions related to the undesirability of charges for library services, the need for continued subsidization of the federal government library depository system for government publications, and a call for a national information policy that would ensure a nation of informed citizens. With the election of Ronald Reagan in 1981, more librarians began to perceive that significant consequences for librarianship and library service could arise out of the political agenda of the government and special-interest groups. The issue of the privatization of information and the increasing budgetary pressures to charge fees for services, an issue that became more explicit with the introduction of commercially available on-line bibliographic search services, emerged as political issues that began to be recognized as forming a pattern. The implications of the myth of the electronic library were becoming more evident.

For example, libraries were increasingly examined primarily as economic entities as economists challenged the "library faith." As one economist claimed, it was necessary, with regard to the public library, to examine from an economic perspective "the myths of its important role in education, in helping the poor, in socializing the immigrants."[20] This approach attempted to assess the value and use of libraries through the use of economic concepts and assumptions such as the motivating force of individual self-interest, the role of rational behavior on economic decision-making, opportunity costs of alternative sources of information, the concepts of scarcity and efficiency, and the distinction between private and public goods. Public libraries were described as constituting an "industry" in that a variety of "inputs are hired" and put together to form a "production process." The industry had to be analyzed to measure costs and efficiency, issues librarians were accused of neglecting.

However, some librarians began to see the issues were not strictly economic but were more appropriate to the realm of political economy. The economic questions relating to the generation of revenue to fund libraries, the issue of who used libraries, and the question of public good had to be dealt with in the broader social and political context. Not all librarians were prepared to give up looking at libraries within the ideology of the library as place. "A specter is haunting this country—the specter of Adam Smith," warned Miriam Braverman, a professor at the Columbia University School of Library Service. She stated emphatically that the economic policies of the Reagan administration were creating an environment favorable to "a queue of market-mechanism worshippers" who "invoke their individual mantras—rugged individualism, free enterprise, free market economy" in an effort to achieve what they perceived as the *laissez-faire* world of Adam Smith. Braverman expressed concern about the "strong evidence in the library field . . . of lemming-like movements to adopt business jargon and methods of evaluation."[21]

The American Library Association felt compelled to form a Commission on Freedom and Equality of Access to Information in 1983, chaired by Dan Lacy, a consultant with McGraw-Hill with a distinguished career in publishing and government information services. The commission's report is an interesting attempt to wed the myths of the library as place and the electronic library. In addressing "The Role of Libraries in an Era of Electronic Information," the report accepted that we live in an Information Society. However, it cautioned that the "marketplace forces that are propelled by the exotic and expensive new information technologies" must be balanced against public interest and needs. It recognized that "of course the free enterprise system must be allowed to function, indeed to flourish, but it must be understood that information need is not always synonymous with the information marketplace."[22] The report asserted that the "community library and information center" must continue to provide access to information regardless of its format. It accepted that "the library as a *place*" of locally owned collections may decline while its role as "community library *service*" increases. The traditional library must become a community information and communications center. The members of the commission expressed concern about what appeared to be a general policy on the part of the government to restrict public information about the government itself and about the dissemination of information gathered by the government. While making the usual reference to the need for informed citizens, the report's authors argued that such a restrictive policy would adversely affect the competitiveness of the entire economy. In short, it adopted the productivity argument promulgated by the Reagan administration.

Librarians were increasingly being given lessons in economic and political theory as they began to examine more closely the economic and political context of libraries. Thus, it was pointed out that as the traditional ownership of capital experiences long-term declines in profit, there is the danger that the ownership of knowledge would be appropriated in the search for private-sector profit.[23] The assumptions and assertions of Bell, Giuliano, and others were scrutinized more closely and questioned. Librarians were warned about the hazards of futuristic predictions. The role of the library as a provider of not only information, but knowledge, in print as well as electronically, was asserted. The possibility of librarians being replaced by private-sector information brokers was disputed. Even Lancaster himself expressed unease in seeing the ownership of information slipping out of the control of the public sector and into that of the private sector, a process encouraged by the information industry.[24]

As librarians explored further the implications of political aspects of the library, they revealed the links between the various elements constituting the myth of the electronic library. By the mid-1980s, sociologist Richard Apostle and library professor Boris Raymond were able to delineate what they called the "information paradigm."[25] The essence of this paradigm is the focus on "information," its commodification and its centrality in concepts of the post-industrial and information societies. While librarians are encouraged to abandon traditional values and roles by the promoters of the paradigm, Apostle and Raymond question several of its elements. The myth of the electronic library was being made ever more explicit.

John Buschman, a librarian at Rider College, New Jersey, explored further these themes in two widely read library journals.[26] He attacked the promulgation of the information broker as an alternative to traditional reference service and defined reference as a service oriented toward people and books. He asserted that there was under way an effortless, subtle shift away from this orientation as librarians strove, in the name of progress, to eliminate a negative professional image. However, the shift to the idea of the information broker generates a number of conflicts with the traditional reference orientation. Implied in the information broker concept is the focus on unrelated bits of information as opposed to the organized knowledge inherent in books. Buschman also expresses concern about the privatization of information embodied in the concept of the information broker. The increased reliance on commercial vendors for computer-based electronic information, combined with more library charges for services and the conception of library service based on the corporate model, threaten librarianship's long-standing commitment to the provision of access to knowledge as a public good. This privatization of information is allied with the reification of information, a process grounded in a zealous enthusiasm for technology and for the methodologies of information retrieval. Buschman accuses librarians, concerned as ever about their image, of being taken in by the hype of information technology, with the result that there is among librarians a lack of a critical attitude toward the political and professional implications of technology and the model of the information broker.

Buschman sees several possibilities arising out of this trend. Instead of an increase in professional status, there is the potential de-skilling of the profession due to an over-reliance on technology, expert systems being an example. The most disturbing aspect for Buschman about adopting the information broker model is the shift to the private entrepreneurial orientation at the expense of the traditional commitment to free and open access to books and information in support of democracy and the general public good. Clearly, we hear here a strong voice for the myth of the library as place.

As librarians began to fill out the lineaments of the myth of the electronic library, they also questioned the presumed neutrality of librarianship. Librarians were accused of asserting their political neutrality in order to join the professional elites of the post-industrial information society.[27] Henry Blanke, reference librarian at Marymount Manhattan College, New York, warned of the danger of such a position: "By perpetuating the myth that their profession should be politically neutral, librarians have created a value vacuum that is easily being filled by the prevailing political and economic ethos. Neutrality, in effect, allows an unquestioned acquiescence to the imperatives of the most powerful and influential elements in society."[28] Blanke attacks the model put forward promoting the information intermediary role and urges librarians to rededicate themselves to serving the information needs of all elements of society. They should not allow themselves to be seduced by the conservative crusade launched by powerful elites. Instead, they should oppose fees for services, the commercialization of information, and abandon their political neutrality in order to fight these trends in the political sphere. Blanke says librarians must defend the values embodied in the principles of equity and public service rather than adopt those values driven by the technological imperative and the marketplace.

The conservative sources of the myth of the electronic library were further explored by Jorge F. Sosa, librarian in the Latin American Faculty of Social Sciences, Quito, Ecuador, and Michael H. Harris, a professor in the College of Library Science at the University of Kentucky. They argue that the neo-conservative utopia of information society adherents such as Daniel Bell and the role of the librarian as information intermediary were foretold in Jose Ortega y Gasset's elitist concept of the mission of the librarian explicated in his address to the International Congress of Bibliographers and Librarians in Paris in 1934. Ortega believed librarians must serve as filters between people and the deluge of books. Sosa and Harris review the debates that have emerged over the issue of intellectual freedom and the role of the librarian as selector, censor, or information intermediary.

They tentatively conclude that the attacks by Blake, Blanke, and others on the information paradigm identified by Apostle and Raymond support a rejection of the paradigm. Thus, by the early 1990s, Sosa and Harris would claim that the debate engendered by the emergence of the myth of the electronic library, with its neo-conservative values, resulted in "the creation of a deep split between those librarians who insist that librarians must remain committed to neutrality and passivity even at the expense of professional status and those who insist librarians must quickly move to establish the foundations of authority within the context of the information paradigm." They believe it is "this contradiction that librarians will continue to debate, and it is clear that the outcome of that debate will have significant implications for the role of the librarian in American society and the structural and functional characteristics of American libraries."[29] In the next chapter we enter that debate.

Libraries and Life Chances

Would life be life if it had to conform to hypothesis?

Milovah Djilas

The political economy of the myth of the electronic library is autonomist liberalism. Liberalism has always been the political framework of librarianship, but the autonomist liberalism of the myth of the electronic library, in contrast to the collectivist liberalism of the myth of the library as place, is in accord with the neo-conservative bent of American political culture since the 1970s, just as the myth of the library as place was in accord with early and mid-twentieth century Progressive and New Deal reformism. The library as place was part of the institution-building of American liberal democracy, bolstered by the bureaucratic professionalization of the public service. The makers of the myth of the electronic library advance the view that the bureaucratic library is an obsolete remnant of industrial society. The information society calls for non-bureaucratic, technically oriented processes—not institutions—free through electronic networks from a sense of place. Examining further the place of the network in the myth of the electronic library, draws us again into the larger cultural and political context.

One of the objectives of this book is to emphasize that there are possibilities beyond those claimed to be inevitable by the myth-makers of the electronic library. I have shown that the information society may not exist to the extent and depth claimed by the myth-makers; that alternative conceptualizations are possible, the therapeutic society as an example; that an alternative role to the information specialist can be posited in that of the therapeutic librarian; that the library as a bureaucratic institution and as a physical place can continue to have relevance for society and librarians; that technology is not the only force for change and the consequences of its development are not inevitable; and that political choices are open to librarians. I believe librarians have the ability to formulate a system of beliefs, norms, and values—in short, a new myth—that allows the library to continue to play a valuable role in a changing society. To do so, we start by returning to the dynamics of social change since the nineteenth century and in particular the dynamic relationship between community and individualism.

We have observed that library ideology included the idea of the public library as an important institutional element identified with the conservative cohesiveness of community while also embodying the more cosmopolitan liberal valuation of individualism. This attempt to encompass both community and individualism contributed to the confusion associated with public library goals. However, I believe librarians can create a myth whose source resides in the library's ability to sustain both community and individualism and to serve as a bridge between them within the context of a liberal ideology.

The interaction between community and the individual in human relations has been a central concern throughout American history. However, it is not easy to find an agreed definition of community or of individualism. Political scientist Mason Drukman states, "In their extreme formulations, individualism and community are irreconcilable principles: to lay heavy emphasis on one is to rule out the inclusion of the other. Whereas individualism is best expressed in terms of *in*dependence, community suggests a condition of *inter*dependence."[1]

Far more attention was given to the issue of community in Europe than in America by the founders of modern sociology who, in the last half of the nineteenth century, were attempting to describe and account for the social change in their midst. Sociologist Robert A. Nisbet states that "the most fundamental and far-reaching of sociology's unit-ideas is community. The rediscovery of community is unquestionably the most distinctive development in nineteenth century thought, a development that extends well beyond sociological theory to such areas as philosophy, history, and theology to become indeed one of the major themes of imaginative writing in the century."[2]

Like community, individualism is a nineteenth-century idea, and its meanings can vary as much as those ascribed to community. In his concise examination of individualism, political scientist Steven Lukes delineates political, economic, religious, ethical, epistemological, and methodological individualism.[3] Many of these elements of individualism are embodied in liberal doctrine. Just as both conservatives and radicals place, in their different ways, great stress on community, so individualism was initially used by them as a term to attack liberalism. In the United States, the term, however, had decidedly positive meanings. According to Lukes, "It was in the United States that 'individualism' primarily came to celebrate capitalism and liberal democracy. It became a symbolic catchword of immense ideological significance, expressing all that has at various times been implied in the philosophy of natural rights, the belief in free enterprise, and the American Dream."[4] This adherence to individualism thrived during the early settlement of America at the expense of community. Americans were very conscious they were breaking away from the traditions of the old world, including those elements constituting communal bonds. During much of the early history of the country, geographic dispersion and the ability to pick up and move on worked against community. Finally, the focus on economic individualism and competition, combined with a relative abundance supporting individual self-sufficiency, fostered individualism. The word "individualism" itself was introduced into English with the translation of Alexis de Tocqueville's famous analysis of American character and society, *Democracy in America*, published in 1840.

The Enlightenment of the eighteenth century advanced the rights of the individual over the multitude of restraints bearing on the individual in the hierarchal community of feudal society. In the nineteenth century, Karl Marx and many others saw industrialization and political revolution as a means of breaking constraints of the mythic rural community. Much American literature of the early twentieth century vividly describes the narrow lives of those confined to the rural small town. Still, people do not want to face alone the alienation, isolation, and estrangement many see as the result of extreme individualism and the collapse of community. Most people want balance in their lives between those bonds we associate with community and the freedom of choice associated with individualism.

Community and individualism are ideals to which we aspire. The family, with all the stresses placed on it in modern society, still remains an enduring institution providing bonds of community. People seek the bonds of community in religious, ethnic, or neighborhood relationships. But people also are involved in more abstract and contractual arrangements related to individualism, such as the professions, citizenship, or the market economy. They strive for self-fulfillment as distinct individuals. The result is that we experience living in a "bifurcated society" in which we simultaneously experience community and individualism, a situation emerging out of the social change of the nineteenth century.[5]

In this bifurcated society, institutions play a critical role, a key point made by Robert Bellah and his colleagues in their follow-up to *Habits of the Heart*. In their attempt to set out an agenda for attaining *The Good Society*, they urge the revitalization of political, religious, and social institutions to counteract anti-institutional American individualism. They believe, as communitarians, that in addition to the typical face-to-face social relations of community, the larger social structures and institutions of contemporary society can be used to address the critical needs, communal and individualistic, of the American people. They assert that America's traditional liberal hopes of individual autonomy from institutions work contrary to the best interests of society. Individuals cannot divorce themselves from institutions. Instead, freedom must be conceived in the context of enabling institutions. In commenting on the role of institutions in the social environment of the market-driven urban milieu, they make an observation that brings us to a consideration of the role of the public library, and other types of libraries to varying degrees. They observe:

And the organizations of the "third sector"—such as schools and universities, religious organizations, theaters, museums, and orchestras, voluntary associations of all kinds—have given the collective purposes of justice, mutual aid, enlightenment, worship, fellowship, and celebration some substance in metropolitan life. They have civilized commerce and enhanced metropolitan life and have saved the market from its own worst consequences. But they have done more. They are points of "focal structure," places where people can meet to focus their attention and gain a sense of the whole of life through the cultivation of memory and orientation.[6]

Here is an institutional role for the public library: a "focal structure" sustaining and serving as a bridge between community and individualism, between the family and local community and the wider world, between communitarianism and liberalism. In this respect, it continues the role it held in the tradition of democratic institution-building that Bellah and others seek to revive.

Is there a possibility that as institutions, libraries can strengthen both community and individualism and serve as a bridge between the two? In a complex urban society, it is not possible that all of one's relationships can be restricted to the communal context. Individuals must deal, at least in certain areas of their daily lives, with outside institutions—the economy being one of the most obvious—in order to survive. Individualism can inject into the community information and a richer organizational life, factors that can help it cope with threats to its cohesiveness. Bridges to the outside are necessary for both the community and individuals. The public library played this role in the past and can continue to do so.

Thomas Bender speculates that the modern public school that emerged in the latter decades of the nineteenth-century served such a bridging function as it supplemented certain socialization processes of the family. The school became a means of enabling the child to adjust to the transition from the supportive role of the family, where one learned about community, to the larger world of individual self-sufficiency. The feminization of education was encouraged in the belief that female teachers would be most adept at guiding children across this bridge.[7] By promoting the best of the world's literature (as they perceived it), good citizenship, Americanism, intellectual freedom, or adult education, nineteenth century librarians also created linkages between community and the larger society. Again, women were perceived as uniquely qualified to establish in the library, as in the schoolroom and the settlement house, a home-like atmosphere, a hospitable way station for those who were moving out of the security of the family and intimate community.[8]

If this bridging role was integral to the mandate of the public library in the closing decades of the nineteenth century, the need remains in the closing decades of the twentieth. A recent example is a report by Ernest L. Boyer, *Ready to Learn: A Mandate for the Nation*, published by the Carnegie Foundation for the Advancement of Teaching in 1991. This is a major study on establishing a learning environment for children before they enter formal schooling. Boyer expresses concern that if children do not have supportive families and other nurturing associations, the schools cannot be expected to compensate for these differences. Boyer believes parents are as concerned as ever about their children. However, he observes, "What *has* changed . . . is the loss of community, the increased fragmentation of family life, the competing, often conflicting, pressures that keep family members on the go and out of touch with one another."[9] Boyer vividly describes the breakdown of community.

Gradually, the protective ring eroded. New work patterns and increased mobility uprooted small-town life. Relatives moved away. Families became isolated, disconnected, struggling alone. Neighbors became strangers, doors were bolted, and friendliness was replaced by fear. A climate of anonymity blanketed communities. Children were warned to avoid people they didn't know, and "reaching out to touch someone" came to mean pushing electronic buttons. Modern life, which offered more conveniences and more options, destabilized former certainties and weakened traditional networks of support.[10]

He advocates creating "neighborhoods for learning" consisting of a variety of "learning stations," including museums, zoos, playgrounds, and libraries. Libraries have a special role, he maintains, in preparing children for school by "offering children entry into the world of books, helping them develop language skills, and stirring the imagination."[11] He notes the irony that while the need for libraries, museums, and other similar agencies is greater than ever, budgets are being reduced drastically.

It is easy to see in Boyer's proposal the public library serving children as a bridge between community and individualism. But can such a role be extended to wider application? We find another example of libraries being asked to do so in *Making Connections: the Humanities, Culture, and Community* (1990), a publication arising out of a conference of the National Task Force on Scholarship and the Public Humanities, written by James Quay and James Veninga, and published by the American Council of Learned Societies and the Federation of State Humanities Councils.[12] They argue that a changing society requires America to become a learning society. One of the consequences of the forces of change is that "Americans will need new ways to see forests instead of trees, to turn information into knowledge, knowledge into wisdom. Computer technology and telecommunications may nourish networks while communities wither."[13] From these trends Quay and Veninga see the need for the humanities to promote three types of literacies: multicultural, civic, and community. With regard to the latter, the humanities are called on to counter the "acids of modernity" that "threaten the connections to place that bind communities together." They recognize that community can be restricting and the freedom offered by much of modern society can be liberating, "but these days, we increasingly have the sense that our communal life is out of balance: we need less acid and more base."[14]

The authors outline how a humanities public scholarship can address these concerns. Of particular interest for our purposes is their assertion of the need for institutional connections providing "opportunities for informal education and cultural conversation." They call these institutions the "parallel school" and include among them public libraries.[15] Clearly, the idea of parallel schools provided by Quay and Veninga is closely allied with Bellah's focal structure and Boyer's neighborhood learning stations. What is also striking is that each of these observers are calling for a *place* for people to go where they can interact with others, a place both providing a sense of community and promoting individualism. They are not talking about individuals isolated in front of a terminal in some remote location. They are talking about the library as place.

Clearly, as well, these studies are calling on libraries to fulfill a cultural role they once proudly pursued in their efforts to Americanize the immigrant, promote adult education, and provide the best literature. However, many librarians, embarrassed by these efforts, which are seen as tools of social control, turn their backs on the humanities and try to attach themselves to science so that they may forget about culture and get on with their "real business," as Margaret Steig so boldly stated it. Those who now look to the special library as the model for librarianship will argue that these calls for assistance from librarianship to serve as a bridge between community and individualism might be applicable to children's or adult services in the public library but have little wider relevance to librarianship. But if one thinks of community and individualism as two poles of a continuum, it is possible to place various types of libraries, or even services, along the continuum. The small-town public library, for example, could be placed at the far end of the community pole as it serves and responds to the needs of the local community. The special library in a multinational private corporation, dedicated to promoting the cosmopolitan, market-driven instrumental ends of the corporation, would be at the far end of the individualism pole. Thus, the two types of library appear to have little in common. However, I am not advocating seeing community/individualism as mutually exclusive forms of social relationships. Both types exist to greater and lesser extents in our lives. We are, in our bifurcated society, constantly moving between them: from family to school and work, from local voluntary group to national professional association, from local neighborhood to national political participation. Consequently, various types of libraries will serve as a bridge to a greater or lesser degree in the pervasive dynamic of community and individualism.

Advocating the relevance of the library as place in the context of the community/individualism nexus does not divorce librarianship from those liberal values, such as intellectual freedom and autonomy from local prejudices, to which it proudly adheres. However, it does require librarians to admit that they and their profession are not value-free and that they must continually examine the validity and consequences of those values.

In addition to the traditional discourse among the political ideologies of liberalism, conservatism, and socialism on the nature of community and individualism, an added perspective is emerging in what has been called the "communitarian critique." This line of thought attempts to break the impasse between welfare liberalism and free-market individualism. It shares with conservatism a suspicion of bureaucracy but extends that suspicion beyond big government to organizations in the private sector as well. It counters liberalism's unencumbered individualism and anti-traditionalism with the view that "the self is situated in and constituted by tradition, membership in a historically rooted community."[16] However, it does not adhere to the nostalgic myth of the little community favored by conservatives. Instead, it claims that "what is missing from the debate about individualism and community, as carried on up until now, is the possibility of a conversational relationship with the past, one that seeks neither to deny the past nor to achieve an imaginative restoration of the past but to enter into a dialogue with the traditions that still shape our view of the world, often in ways in which we are not even aware."[17] This is not an advocacy of conservatism's reliance on tradition as authority but an acknowledgment of the conflicts as well as consensus embodied in traditions. The communitarian critique encourages a "public conversation" drawing on the richness of tradition and, in doing so, expands the discussion beyond purely economic consideration to ones involving morality, religion, and culture.

Gillian Gremmels attempts to introduce a communitarian perspective into recent concerns about the ethics of library reference service. Gremmels, coordinator of public services at the Depauw University Library, urges librarians to recognize that librarianship is not value-free, but rooted in liberal individualism. Librarians must stop hiding behind an unattainable neutrality and recognize that the reference encounter is a complex interchange between the client, the librarian, and the information source, each of which embodies various values within a social and institutional context. Librarians must continually assess the rights of the individual and of the public interest, attempting always the difficult and complex task of seeking an appropriate balance.[18]

While librarians must engage in such difficult assessments, this is not a case of opting for either liberal individualism or conservative or socialist communitarianism. Rather, librarians can recognize that librarianship operates in the sphere where these areas touch and debate ensues. Libraries are an institutional bridge offering, on the communitarian side, resources contributing to the formulation of a shared culture, an organization of knowledge that serves as a "community of memory,"[19] and, on the individualism side, a window to the world of experience, ideas, and values beyond the local. This is a difficult position to be in, to be sure. It means librarians will continue to operate in a political and moral sphere fraught with ambiguity. They will not have available the narrow, precise, and neutral stance promised, unrealistically, by the myth of the electronic library. Neither does it mean that the liberal traditions of librarianship must be abandoned. The self-fulfillment of the individual will remain a primary social objective to which librarianship contributes. Can we formulate a conceptual framework reconciling a liberal commitment to individualism with the need for community when formulating a new myth for librarianship?

Liberals are not unaware that they must address the issue of community and individualism in the age of modernity. In doing so, the liberal political philosopher Ralf Dahrendorf provides in his concept of "life chances" a framework for incorporation into a new myth of the library. Dahrendorf wants "a liberal society that is not libertine, a structure of authority that is not authoritarian, a social order that is not informed by law-and-order hysteria, thus a world in which choices are more than an invitation for endless *actes gratuities*, and bonds are more than painful restrictions of individual development."[20] Dahrendorf is committed to the individualism of liberalism and modernity but recognizes, as have others we have cited, that it has created its own problems: anomie, lack of appreciation for history, a reduced role for religion, a valuing of mobility over local loyalties, the family placed under extreme stress.

To address the dilemma of modern liberal individualism, Dahrendorf proposes thinking in terms of "life chances," a concept consisting of two critical elements: " options" and "ligatures" (or, as he sometimes refers to them, choices and linkages). Life chances are "the sum total of opportunities offered to the individual by his society, or by a specific position occupied in society."[21] They are those opportunities provided by social structures that allow for individual growth and the realization of one's talents and dreams. Life chances are a function of the two factors: options and ligatures. Options are the possibility of choice or alternatives. They may be available because of, for example, money, mobility, the cultural opportunities of the city, or education. They are in simple terms the opportunities open to individuals. Options, as choices, represent that aspect of individual freedom liberals value so highly. Liberalism and modernity have extended the range of options for many people. However, Dahrendorf acknowledges that a point is reached at which "choices begin to lose their meaning because they take place in a social vacuum, or better perhaps, a social desert, in which no known co-ordinates make any direction preferable to any other."[22] At that point there exists an imbalance of options to ligatures.

Dahrendorf defines ligatures as allegiances, bonds, or linkages, including those bonds often associated with community such as religion, the responsibilities of the social contract, an awareness of history, patriotism, or the sense of family. There can be an imbalance of ligatures as well as options with the result that they become excessively restrictive. Nevertheless, Dahrendorf asserts that "a liberal position which aims at the extension of human life chances must have the formation of ligatures as much (and at times perhaps more) in mind as the opening-up of options."[23] As he states, where there is a predominance of ligatures over options there is oppression; however, a predominance of options without ligatures is meaninglessness. He rejects the usual zero-sum game implied in this type of typology in which an increase in one element requires a decrease in the other. He maintains that an increase in options should not have to result in a decrease in ligature, although that often appears to be the case. Instead, ways must be found to enhance life chances by increasing both options and ligatures and maintaining an appropriate balance between them. It is in this way that the liberal commitment to advancing liberty can best be achieved in the context of community.

Dahrendorf's concept of life chances, consisting of options and ligatures, provides a conceptual framework preserving librarianship's liberal commitment to individualism and responding as well to communitarian concerns. We noted earlier that the myth of the library as place includes elements often identified with conservatism and community—in short, ligatures. But there are also elements relating to liberalism's focus on the free choices and equal opportunities of individuals, that is, options. I believe the objective of librarianship is the extension of life chances through the enhancement of ligatures and options. This extension of life chances is achieved through the institutional structure of the library providing access to an organized body of knowledge. The library as an institution meets a social need through the provision of access to organized bodies of knowledge. It supports ligatures by serving as a community of memory and options by enhancing the learning opportunities of individuals. It also serves the individual and the community by providing a bridge for the individual between community and the wider world of the bifurcated society.

If we accept that the role of the library is that of a dynamic institution providing a bridging function that enhances life chances in the context of both ligatures and options, then we can expect, as in the past, that the objectives of the public library will remain diverse and multiple. Rather than seeing this situation as a weakness, a lack of focus, it should be recognized as a strength appropriate in a complex bifurcated society. The persistent need in people for both communal bonds and individual liberty will continue and result in a multiplicity of social structures and institutions supporting these ends. Libraries gain from this interaction of community and individualism not a confusion but a profusion of goals. This profusion of goals serving a bridging function between community and individualism is precisely what we find when we examine *Planning and Role Setting for Public Libraries: A Manual of Operations and Procedures*, published in 1987 by the American Library Association for the Public Library Development Project. The manual sets out eight basic goals for the public library that represent an extensive range of services directed to a diverse clientele. These roles, I believe, also illustrate how the public library is attempting to meet the objectives that Boyer and others call for; how, in doing so, it supports both ligatures and options; how it serves as a bridge between community and individualism. The goals are:

Community Activities Center: The library is a central focus point for community activities, meetings, and services.

Community Information Center: The library is a clearinghouse for current information on community organizations, issues, and services.

Formal Education Support Center: The library assists students of all ages in meeting educational objectives established during their formal courses of study.

Independent Learning Center: The library supports individuals of all ages pursuing a sustained program of learning independent of any educational provider.

Popular Materials Library: The library features current, high-demand, high-interest materials in a variety of formats for persons of all ages.

Preschoolers' Door to Learning: The library encourages young children to develop an interest in reading and learning through services for children, and for parents and children together.

Reference Library: The library actively provides timely, accurate, and useful information for community residents.

Research Center: The library assists scholars and researchers to conduct in-depth studies, investigate specific areas of knowledge, and create new knowledge.[24]

In elaborating on the benefits to the community of these roles, the manual speaks of the opportunities provided to members of the community "to explore their common heritage, discuss their divergent views on issues and current topics, and receive some social services." The library will provide access to information that "helps individuals to become self-sufficient, control their lives, and better understand community issues." The library is described as a formal educational opportunity supplementing other educational institutions and, as called for by Boyer, as a door to learning for preschoolers that will contribute to success when children move into formal schooling. The library further promotes ligatures and options and serves as a bridge in its provision of services to those independent learners who want to improve their work opportunities, "to clarify their values, to learn something new," or to adjust to changes in their lives. In this way, "the library supports an educated, self-reliant, and productive citizenry, thus contributing to the stability, attractiveness, and economic well-being of the community."[25] As we see, the roles are aimed at the general community as well as specific groups, although, as in the past and in accord with liberal tenets, the ultimate target is the individual. Nevertheless, the library is identified as an important resource contributing to community and individualism, ligatures, and options. The roles also delineate how the library serves as a bridging instrument for those ranging from preschoolers to scholarly researchers.

The community/individualism nexus, then, should be seen as a source of constant creative revitalization of the public library, garnering it widespread support and ensuring its continued existence as a bridge between these two fundamental modes of social interaction. Librarians may be attracted to the myth of the electronic library because they see it as one explicitly and narrowly defining the role of the librarian, primarily as a provider of access to information. This stance may be intellectually satisfying and may alleviate some of the anxiety perpetually surrounding the question of library goals and the purpose of librarianship. But such an approach ignores the complexity and ambiguity of the real world, especially during a time of change. Instead, librarians should welcome a multiplicity of goals despite the uncertainty that entails. Such diversity can make the library a stronger institution and librarianship a stronger profession. A student of higher education, Burton Clark, makes the point in his analysis of universities that a multiplicity of goals, some of which are contradictory, can ensure greater institutional flexibility, vitality, and survival. He advocates the acceptance of ambiguity, disorder, decentralization, and variety in the goals of university systems as a means of enhancing institutional effectiveness. The impulse for consistency and simplicity should be resisted.[26] Like complex natural ecological systems, complex institutions are more apt to survive trauma than are simple systems. Thus, a flexible diversity of goals can strengthen the institutional foundations of the public library and broaden its range of support and clientele.

Turning to the role of the librarian, I see it continuing within the institutional framework of the library. I am insisting that that role, and any myth of the library, must revolve around an institution rather than, as with the myth of the electronic library, a technology or an abstract concept of the electronic library. It is within an institutional framework that librarianship will achieve greater professional status and, more important, make a substantive contribution to a liberal democratic society. I argue that the concept of a therapeutic society offers more potential for discerning the role of the librarian than does the information society. I advance the view that the role of the librarian is therapeutic in that librarians share their expertise with their clients in order to allow clients to increase their own personal growth and self-sufficiency. This therapeutic role is in accord with the bridging function of libraries between ligatures and options.

We have examined the institutional implications of the library and the role of the librarian in the context of enhancing life chances in a therapeutic society. Let's now examine the library, not as an institution, but as a physical place in that context as well. The myth-makers replace the material library as place with the abstract electronic library, a node on an electronic super highway. The library and the network are seen as one and the same thing. The concept of the network can be seen as another metaphor arising out of the social change of modernity of the last and current century. We noted earlier the utopian values associated with the myth of the electronic revolution and how technological utopians saw the electronic grid as a metaphor for social and institutional relations. Robert Fishman sees the power of this metaphor in the emergence of what he calls the technoburbs that make up the techno-city. The technoburb, in contrast to the older suburbia contingent to a central city, is a peripheral zone around major urban centers that are self-sufficient and independent of the central city. This socio-economic unit is made possible by the communication technologies that have made the face-to-face communication of the traditional city dispensable. The technoburb is decentralized, multidirectional, formless. It consists not of a central core but of a multiplicity of destinations of urban services and jobs close to each dwelling. A collection of technoburbs transforms a metropolitan region into the techno-city. The technoburb is the culmination of American liberalism's autonomist individual pursuing her own self-interest on the electronic highway. Its primary cultural instrument is television, a technology decentralized and home-centered, like the technoburb itself. Many now anticipate that the home computer terminal will become as ubiquitous as the TV receiver. The technoburb—formless, decentralized, home-centered—is the milieu in which the myth-makers see the electronic or virtual library thriving.[27] Will the electronic library be part of a society that lacks any coherence or community, that serves alone the ends of totally liberated, free-floating individuals?

Some hope the development of the telecommunications technologies will actually be a means of restoring the sense of community destroyed by the Industrial Revolution. Anthony Smith, a student of communications, agrees that "the perfect information society should be totally self-transparent: in it everyone can find out and know everything; it is in this sense a perfect community."[28] However, Smith warns that an information society, in which relationships are defined only by one's relation to links in the flow of information, can lead to a shattering of community. As we move from the era of Gutenberg to the era of Shannon, we risk believing that we can disregard history itself through the use of "artificial intelligence" in a network environment. According to Smith, if we live in an electronic "virtual" information society transcending space and time, we live without memory or history—in short, without community. This sterile prospect draws us back to the need for those institutions, like the library, that will play the cultural role Bellah and others hope to see in a revitalization of democratic institutions. Networks, it appears, can offer the possibility of some degree of community for those seeking it and greater individualism for others. These two possibilities do not exclude the further possibility that the seekers of both types of social relations will not require an institutional support to achieve their ends. And while institutions can be social forms separate from any particular material representation, most are manifested in an objective way: the corporate skyscraper, the school, the church, the courthouse, the library. Not only will people want the library as place to remain as a focus for sensual delight and social interaction, but because it is essential as a means of preserving and maintaining important cultural and political values and objectives.

To accept this perspective does not require a rejection of the importance of the electronic network environment and the communications theory that underlies it. But it is important, as James Carey asserts, to view communications in American culture differently from the way they are used within the myth of the electronic library. The myth-makers placed the development of information technology in a framework derived from communications theory. The results of this effort need not be abandoned, but we do need to look on communications theory in a broader respect. According to Carey, since the word "communication" became commonly used in nineteenth-century America, it has had two alternative conceptions: a transmission view and a ritual view. The transmission view, the sending or transmitting of information, is the most widely used conception of communication, relating initially to the transmission of goods, people, and information over geographic space to meet the needs of the Industrial Revolution. The speed of this transmission was vastly accelerated with the discovery of the telegraph. The introduction of electronic communications cut the link between communication and transportation. Carey notes that in the nineteenth century, the technology of communication was often enveloped in religious metaphors and a rhetoric of morality. It was perceived as a means of spreading the word of God faster than ever before, thereby expediting the long-awaited day of salvation. In the twentieth century, the explicit religious references fell away. Despite the secularization of communication technologies, the moral overtones have remained. As Carey states:

From the telegraph to the computer the same sense of profound possibility for moral improvement is present whenever these machines are invoked. And we need not be reminded of the regularity with which improved communication is invoked by an army of teachers, preachers, and columnists as the talisman of all our troubles. More controversially, the same root attitudes, as I can only assert here rather than demonstrate, are at work in most of our scientifically sophisticated views of communication.[29]

As we discussed earlier, it is this "transmission" view of communication—the electronic sending of bits—that prevails in the myth of the electronic library.

The "ritual" view of communication is far less recognized in public and scholarly discussions of communication, although its roots go back as far, if not further, than those of the transmission view. Nevertheless, it is the view of communications that I believe is relevant to our consideration of the library's role in strengthening and bridging ligatures and options. Carey defines the ritual view of transmission as a view of communications that is not concerned with the sending of messages in space, but relates to the "maintenance of society in time; not the act of imparting information but representation of shared beliefs." This definition has its own religious sources and draws on the shared roots of such concepts as communion, community, and communication. The ritual view does not see the transmission of information as the highest order of communication. Rather, communication is recognized as "the construction and maintenance of an ordered, meaningful cultural world that can serve as a control and container for human action."[30] Carey helps us understand how the ritual view differs from the transmission view by applying it to the newspaper. The transmission view of the newspaper is straightforward: The newspaper is a means of disseminating news and information. Communications research is typically concerned about the effectiveness of the newspaper as a medium of transmission, its use relative to other media, and so forth. The ritual view takes a different look at the newspaper. The newspaper is not perceived as solely a source of information but as a highly dramatic presentation of the world. As Carey states, "The model here is not that of information acquisition, though such acquisition occurs, but of dramatic action in which the reader joins a world of contending forces as an observer at a play."[31] In this context, reading the newspaper becomes a ritual act, not solely the imparting of information but, even more, a drama.

This view of communication—the dramatic provision of an ordered and meaningful cultural world for the purposes of human action—represents a more profound view of the role of the library than does the transmission view alone. This strategy does not require the exclusion of the transmission view, but instead the reversal of its dominance—a recognition that the transmission view must be incorporated into the ritual view of communication. With the ritual view of communication we see the library, not unlike the newspaper, as a ritual drama, a presentation of contending spheres of knowledge brought together in a communal ritual place for the total sensual and intellectual satisfaction of the individual. Is it any wonder people want the monumental library, the awe-inspiring reading rooms? Like the newspaper, the library "is a presentation of reality that gives life an overall form, order, and tone."[32] Hence, the need for the library as physical communal space remains. As the adoption of the ritual view of communication does not require the rejection of the transmission view, so the perpetuation of the library as place does not require the complete rejection of the myth of the electronic library. As the transmission view is subordinated and incorporated into the ritual view of communication, so we may expect the electronic library will be subordinated and incorporated into the myth of the library as place.

Can the library as a communal ritual place, the library *with* walls, incorporate the electronic library? We find in the proposed new San Francisco Public Library a vivid example of the enduring qualities of the library as place as a communal center promoting life chances while also incorporating elements of the electronic library. We also find, not without irony, that the library director behind the plans for the new library is one of our most prominent myth-makers, Kenneth Dowlin.

In 1987, Dowlin left the Pikes Peak Library in Colorado Springs and went to the San Francisco Public Library where he became involved in planning a 375,000-square-foot, $100 million main library. After widespread consultation with the community, the concept of a decentralized branch system, as advocated by Charles Robinson at the Baltimore County Library, was rejected in favor of a central library located at the "cultural nexus of the city."[33] Dowlin has not given up the rhetoric of the myth of the electronic library by any means. But it is expressed in the context of the library as place as well. The new library will be an "intelligent building" wired for a "telecommunications grid" housing about 800 terminals. However, he emphasizes that books remain the primary format, at least for the near future. Thus, a collection of 1.3 million volumes is projected for the year 2010, a substantial increase over the current collection of 750,000 volumes. The library is expected to serve as a communications center, a "global village library," but one providing "the ambience and sense of the community with instantaneous connections."[34] Its exterior turns to the past and present with a Beaux Arts design to blend with the public architecture of the facing Civic Center, while the style of its other facades mesh with those of the surrounding commercial district.

The interior also preserves elements of the library as place, with a grand staircase and large reading room. One of the architects maintains: "I believe that having a great reading room in your library is important, because that's the place where the relationship among community, scholarship, and the individual as part of that community is explored and experienced."[35] Here is a graphic description of the library serving as a communal ritual place, providing a bridge between community and individualism, providing ligatures and options. But the library is planned to incorporate current and potential information technologies as well. Those responsible for the 1987 public library planning manual now rightly call for its revision in light of the availability of the Internet and National Research and Education Network (NREN).[36] No doubt these technological developments open up the potential for enhanced library services. The San Francisco Public Library appears to preserve the best of the library as place while being poised to take advantage of such new technological developments and the new roles they can generate. The ritual library as place incorporates the transmissional electronic library.

Conclusion: The Second Century

> Instead of creating a "new future," modern technology invites the
> public to participate in a ritual of control in which fascination with
> technology masks the underlying factors of politics and power.
>
> James W. Carey

It was 1979 when Vincent Giuliano issued his manifesto for librarians,
proclaiming many of the tenets of the emerging myth of the electronic
library. By 1992, the myth of the electronic library was the foundation for
another manifesto, this one published by the American Library Association.
In *Redesigning Library Services: A Manifesto*, Michael Buckland explores the
transition from the "Paper Library" to the "Electronic Library."[1] Not unlike
other adherents to the myth of the electronic library, Buckland ignores
political and social issues related to the electronic library. He considers only
the implications of information technology, which he accepts as the primary
influence on the future of libraries.

Although Buckland adheres to the electronic library myth, the revolutionary rhetoric of his manifesto is more subdued than Giuliano's. He does
not argue for the abandonment of print materials and local collections. But
he does conclude that the new information technology requires librarians
"to think again the mission of the library, the role of the library, and the
means of providing service." He notes, "For the first time in one hundred
years we face the grand and difficult challenge of redesigning library
services."[2]

I have argued that the first century of modern librarianship was propelled by the myth of the library as place. The second century, Buckland

and others argue, will be driven by the myth of the electronic library. Although recent reports from Carnegie-Mellon University predict that it will take twenty-five years to achieve their electronic library, the electronic library myth is increasingly accepted as the myth for the second century of modern librarianship.[3] That being so, when we think about the mission and role of the library and methods of providing service, as Buckland urges us to do, we cannot limit ourselves, as he and others tend to do, to technological issues alone. The thrust of this book has been an attempt to broaden the consideration of the myth of the electronic library to its political, cultural, and social implications. As a means of stimulating further debate, I conclude with a series of propositions based on the issues addressed in the previous chapters.

1. Librarians should not accept the inevitability of a technologically dominated information society. Alternative conceptions and/or social trends can have greater relevance to the role of the library and librarians. The idea of the therapeutic society is one alternative.

2. The library will continue to serve as a crucial social institution providing a place for social interaction, communal and cultural authenticity, and sensory and intellectual stimulation. Librarians should not adopt an abstract, idealist concept of the library, as represented by the electronic library, over a materialistic concept, as represented by the library as place, as a philosophical foundation for librarianship. Society continually reaffirms its desire for such a physical institutional presence through the construction of new libraries and the preservation of libraries as a part of the American heritage.

3. Assuming, then, that libraries will remain for the foreseeable future, librarians should not abandon their identification with the library. Aside from the important role librarians continue to play in meeting society's knowledge needs, they should maintain a strong identification with the library as a means of maintaining and increasing their professional status.

4. Librarians should reject outmoded models of professionalism and adopt the conceptualization of the personal service professions. Librarianship's bureaucratic base, body of techniques, and therapeutic role are more akin to the needs of a society undergoing change than those of the autonomous impersonal professions.

5. Accordingly, librarians should adhere to the therapeutic objective of promoting client self-sufficiency. This does not require a complete rejection of the role of intermediary. Nonetheless, the instructional model should be the prominent outlook of librarians.

6. Librarians should be identified with a broad concern for the collection, organization, and dissemination of knowledge, rather than a narrower focus on information. Many occupations in society are clearly concerned in one way or another with information, as Fritz Machlup and others have demonstrated. However, librarianship is among the few occupations with the experience in organizing books, journals, and other media into coherent bodies of knowledge.

7. Librarians should exploit the contributions of information science for what they can offer to improve the effectiveness of librarianship. However, the knowledge base of librarianship must continue to rely on a multiplicity of disciplines, not information or communications theory alone. Not only the social sciences, but the humanities and the arts can serve as fertile sources of knowledge and understanding during a time of dynamic change.

8. Librarians should recognize that their professional ideology embodies political values and reject the market-driven, neo-conservative politics of the myth of the electronic library. They must remain committed to promoting the widest possible access to knowledge by opposing censorship, fees for service, and the monopolization of information by any public or private group or organization. However, they should also examine the liberal tenets of librarianship in the light of the communitarian critique of liberalism.

9. Librarianship's commitment to client self-sufficiency should be promoted in the context of the library serving as a bridge between community and individualism, reinforcing ligatures and providing options with the social objective of promoting life chances for all members of society.

It is hoped that the explicit assertion of these propositions contributes to the need for librarians to critically assess the role of libraries and librarianship in a time of social change and, in particular, to explore and debate more fully the implications of the myth of the electronic library.

Notes

PREFACE

1. Wilson P. Dizard, Jr. *The Coming Information Age: An Overview of Technology, Economics and Politics*. New York: Longman, 1982, p. 3.

2. Bill Bourne, Udi Eichler, and David Herman, eds. *Modernity and Its Discontents (Voices)*. Nottingham, England: Spokesman, 1987, p. 11.

3. Richard R. Rowe. "You, the CIO." *American Libraries*, 18 (April 1987), p. 297.

4. Archibald MacLeish. "The Premise of Meaning." In *The University—The Library*. Edited by Samuel Rothstein. Oxford: Shakespeare Head Press, 1972, p. 52 (emphasis in the original).

5. Charles Robinson. "The Public Library Vanishes." *Library Journal*, 117 (March 15, 1992), pp. 51–54.

6 Margaret F. Steig. *Change and Challenge in Library and Information Science Education*. Chicago: American Library Association, 1992, p. 3.

7. Bryan Pfaffenberger. *Democratizing Information: Online Databases and the Rise of End-User Searching*. Boston: G. K. Hall, 1990, p. 57.

CHAPTER 1

1. Thomas S. Kuhn. *The Structure of Scientific Revolutions*. 2nd edn. Chicago: University of Chicago, 1970, p. viii.

2. William H. McNeill. *Mythistory and Other Essays*. Chicago: University of Chicago Press, 1986, p. 19.

3. Berry A. Turner, ed. *Organizational Symbolism*. Berlin: Walter de Gruyter, 1990, p. 2.

4. Virginia Ingersoll and Guy B. Adams. "Beyond Organizational Boundaries, Exploring the Managerial Myth." *Administration and Society*, 18 (November 1986), p. 361 (emphasis in the original).

5. Ibid., p. 364.

6. Chris Warntz. "Some Promises Kept: The Peterborough Town Library." *Wilson Library Bulletin*, 56 (January 1982), pp. 342–46.

7. Jesse H. Shera. *Foundations of the Public Library*. Chicago: University of Chicago, 1949, p. 169.

8. See Patrick Williams. *The American Public Library and the Problem of Purpose*. New York: Greenwood Press, 1988.

9. Douglas Knight and Morse E. Shipley, eds. *Libraries at Large*. New York: Bowker, 1969, p. 273.

10. More recently there has been some displacement of the term "electronic library" by "virtual library." The change in jargon does not change the argument of this book. Therefore, I will continue using "electronic library" as it remains the term most commonly used.

CHAPTER 2

1. Irene S. Farkas-Conn, *From Documentation to Information Science*. Westport, Conn.: Greenwood Press, 1990; W. Boyd Rayward, "Library and Information Science: An Historical Perspective." *Journal of Library History*, 20 (Spring 1985), pp. 120–36.

2. Michael K. Buckland, "Emanuel Goldberg, Electronic Document Retrieval, Vannevar Bush's Memex." *Journal of the American Society for Information Science*, 43 (May 1992), pp. 284–94; Susan A. Cady, "The Electronic Revolution in Libraries: Microfilm Déja Vu?" *College and Research Libraries*, 51 (July 1990), pp. 374–86; James M. Nyce and Paul Kahn, "Innovation, Pragmatism, and Technological Continuity: Vannevar Bush's Memex." *Journal of the American Society for Information Science*, 40 (May 1989), pp. 214–20.

3. Robert C. Binkley. *Manual of Methods of Reproducing Research Materials*. Ann Arbor, Mich.: Edward Brothers, 1936, pp. 201–202.

4. Farkas-Conn, *From Documentation*, pp. 41–42; Binkley, *Manual*, pp. 134–35.

5. Fremont Rider. *The Scholar and the Future of the Research Library*. New York: Hadham Press, 1944.

6. Buckland. "Emanuel Goldberg," p. 285; Nyce and Kahn, "Innovation," p. 215.

7. Vannevar Bush. "As We May Think." *Atlantic Monthly*, 176 (July 1945), pp. 101–108.

8. Linda C. Smith. "'Memex' as an Image of Potentiality in Information Retrieval Research and Development." In R. N. Oddy et al. *Information Retrieval Research*. London: Butterworths, 1981, pp. 345-69.

9. Bush. "As We May Think," p. 105.

10. See Nyce and Kahn, "Innovation," for an illustration.

11. Bush. "As We May Think," p. 107.

12. Smith. " 'Memex.' " p. 353.

13. *Bibliography in an Age of Science*. Urbana: University of Illinois Press, 1952.

14. Louis Ridenour. "Bibliography in an Age of Science." In ibid., p. 13.

15. Ridenour. "Bibliography," p. 26.

16. Ridenour. "Bibliography," p. 26.

17. Ridenour. "Bibliography." pp. 28–29.

18. Albert G. Hill. "The Storage, Processing and Communication of Information." In ibid., pp. 73–90.

19. Ralph R. Shaw. "Machines and the Bibliographical Problems of the Twentieth Century." In ibid., footnote 18, p. 58.

20. John Kemeny. "A Library for 2000 A.D." In *Computers and the World of the Future*. Edited by Martin Greenberger. Cambridge, Mass.: MIT Press, 1965.

21. J.C.R. Licklider. *Libraries of the Future*. Cambridge, Mass.: MIT Press, 1965.

22. Licklider. *Libraries*, p. 4.

23. J.C.R. Licklider. "A Crux in Scientific and Technical Communication." *American Psychologist*, 21 (1966), p. 1044.

24. Robert S. Taylor. "Review of *Libraries of the Future*." *College and Research Libraries*, 26 (September 1965), p. 407.

25. Franklin K. Patterson. *The Making of a College*. Cambridge, Mass.: MIT Press, 1966.

26. Ibid., p. 24.

27. Robert S. Taylor. *The Making of a Library*. New York: Becker and Hayes, 1972.

28. Ibid., p. 200.

29. Ibid., p. 92.

30. Ibid., p. 57.

31. Edwin B. Parker. "Information and Society." In *Annual Review of Information Sciences and Technology*, vol. 8. Edited by Carlos A. Cuadra. Washington, D.C.: American Society for Information Science, 1973, pp. 345-73.

32. Edwin B. Parker. "The New Communication Media." In *Toward Century 21: Technology, Society, and Human Values*. Edited by C. S. Wallis. New York: Basic Books, 1970.

33. Philip H. Ennis. "Technological Change and the Professions: Neither Luddite nor Technocrat." *Library Quarterly*, 32 (July 1962), pp. 189–98.

34. Louis A. Schultheiss et al. *Advanced Data Processing in the University Library*. New York: Scarecrow Press, 1962.

35. Gilbert W. King. *Automation and the Library Congress*. Washington, D.C.: Library of Congress, 1963.

36. Barbara E. Markuson, ed. *Libraries and Automation*. Washington, D.C.: Library of Congress, 1964.

37. J.C.R. Licklider. "An On-Line Information Network." In *Intrex: Report of a Planning Conference on Information Transfer Experiments*. Edited by Carl F. J. Overhage and R. Joyce Harmon. Cambridge, Mass.: MIT Press, 1965, pp. 147-55.

38. Vannevar Bush. "Memex Revisited." In *Science is Not Enough*. Edited by Vannevar Bush. New York: William Morrow, 1967, p. 81.

39. Edwin B. Parker. "Developing a Campus Information Retrieval System." In *Proceedings of a Conference Held at Stanford University Libraries October 4–5, 1968*. Edited by Allen B. Veaner and Paul J. Fasana. Stanford, Calif.: Stanford University Libraries, 1969, pp. 213–30.

40. J.C.R. Licklider. "A Hypothetical Plan for a Library-Information Network." In *Conference on Interlibrary Communications and Information Networks*. Edited by Joseph Becker. Chicago: American Library Association, 1971, pp. 313–15.

41. Gordon Martin and Irving Lieberman. "Library 21: ALA Exhibit at the World's Fair." *ALA Bulletin*, 56 (March 1962), pp. 230–32.

42. President's Science Advisory Committee. *Improving the Availability of Scientific and Technical Information in the United States*. Washington, D.C.: The White House, 1958.

43. L. Carter et al. *National Document-Handling Systems for Science and Technology*. New York: John Wiley, 1967, pp. 129–89, 309.

44. President's Science Advisory Committee. *Science, Government, and Information*. Washington, D.C.: The White House, 1963, p. 14.

45. Ibid., p. 13.

46. Computer Science and Engineering Board, National Academy of Sciences. *Libraries and Information Technology: A National System Challenge*. Washington, D.C.: National Academy of Sciences, 1972, pp. 11, 15.

47. Fritz Machlup. *The Production and Distribution of Knowledge in the United States*. Princeton, N.J.: Princeton University Press, 1962.

48. Peter F. Drucker. *The Age of Discontinuity*. New York: Harper, 1968.

49. Daniel Bell. *The Coming of Post-Industrial Society*. New York: Basic Books, 1976.

50. Philip Marchand. *Marshall McLuhan: The Medium and the Messenger*. Toronto: Random House, 1989.

51. Joshua Meyrowitz. *No Sense of Place: The Impact of Electronic Media on Social Behavior*. New York: Oxford University Press, 1985, p. 308.

52. K. J. McGarry. *Communication, Knowledge, and the Librarian*. London: Clive Bingley, 1975, p. 158.

53. Alvin Toffler. *The Third Wave*. New York: Morrow, 1980.

54. Wilson P. Dizard, Jr. *The Coming Information Age*. New York: Longman, 1982, pp. 4, 91–93.

55. Bryan Pfaffenberger. *Democratizing Information*. Boston: G.K. Hall, 1990, pp. 61–62.

56. Norbert Wiener. *Cybernetics or Control and Communication in the Animal and the Machine*, 2nd ed. Cambridge, Mass.: MIT Press, 1961.

57. Donald P. Hammer, ed. *The Information Age: Its Development and Impact*. Metuchen, N.J.: Scarecrow Press, 1976, p. vii.

58. Ibid., pp. ix, xi.

59. Vincent E. Giuliano. "A Manifesto for Librarians." *Library Journal*, 104 (September 15, 1979), pp. 1837–42.

60. Joseph Boisse and Carla J. Stoffle. "Epilogue: Issues and Answers: The Participants Views." In *The Information Society: Issues and Answers*. Edited by E. J. Josey. Phoenix: Oryx Press, 1978, pp. 115, 120–21.

CHAPTER 3

1. Robert D. Leigh. *The Public Library in the United States*. New York: Columbia University Press, 1950, p. vii.

2. Robert S. Taylor. *The Making of a Library*. New York: Becker and Hayes, 1972, p. 92.

3. Robert S. Taylor. "Patterns Toward a User-Centered Academic Library." In *New Dimensions for Academic Library Service*. Edited by E. J. Josey. Metuchen, N.J.: Scarecrow Press, 1975, p. 299. See also Taylor, "Technology and Libraries." *EDUCOM Bulletin*, 5 (May 1970), pp. 4–5.

4. James F. Govan. "Fluidity and Intangibility: The Stunning Impact of an Expanded Information Base." *Journal of Library Administration*, 8 (Summer 1987), p. 17.

5. Patricia Battin. "The Electronic Library—A Vision for the Future." *EDUCOM Bulletin*, 19 (Summer 1984), p. 17.

6. John R. Sack. "Open Systems for Open Minds: Building the Library Without Walls." *College and Research Libraries*, 47 (November 1986), p. 535.

7. Brigitte L. Kenney. "Library Information Delivery Systems: Past, Present, and Future." *Drexel Library Quarterly*, 17 (Fall 1981), p. 61.

8. M. Kibby and N. H. Evans. "The Network is the Library." *EDUCOM Bulletin*, 24 (Fall 1989), p. 15.

9. Kenneth E. Dowlin. *The Electronic Library: The Promise and the Process*. New York: Neal-Schuman, 1984. See also his "The Electronic Library," *Library Journal*, 105 (November 1, 1980), pp. 2265-70.

10. See Denise A. Troll. *Library Information System II: Progress Report and Technical Plan*. Mercury Technical Report Series No. 3. Pittsburgh: Carnegie-Mellon University, 1990, especially bibliography on pp. 38–42; William Y. Arms, et al., "The Design of the Mercury Electronic Library." *EDUCOM Review*, 27 (November/December 1992), pp. 38–41.

11. Caroline R. Arms, ed. *Campus Strategies for Libraries and Electronic Information*. Rockport, Mass.: Digital Press, 1990, p. 267.

12. Nancy Evans et al. *The Vision of the Electronic Library*. Mercury Technical Report Series No. 1. Pittsburgh: Carnegie-Mellon University, 1989, p. 22.

13. Kibbey and Evans. "The Network is the Library," p. 16.

14. Frederick W. Lancaster. "Whither Libraries? Or Wither Libraries?" *College and Research Libraries*, 39 (September 1978), pp. 345-57; reprinted in 50 (July 1989), pp. 406–19.

15. Frederick W. Lancaster. *Toward Paperless Information Systems*. New York: Academic Press, 1978; *Libraries and Librarians in an Age of Electronics*. Arlington, Va.: Information Resources, 1982.

16. Lancaster. *Libraries and Librarians*, p. 139 (emphasis in the original).

17. Ibid., p. 144.

18. Frederick W. Lancaster. "Implications for Library and Information Science Education." *Library Trends*, 32 (Winter 1984), p. 341.

19. Lancaster. "Whither Libraries? Or Wither Libraries?" pp. 407, 418; Vincent E. Giuliano, "A Manifesto for Librarians." *Library Journal*, 104 (September 15, 1979), p. 1839; Lancaster, *Libraries and Librarians*, p. 137; Robert S. Taylor, "Reminiscing About the Future: Professional Education and the Information Environment." *Library Journal* 104 (September 15, 1979), p. 1871; Dennis A. Lewis, "Today's Challenge—Tomorrow's Choice: Change or Be Changed Or the Doomsday Scenario Mk2." *Journal of Information Science*, 2 (September 1980), p. 68.

20. Taylor. "Reminiscing." p. 1871.

21. Giuliano. "A Manifesto." p. 1840.

22. Dowlin. *The Electronic Library*. pp. v, 130.

23. James Thompson. *The End of Libraries*. London: Clive Bingley, 1982, p. 16.

24. Susan S. Cherry. "Electronic Library Association Born at Columbus Forum." *American Libraries*, 12 (May 1981), pp. 275-76.

25. Alan F. Westin and Anne L. Finger. *Using the Public Library in the Computer Age*. Chicago: American Library Association, 1991, p. 9.

26. Ibid., p. 55.

27. William Y. Arms. *Electronic Publishing and the Academic Library*. Pittsburgh: Carnegie-Mellon University, n.d., p. 2.

28. Charles R. McClure et al. *Public Libraries and the Internet/NREN: New Challenges, New Opportunities*. Syracuse, N.Y.: Syracuse University, 1992; Carola Parkhurst, ed., *Library Perspectives on NREN: The National Research and Education Network*. Chicago: Library and Information Technology Association, 1990.

29. Spencer E. Watts and Alan R. Samuels. "What Business Are We In? Perceptions of the Roles and Purposes of the Public Library in Professional Literature." *Public Libraries*, 23 (Winter 1984), p. 133.

30. Ernestine Rose. *The Public Library in American Life*. New York: Columbia University Press, 1954, p. 7.

31. Ibid., p. 51.

32. Kathleen R. Molz. *The Knowledge Institutions in the Information Age: The Case of the Public Library*. Washington, D.C.: Library of Congress, 1988.

33. Dowlin. *The Electronic Library*, p. 134.

34. Giuliano. "A Manifesto for Libraries," pp. 1839, 1842.

35. Lancaster. *Toward Paperless Information Systems*, p. 110.

36. Tom Suprenant. "Future Libraries: the Electronic Environment." *Wilson Library Bulletin*, 56 (January 1982), p. 341.

37. William Y. Arms and Dana S. Scott. *Brief Review of Research on the Electronic Library at Carnegie-Mellon University*. Mercury Technical Report Series No. 2. Pittsburgh: Carnegie-Mellon University, 1990, p. 2.

38. Thompson. The *End of Libraries*, p. 13.

39. Frederick W. Lancaster. "Information Professionals in the Information Age." Bertha Bessom Lecture in Librarianship No. 6. Toronto: University of Toronto Faculty of Library and Information Science, 1982, p. 2.

40. Roger W. Christian. *Electronic Library: Bibliographic Data Bases, 1975-76*. White Plains, N.Y.: Knowledge Industry Publications, 1975, p. 9.

41. Hugh F. Cline and Loraine T. Sennett. *The Electronic Library: The Impact of Automation on Academic Libraries*. Lexington, Mass.: D.C. Heath, 1983, p. 173.

42. Lancaster. "Whither Libraries?" p. 418.

43. Lancaster. *Libraries and Librarians*, p. 179.

44. Dowlin. *The Electronic Library*, p. 137.

45. Nora Rawlinson. "The Central Library—A Fatal Attraction." *Library Journal*, 115 (June 1, 1990), p. 6; John N. Berry, "The Central Library—Beyond Symbolism." *Library Journal*, 115 (June 1, 1990), p. 7.

46. Dottie Lamm. "Should the Denver Public Library Be Expanded? Yes." *Denver Post*, August 12, 1990, pp. 1H, 5H; Marj Mickum, "Should the Denver Public Library Be Expanded? No." *Denver Post*, August 12, 1990, pp. 1H, 5H.

47. James M. Kusack. "Librarians and the Information Age: An Affair on the Rocks?" *Bulletin of the American Society for Information Science*, 14 (December/January 1988–1989), pp. 26–27.

CHAPTER 4

1. Daniel Bell. *The Coming of the Post-Industrial Society*. New York: Basic Books, 1976, p. 467.

2. Krishan Kumar. *Prophecy and Progress*. Harmondsworth, Britain: Penguin, 1978, p. 223.

3. Victor Ferkiss. "Daniel Bell's Concept of Post-Industrial Society: Theory, Myth, and Ideology." *Political Science Review*, 9 (Fall 1979), p. 74.

4. Thomas Ballard. "The Information Age and the Public Library." *Wilson Library Bulletin*, 62 (June 1988), p. 74. The Porat and Rubin study in U.S. Department of Commerce, *The Information Economy*, 9 vols. Office of Telecommunications Special Publication 77–12. Washington, D.C.: Government Printing Office, 1971.

5. Michael R. Rubin et al. *The Knowledge Industry in the United States, 1960–1980*. Princeton, N.J.: Princeton University Press, 1986, p. 16.

6. Ibid., p. 192.

7. Ibid., pp. 12–13.

8. Robert M. Hayes, ed. *Libraries and the Information Economy of California*. Los Angeles: Graduate School of Library and Information Science, University of California at Los Angeles, 1985, p. 6.

9. Stephen S. Cohen and John Zysman. *Manufacturing Matters: The Myth of the Post-Industrial Society*. New York: Basic Books, 1987, p. 4.

10. Ibid., p. 14.

11. Ibid., p. 56.

12. Rubin. *The Knowledge Industry*, Table III-2, p. 19.

13. Ibid., p. 3.

14. Michael R. Rubin. "The Emerging World-Wide Information Economy." *Library Hi Tech*, 4 (Winter 1986), p. 79.

15. Marc U. Porat. "Global Implications of the Information Society." *Journal of Communication*, 28 (Winter 1978), p. 74.

16. Rubin. *The Knowledge Industry*, Table IX-3, p. 196.

17. George Silvestri and John Lukasiewicz. "Projections of Occupational Employment, 1988–2000." *Monthly Labor Review*, 112 (November 1989), Table 4, p. 52.

18. Porat. "Global Implications," p. 79.

19. Patricia G. Schuman. "Reclaiming Our Technological Future." *Library Journal*, 115 (March 1, 1990), p. 35.

20. Langdon Winner. *The Whale and the Reactor*. Chicago: University of Chicago Press, 1986, p. 113.

21. Kumar. *Prophecy and Progress*, pp. 228–29.

22. Heinz von Foerster. "Epistemology of Communication." In *The Myths of Information: Technology and Postindustrial Culture*. Edited by Kathleen Woodward. Madison, Wis.: Coda Press, 1980, p. 19.

23. Ibid., p. 21.

24. Theodore Roszak. *The Cult of Information*. New York: Pantheon, 1986, p. xi.

25. David Lyon. *The Information Society: Issues and Illusions*. Cambridge, Britain: Polity Press, 1988, p. 53.

26. Frederick W. Lancaster. *Toward Paperless Information Systems*. New York: Academic Press, 1978, p. 54.

27. Langdon Winner. *Autonomous Technology: Technics-Out-of-Control as a Theme in Political Thought*. Cambridge, Mass.: MIT Press, 1977, p. 46.

28. Frederick W. Lancaster. "Information Professionals in the Information Age." Bertha Bassam Lecture in Librarianship No. 6. Toronto: University of Toronto Faculty of Library and Information Science, 1982, p. 17.

29. James W. Carey and John J. Quirk. "The Mythos of the Electronic Revolution." *American Scholar*, 39 (Spring 1970), pp. 219–41; (Summer 1970), 395-424.

30. Howard P. Segal. *Technological Utopianism in American Culture*. Chicago: University of Chicago Press, 1985, p. 26; see also Delores Greenberg, "Energy, Power, and Perceptions of Social Change in the Early Nineteenth Century." *American Historical Review*, 95 (June 1990), pp. 693–714.

31. Karen Wright. "The Road to the Global Village." *Scientific American*, 262 (March 1990), pp. 83–94.

32. Carey and Quirk. "The Mythos of the Electronic Revolution," p. 222.

33. David E. Nye. *Image Worlds: Corporate Identities at General Electric, 1850–1930*. Cambridge, Mass.: MIT Press, 1985, p. 21.

34. David E. Nye. *Electrifying America: Social Meaning of a New Technology, 1880–1940*. Cambridge, Mass.: MIT Press, 1990.

35. Quoted in Carey and Quirk. "The Mythos of the Electronic Revolution," p. 397.

36. Ibid., p. 402.

37. Winner. *The Whale and the Reactor*, p. 105.

38. Thomas Hughes. *Networks of Power: Electrification in Western Society, 1880–1930*. Baltimore, Md.: Johns Hopkins University Press, 1983, p. 1.

39. Ibid., p. 2.

40. Raymond Williams. *Television: Technology and Cultural Form*. New York: Schocken Books, 1975, p. 128.

41. Lyon. *The Information Society*, pp. 41–42.

CHAPTER 5

1. Hans Jonas. *Philosophical Essays: From Ancient Creed to Technological Man*. Englewood Cliffs, N.J.: Prentice-Hall, 1974, p. 75.

2. Ibid., p. 78 (emphasis in the original).

3. Kathleen Woodward, ed. *The Myths of Information: Technology and Post-Industrial Culture*. Madison, Wis.: Coda Press, 1980, p. 175.

4. Lewis Mumford. *The City in History*. New York: Harcourt, Brace and World, 1961, pp. 563–67.

5. Hazel Henderson. "The Age of Light: Beyond the Information Age." *Futurist*, 20 (July-August 1986), p. 56.

6. William Dickey. "Poem Descending a Staircase: Hypertext and the Simultaneity of Experience." In Paul Delany and George P. Landow, eds., *Hypermedia and Literary Studies*. Cambridge, Mass.: MIT Press, 1991, p. 144.

7. Marshall Berman. *All That is Solid Melts Into Air: The Experience of Modernity*. New York: Penguin Books, 1988, p. 15.

8. Annie Dillard. *An American Childhood*. New York: Harper & Row, 1987, p. 81.

9. Ibid., p. 85.

10. "The Talk of the Town." *The New Yorker* (February 18, 1990), p. 21.

11. Timothy Steele. "The Library." *Poetry*, 143 (December 1983), p. 129.

12. Susan Allen Toth and John Coughan, eds. *Reading Poems*. New York: Doubleday, 1991, p. 3.

13. Edward Hall. *The Hidden Dimension*. New York: Doubleday, 1966, p. ix.

14. William H. Whyte. *City: Discovering the Center*. New York: Doubleday, 1988.

15. George S. Bobinski. "Carnegies." *American Libraries*, 21 (April 1990), p. 296.

16. Joseph Falgione. "Pittsburgh Makes Its Carnegie Work." *American Libraries*, 21 (April 1990), p. 303.

17. Edward Relph. *Place and Placeness*. London: Pion Limited, 1976, p. 141.

18. Tony Hiss. *The Experience of Place*. New York: Knopf, 1990, p. 18.

19. Ibid., p. 28.

20. Steele. "The Library," p. 129.

21. Whyte. *City*, p. 341.

22. Hiss. *The Experience of Place*, pp. 27, 34.

23. Wilbur Zelinsky. "The Imprint of Central Authority." In Michael P. Conzen, ed. *The Making of the American Landscape*. Boston: Unwin Hyman, 1990, p. 316.

24. Ibid., p. 320.

25. Wheeler, Joseph L. and Alfred M. Githens. *The American Public Library Building*. New York: C. Scribner's, 1941, p. 7.

26. Ibid., pp. 11–12.

27. Ibid., pp. 1–2.

28. Art Plotnik. "Chicago to Build Nation's Largest Municipal Library: Classical Design Triumphs in International Competition." *American Libraries*, 19 (July/August 1988), pp. 565-66.

29. Kevin Lynch. *The Image of the City*. Cambridge, Mass.: MIT Press, 1960, p. 9.

30. Ibid., p. 76 (emphasis added).

31. Hiss. *The Experience of Place*, p. xiii.

32. Quoted in Donald E. Riggs and Gordon A. Sabine. *Libraries in the '90s: What the Leaders Expect*. Phoenix, Ariz.: Oryx Press, 1988, p. 91.

33. Caroline R. Arms. ed. *Campus Strategies for Libraries and Electronic Information*. Rockport, Mass.: Digital Press, 1990.

34. Kenneth Dowlin. "Maggie III: The Prototypical Library System." *Library Hi Tech*, 4 (1986), p. 7.

CHAPTER 6

1. Samuel P. Hays. *The Response to Industrialism: 1885-1914*. Chicago: University of Chicago Press, 1957, p. 1.

2. Robert N. Bellah et al. *Habits of the Heart: Individualism and Commitment in American Life*. New York: Harper, 1985, p. 34.

3. These themes are explored in Bruce Mazlish, *A New Science: the Breakdown of Connections and the Birth of Sociology*. New York: Oxford University Press, 1989.

4. T. J. Jackson Lears. "From Salvation to Self-Realization: Advertising and the Therapeutic Roots of the Consumer Culture, 1880–1930." In *The Culture of Consumerism: Critical Essays in American History, 1880–1980*. Edited by Richard Wightman Fox and T. J. Jackson Lears. New York: Pantheon Books, 1983, p. 4; see also his *No Place of Grace*. New York: Pantheon Books, 1981.

5. Edith Kurzweil. *The Freudians: A Comparative Perspective*. New Haven, Conn.: Yale University Press, 1989, pp. 23–27.

164   Notes

6. Ibid., p. 34.

7. Rollo R. May. "Therapy in Our Day." In *The Evolution of Psychotherapy*. Edited by Jeffrey K. Zeig. New York: Brunner/Mazel, 1987, p. 212.

8. Richard I. Evans. *Carl Rogers: The Man and His Ideas*. New York: Dutton, 1975.

9. Sarah Fine. "The Librarian As Youth Counselor." *Drexel Library Quarterly*, 14 (January 1978), p. 38.

10. Kurzweil. *The Freudians*, p. 255.

11. Joseph Veroff et al. *The Inner American: A Self-Portrait From 1957–1976*. New York: Basic Books, 1981, p. 14.

12. Daniel Yankelovich. *New Rules: Searching for Self-fulfilment in a World Turned Upside Down*. New York: Random House, 1981, pp. xix-xx.

13. Ibid., p. 5.

14. Bellah et al. *Habits of the Heart*, p. 113.

15. Terry A. Kupers. *Ending Therapy: The Meaning of Termination*. New York: New York University Press, 1988, pp. 123–33.

16. Philip Rieff. *The Triumph of the Therapeutic*. London: Chatto and Windus, 1966.

17. Alasdair MacIntyre. *After Virtue*. Notre Dame, Ind.: University of Notre Dame, 1981, pp. 28–29.

18. Bellah et al. *Habits of the Heart*, p. 39.

19. Ibid., p. 47.

20. Paul Halmos. *The Faith of the Counsellors*. London: Constable, 1965. See also his *The Personal Service Society*. London: Constable, 1970.

21. William S. Bennett, Jr. and Merl C. Hokenstad, Jr. "Full-Time People Workers and Conceptions of Professional." In *The Sociological Review Monograph, 20*. Edited by Paul Halmos. Keele, Britain: University of Keele, 1973.

22. Ibid., p. 23.

23. Ibid., p. 35 (emphasis in the original).

24. Mary L. Bundy and Paul Wasserman. "Professionalism Reconsidered." *College and Research Libraries*, 29 (January 1968), pp. 5–26; William J. Goode, "The Librarian: From Occupation to Profession?" *Library Quarterly*, 31 (October 1961), pp. 306–20.

25. Bennett and Hokenstad. "Full-Time People Workers," p. 34.

26. Samuel S. Green. "Personal Relations Between Librarians and Readers." *Library Journal*, 1 (October 1876), pp. 74–81.

27. Robert Wagers. "American Reference Theory and Information Dogma." *Journal of Library History*. 13 (Summer 1978), pp. 265–81.

28. James I. Wyer. *Reference Work: A Textbook for Students of Library Work and Librarians*. Chicago: American Library Association, 1930, p. 101.

29. Ibid., p. 98.

30. Ibid., pp. 100–101.

31. Alice I. Bryan. "The Psychology of the Reader." *Library Journal*, 64 (January 1, 1939), p. 9.

32. Ernestine Rose. *The Public Library in American Life*. New York: Columbia University Press, 1954.

33. Margaret Hutchins. *Introduction to Reference Work*. Chicago: American Library Association, 1944.

34. David K. Maxfield. *Counselor Librarianship: A New Departure*. Occasional Papers No. 38 (March 1954). Champaign-Urbana, Ill.: University of Illinois Library School, 1954; see also his "Counselor Librarianship at U.I.C." *College and Research Libraries*, 15 (April 1954), pp. 161–66, 179.

35. Maxfield. *Counselor Librarianship*, pp. 11–12 (emphasis in the original).

36. Ibid., pp. 22–23.

37. Ibid., p. 8 (emphasis in the original).

38. Ibid., p. 19.

CHAPTER 7

1. Brian Nielsen. "Teacher or Intermediary: Alternative Professional Models in the Information Age." *College and Research Libraries*, 43 (May 1982), p. 185.

2. John M. Tucker. "User Education in Academic Libraries: A Century in Retrospect." *Library Trends*, 29 (Summer 1980), p. 20.

3. James I. Wyer. *Reference Work: A Textbook for Students of Library Work and Librarians*. Chicago: American Library Association, 1930.

4. Samuel Rothstein. *The Development of Reference Services Through Academic Traditions, Public Library Practice and Special Librarianship*. ACRL Monographs No. 14. Chicago: Association of College and Reference Libraries, 1955.

5. Robert S. Taylor. "The Process of Asking Questions." *American Documentation*, 13 (October 1962), pp. 391–96; "Question Negotiation and Information Seeking in Libraries." *College and Research Libraries*, 29 (May 1968), pp. 178–94.

6. Taylor. "Question Negotiation," p. 179 (emphasis in the original).

7. Anthony Smith. "Technology, Identity, and the Information Machine." *Daedalus*, 115 (Summer 1986), p. 161.

8. Taylor. "Question Negotiation," p. 194.

9. Bernard F. Vavrek. "The Nature of Reference Librarianship." *RQ* 13 (Spring 1974), p. 214; see also his "The Emergence of a New Reference?" *Journal of Education for Librarianship*, 10 (Fall 1969), pp. 109–15; "A Theory of Reference Service." *College and Research Libraries*, 29 (November 1968), pp. 508–10.

10. Helen Gothberg. "Communication Patterns in Library Reference and Information Service." *RQ*, 13 (Fall 1973), pp. 7–13.

11. James Benson and Ruth K. Maloney. "Principles of Searching." *RQ*, 14 (Summer 1975), pp. 316–20; Charles A. Bunge, "Charting the Reference Query." *RQ*, 8 (Summer 1969), pp. 245–50; Gerald Jahoda and Paul E. Olson, "Models of Reference: Analyzing the Reference Process." *RQ*, 12 (Winter 1972), pp. 148–56; and James Rettig, "A Theoretical Model and Definition of the Reference Process." *RQ*, 18 (Fall 1978), pp. 19–29.

12. Brenda Dervin and Patricia Dewdney. "Neutral Questioning: A New Approach to the Reference Interview." *RQ*, 25 (Summer 1986), pp. 506–13; Thomas L. Eichman, "The Complex Nature of Opening Reference Questions." *RQ*, 17 (Spring 1978), pp. 212–22; Geraldine King, "Open and Closed Questions: The Reference Interview." *RQ*, 12 (Winter 1972), pp. 157–60; and Barbara Robinson, "Reference Services: A Model of Question Handling." *RQ*, 29 (Fall 1989), pp. 418–61.

13. Barron Holland. "Updating Reference Services Through Training for Interpersonal Competence." *RQ*, 17 (Spring 1978), pp. 207–21; Benita Howell et al., "Fleeting Encounters—A Role Analysis of Reference Librarian-Patron Interac-

tion." *RQ*, 16 (Winter 1976), pp. 124–29; Theodore P. Peck, "Counseling Skills Applied to Reference Services." *RQ*, 14 (Spring 1975), pp. 233–35; and Marilyn D. White, "The Dimensions of the Reference Interview." *RQ*, 20 (Summer 1981), pp. 373–81.

14. Virginia Boucher. "Non-Verbal Communication and the Reference Interview." *RQ*, 16 (Fall 1976), pp. 27–32; and Joanna L. Munoz, "The Significance of Nonverbal Communication in the Reference Interview." *RQ*, 16 (Spring 1977), pp. 220–24.

15. Kerry Johnson and Marilyn D. White. "The Cognitive Style of Reference Librarians." *RQ*, 21 (Spring 1982), pp. 239–46; and R. Errol Lam, "The Reference Interview: Some Intercultural Considerations." *RQ*, 27 (Spring 1988), pp. 390–95.

16. Ethel Auster. "User Satisfaction With the Online Negotiation Interview: Contemporary Concern in Traditional Perspective." *RQ*, 23 (Fall 1983), pp. 47–59; Elaine Z. Jennerich, "Before the Answer: Evaluating the Reference Process." *RQ*, 19 (Summer 1980), pp. 360–66; Lisa L. Smith, "Evaluating the Reference Interview: A Theoretical Discussion of the Desirability and Achievability of Evaluation." *RQ*, 31 (Fall 1991), pp. 75–79; Marilyn Von Seggern, "Evaluating the Interview." *RQ*, 29 (Winter 1989), pp. 260–65; and Marilyn D. White, "Evaluation of the Reference Interview." *RQ*, 25 (Fall 1985), pp. 76–84.

17. Charles A. Bunge. "Interpersonal Dimensions of the Reference Interview: A Historical Review of the Literature." *Drexel Library Quarterly*, 20 (Spring 1984), pp. 4–23.

18. Patrick R. Penland. *Communication for Librarians*. Pittsburgh, Pa.: University of Pittsburgh, 1971, p. 12.

19. Patrick R. Penland. *Interviewing for Counselor and Reference Librarians*. Pittsburgh, Pa.: University of Pittsburgh, 1970, p. 4.

20. Estelle Jussim. "Review of *Communication Science and Technology Series*." *Library Journal*, 100 (February 15, 1975), p. 374.

21. K. J. McGarry. *Communication, Knowledge, and the Librarian*. London: Clive Bingley, 1975, p. 20.

22. See, for example, "Foundations of Library Practice." Charles H. Buska, issue editor. *Drexel Library Quarterly*, 19 (Spring 1983), entire issue.

23. William A. Katz. *Introduction to Reference Work*. Vol. 2, *Reference Services and Reference Processes*. New York: McGraw-Hill, 1992.

24. Thomas Suprenant and Claudia Perry-Holmes. "The Reference Librarian of the Future: A Scenario." *RQ*, 25 (Winter 1985), pp. 234–38.

25. Ibid., p. 238.

26. Quoted in Rothstein. *The Development of Reference Services*, p. 54.

27. Emily G. Fayen. "Beyond Technology: Rethinking 'Librarian.' " *American Libraries*, 17 (April 1986), p. 240.

28. Constance Miller and Patricia Tegler. "In Pursuit of Windmills: Librarians and the Determination to Instruct." *Reference Librarian*, 18 (Summer 1987), p. 57.

29. Richard Derr. "Questions: Definitions, Structure, and Classification." *RQ*, 24 (Winter 1984), pp. 186–90.

30. Patrick Wilson. "The Face Value Rule in Reference Work." *RQ*, 25 (Summer 1986), pp. 468, 470–71.

31. Katz. *Introduction to Reference Work*, Vol. 2, pp. 74–76.

32. Elaine Z. Jennerich and Edward J. Jennerich. *The Reference Interview as a Creative Art*. Littleton, Colo.: Libraries Unlimited, 1987, p. xii.

33. Judith W. Powell and Robert B. LeLieuvre. *Peoplework: Communications Dynamics for Librarians*. Chicago: American Library Association, 1979, pp. 21–22.

34. A recent example is Brent D. Rubin. "The Communication-Information Relationship in System Theoretic Perspective." *Journal of the American Society for Information Science*, 43 (January 1992), pp. 15–27.

35. James D. Anderson et al. "Information Science at Rutgers: Establishing New Inter-Disciplinary Connections." *Journal of the American Society for Information Science*, 39 (September, 1988), pp. 377–84.

36. Herbert S. White. *Librarians and the Awakening From Innocence*. Boston: G. K. Hall, 1989, pp. 128–29, 166–67.

37. Herbert S. White. "Bibliographic Instruction, Information Literacy, and Information Empowerment." *Library Journal*, 117 (January 1992), p. 78.

38. Anita R. Schiller. "Instruction and Information: What's Changed." *Reference Librarian*, 1/2 (Fall/Winter 1981), p. 5; "Reference Service: Instruction or Information." *Library Quarterly*, 35 (January 1965), pp. 52–60.

39. Brian Nielsen. "The Role of the Public Service Librarian: The New Revolution." In *Rethinking the Library in the Information Age*. Vol. 3, *Issues in Library Research: Proposals for the 1990s*. Washington, D.C.: U.S. Department of Education, Government Printing Office, 1989, p. 190.

40. Mary E. Larson. "Connecting to the Electronic Library: A Paradigm Shift in Training Reference Librarians." *The Reference Librarian*, 30 (1990), p. 101.

41. Elaine Z. Jennerich. "Before the Answer: Evaluating the Reference Process." *RQ*, 19 (Summer 1980), p. 361.

CHAPTER 8

1. Mary L. Bundy and Paul Wasserman. "Professionalism Reconsidered." *College and Research Libraries*, 29 (January 1968), pp. 5–26.

2. Marcia J. Nauratil. *The Alienated Librarian*. New York: Greenwood Press, 1989, pp. 54–55.

3. Lee W. Finks. "Values Without Shame." *American Libraries*, 20 (April 1989), p. 356.

4. Vincent E. Giuliano. "The Relationship of Information Science to Librarianship—Problems and Scientific Training." *American Documentation*, 20 (October 1969), p. 344.

5. Frederick W. Lancaster. "Future Librarianship: Preparing for an Unconventional Career." *Wilson Library Bulletin*, 57 (May 1983), p. 748.

6. Ira Katznelson. *City Trenches: Urban Politics and the Patterning of Class in the United States*. New York: Pantheon Press, 1981.

7. Michael F. Winter. *The Culture and Control of Expertise*. New York: Greenwood Press, 1988, p. 15.

8. Joseph A. Raelin. *The Clash of Cultures*. Boston: Harvard Business School Press, 1986, p. 7.

9. John B. McKinlay. "Toward the Proletarianization of Physicians." In *Professionals as Workers: Mental Labor in Advanced Capitalism*. Edited by Charles Derber. Boston: G. K. Hall, 1982, pp. 39–40.

10. Michael Lipsky. "Street-Level Bureaucracy and the Analysis of Urban Reform." *Urban Affairs Quarterly*, 6 (June 1971), pp. 391–409.

11. Jane Robbins. "The Reference Librarian: A Street Level Bureaucrat?" *Library Journal*, 97 (April 15, 1972), pp. 1389–92.

12. Robert S. Taylor. *The Making of a Library*. New York: Becker and Hayes, 1972, p. 47.

13. George W. Brown et al. *EDUNET: Report of the Summer Study on Information Networks Conducted by the Interuniversity Communications Council (EDUCOM)*. New York: John Wiley, 1967, p. 6.

14. "A Look at where EDUCOM Now Stands and the Goals it Hopes to Accomplish." *EDUCOM*, 2 (January 1967), p. 2.

15. Ibid., p. 3.

16. Brown et al. *EDUNET*, p. 185.

17. Helen A. Howard. *Administrative Integration of Information Resources in Universities in Canada and the United States: A Report to the Council on Library Resources*. ERIC Document ED 096–945. Arlington, Va.: ERIC Document Reproduction Center, 1974, p. 1974; see also her "Innovation in University Organization: The Communication Model." *Journal of Academic Librarianship*, 6 (May 1980), pp. 77–82.

18. *Dalhousie University Libraries, 1867–1970*. Halifax, Nova Scotia: n.p., n.d., p. 16.

19. Anne Woodsworth. *Patterns for Managing Information Technology on Campus*. Chicago: American Library Association, 1991.

20. Patricia Battin. "The Electronic Library—A Vision for the Future." *EDUCOM Bulletin*, 19 (Summer 1984), pp. 12–17, 34; C. Lee Jones, "Academic Libraries and Computing: A Time of Change." *EDUCOM Bulletin*, 20 (Spring 1985), pp. 9–12; Raymond K. Neff. "Merging Libraries and Computer Centers: Manifest Destiny or Manifestly Deranged." *EDUCOM Bulletin*, 20 (Winter 1983), pp. 8–12, 16.

21. Pat Molholt. "On Converging Paths: The Computing Center and the Library." *Libraries and Computing Centers*, No. 1 (March 1987). Insert in *Journal of Academic Librarianship*, 13 (March 1987).

22. Jones. "Academic Libraries and Computing," p. 10.

23. Battin. "The Electronic Library," pp. 12, 16.

24. Pat Molholt. "What Happened to the Merger Debate?" *Libraries and Computing Centers*, No. 13 (May 1989). Insert in *Journal of Academic Librarianship*, 15 (May 1989).

25. Richard P. West and Richard N. Katz. "Implementing the Vision: A Framework and an Agenda for Investing in Academic Computing." *EDUCOM Review*, 25 (Winter 1990), pp. 32–33.

26. Woodsworth. *Patterns*, p. 23.

27. See, for example, Marilyn J. Martin, "Academic Libraries and Computing Centers: Opportunities for Leadership." *Library Administration and Management*, 6 (Spring 1992), pp. 77–81.

CHAPTER 9

1. Oliver Garceau. *The Public Library in the Political Process*. New York: Columbia University Press, 1949, p. 239.

2. E. J. Josey, ed. *Libraries in the Political Process*. Phoenix, Ariz.: Oryx Press, 1980, p. x.

3. E. J. Josey and Kenneth D. Shearer, eds. *Politics and the Support of Libraries*. New York: Neal-Schuman, 1990.

4. American Library Association. *Handbook of Organization and Membership Directory, 1991/92*. Chicago: American Library Association, 1991, pp. 146–59.

5. Quoted in Evelyn Geller. *Forbidden Books in American Public Libraries, 1876– 1939*. New York: Greenwood Press, 1984, p. 149.

6. Jesse H. Shera. *The Foundation of Education for Librarianship*. New York: John Wiley, 1972, pp. 295–97.

7. Garceau. *The Public Library*, p. 117.

8. Mary L. Bundy and Frederick J. Stielow, eds. *Activism in American Librarianship, 1962–1973*. Chicago: American Library Association, 1987.

9. Manfred Kochen and Joseph C. Donahue, eds. *Information for the Community*. Chicago: American Library Association, 1976, p. 9.

10. Jane Robbins-Carter. "Political Science: Utility for Research in Librarianship." *Library Trends*, 32 (Spring 1984), p. 436.

11. Lee W. Finks. "Values Without Shame." *American Libraries*, 20 (April 1989), p. 353.

12. Alice Bryan. *The Public Librarian*. New York: Columbia University Press, 1952, p. 50.

13. Seymour M. Lipset. *Political Man*. New York: Doubleday, 1963, pp. 338–39.

14. Pauline E. Wilson. *Stereotype and Status: Librarians in the United States*. Westport, Conn.: Greenwood Press, 1982, p. 8.

15. Kenneth E. Dowlin. *The Electronic Library: The Promise and the Process*. New York: Neal-Schuman, 1984, p. 129.

16. Gunnar Myrdal. *An American Dilemma*. New York: Harper, 1944, p. 7 (emphasis in original).

17. Warren I. Susman. *Culture as History*. New York: Pantheon, 1985, p. 63.

18. Robert P. Wolff. *The Poverty of Liberalism*. Boston: Beacon Press, 1968, p. 3.

19. Louis Hartz. *The Liberal Tradition in America*. New York: Harcourt, Brace, & World, 1955, p. 50.

20. John C. Colson. "Form Against Function: The American Public Library and Contemporary Society." *Journal of Library History*, 18 (Spring 1983), pp. 111–42.

21. Stephen Hardy. *How Boston Played: Sports, Recreation, and Community, 1865– 1915*. Boston: Northeastern University Press, 1982.

22. Standard works on this theme are Samuel P. Hays, *The Response to Industrialism: 1885–1914*. Chicago: University of Chicago Press, 1957; and Robert H. Wiebe, *The Search for Order, 1877–1920*. New York: Hill and Wang, 1967.

23. Robert D. Leigh. *The Public Library in the United States*. New York: Columbia University Press, 1950, p. 9.

24. Rosemary R. DuMont. *Reform and Reaction: The Big City Public Library in American Life*. Westport, Conn.: Greenwood Press, 1977, p. 78.

25. Carlton Rochell. *Wheeler and Goldhor's Practical Administration of Public Libraries*. New York: Harper, 1981, p. 5.

26. DuMont. *Reform and Reaction*, p. 79.

27. Public Library Association. *The Library Connection: Essays Written in Praise of Public Libraries*. Chicago: American Library Association, 1977.

28. Edward Shils. "The Autonomies of Liberalism." In *The Relevance of Liberalism*. Edited by the Research Institute on International Change, Columbia University. Boulder, Colo.: Westview Press, 1978, p. 135.

29. Anthony Arblaster. *The Rise and Decline of Western Liberalism*. Oxford: Basil Blackwood, 1984, p. 6.

30. Lipset. *Political Man*, p. 318.

31. Benjamin R. Barber. *Strong Democracy: Participatory Politics for a New Age*. Berkeley, Calif.: University of California Press, 1984, p. 5.

32. Ibid., p. 68.

33. Gerald Gaus. *The Modern Liberal Theory of Man*. London: Croom Helm, 1983, p. 187.

34. Amy Gutman. *Liberal Equality*. Cambridge, Britain: Cambridge University Press, 1980, p. 25.

35. Vernon E. Palmour et al. "A Planning Process for Public Libraries: Introduction and Overview." In *Public Librarianship: A Reader*. Edited by Jane Robbins-Carter. Littleton, Colo.: Libraries Unlimited, 1983, p. 147.

36. Ernestine Rose. *The Public Library in American Life*. New York: Columbia University Press, 1954, p. 47.

37. Ralph A. Ulveling. "The Public Library in the Large Community." In *The Library in the Community*. Edited by Leon Carnovsky and Lowell Martin. Chicago: University of Chicago Press, 1940, p. 26.

38. Rochell. *Wheeler and Goldhor's Practical Administration*, p. 16.

39. Ibid., p. 24.

40. Leigh. *The Public Library*, pp. 234–35.

41. Peter Hall. *The Organization of American Culture*. New York: New York University Press, 1982, p. 3.

42. Benjamin R. Barber. *The Conquest of Politics: Liberal Philosophy in Democratic Times*. Princeton, N.J.: Princeton University Press, 1988, p. 177.

43. Charles Frankel. "Does Liberalism Have a Future?" In *The Relevance of Liberalism*, p. 119.

44. Peter Clecak. *Crooked Paths: Reflections on Socialism, Conservatism, and the Welfare State*. New York: Harper, 1983, p. 13.

CHAPTER 10

1. Langdon Winner. *The Whale and the Reactor*. Chicago: University of Chicago Press, 1986, p. 19.

2. Ibid., p. 23.

3. Ibid., p. 29.

4. Ibid., p. 38.

5. Joseph Weizenbaum. *Computer Power and Human Reason: From Judgment to Calculation*. San Francisco: W. H. Freeman, 1976, pp. 31–32.

6. Edward Shils. "The Autonomies of Liberalism." In *The Relevance of Liberalism*. Edited by the Research Institute on International Change, Columbia University. Boulder, Colo.: Westview Press, 1978, p. 138.

7. Patrick R. Penland. *Advisory Counseling for Librarians*. Pittsburgh, Pa.: University of Pittsburgh, 1969, p. 25.

8. Ibid., p. 26.

9. Vincent E. Giuliano. "A Manifesto for Librarians." *Library Journal*, 104 (September 15, 1979), p. 1839.

10. Ronald Reagan. "Inaugural Address, January 20, 1981." *Public Papers of the Presidents of the United States, Ronald Reagan, 1981.* Washington, D.C.: U.S. Government Printing Office, 1982, p. 2.

11. David Dickson and David Noble. "By Force of Reason: The Politics of Science and Technology Policy." In *Hidden Election: Politics and Economics in the 1980 Presidential Campaign.* Edited by Thomas Ferguson and Joel Rogers. New York: Pantheon, 1981, p. 261.

12. Ibid., p. 267.

13. Ibid., p. 304.

14. Herbert I. Schiller. *Who Knows: Information in the Age of the Fortune 500.* Norwood, N.J.: Ablex Publishing, 1981, pp. xiv-xv.

15. Victor Ferkiss. "Daniel Bell's Concept of Post-Industrial Society: Theory, Myth, and Ideology." *Political Science Reviewer*, 9 (Fall 1979), pp. 61–102; see also Kevin Robins and Frank Webster, "Information As Capital: A Critique of Daniel Bell." In *The Ideology of the Information Age.* Edited by Jennifer D. Slacks and Fred Fejes. Norwood, N.J.: Ablex, 1987, pp. 95–117.

16. Ferkiss. "Daniel Bell's Concept." pp. 67–68.

17. R. E. Lane. "The Decline of Politics and Ideology in a Knowledgeable Society." *American Sociological Review*, 13 (October 1966), pp. 649–62.

18. Fred Fejes and James Schwach. "A Competing Ideology for the Information Age: A Two-Sector Model for the Information Society." In *The Ideology of the Information Age*, p. 159.

19. Fay M. Blake. "Let My People Know: Access to Information in a Post-Industrial Society." *Wilson Library Bulletin*, 52 (January 1978), pp. 392–99.

20. Lawrence J. White. *Public Library in the 1980s.* Lexington, Mass.: Lexington Books, 1983, p. 12; see also Malcolm Getz, *Public Libraries: An Economic View.* Baltimore, Md.: Johns Hopkins, 1980; Pete Giacoma. *The Fee or Free Decision.* New York: Neal-Schuman, 1989.

21. Miriam Braverman. "From Adam Smith to Ronald Reagan: Public Libraries as a Public Good." *Library Journal*, 107 (February 15, 1982), p. 397. See also James F. Govan, "The Creeping Hand: Entrepreneurial Librarianship." *Library Journal*, 113 (January 1988), pp. 35–38.

22. American Library Association Commission on Freedom and Equality of Access to Information. *Freedom and Equality of Access to Information.* Chicago: American Library Association, p. 100.

23. Leigh Estabrook. "Productivity, Profit, and Libraries." *Library Journal*, 106 (July 1981), pp. 1377–80.

24. Richard DeGennaro. "Libraries, Technology, and the Information Marketplace." *Library Journal*, 107 (June 1, 1982), pp. 1045–54; Svend Larsen, "The Idea of an Electronic Library: A Critical Essay." *Libri*, 38 (September 1988), pp. 159–77; Patricia G. Schuman, "Reclaiming Our Technological Future." *Library Journal*, 115 (March 1, 1990), pp. 34–38; Frederick W. Lancaster, "The Impact of Technology on the Use of Information Sources." In *Information Technology and Information Use.* Edited by Peter Ingwersen et al. London: Taylor Graham, 1986.

25. Richard Apostle and Boris Raymond. "Librarianship and the Information Paradigm." *Canadian Library Journal*, 43 (December 1986), pp. 377–84.

26. John Buschman. "Asking the Right Questions About Information Technology." *American Libraries*, 21 (December 1990), pp. 1026–30; "A Critique of the Information Broker: Context of Reference Services." *Reference Librarian*, 31 (1990), pp. 131–35.

27. William F. Birdsall. "The Political Persuasion of Librarianship." *Library Journal*, 113 (June 1, 1988), pp. 75–79; Henry T. Blanke, "Librarianship and Political Values: Neutrality or Commitment?" *Library Journal*, 114 (July 1989), pp. 39–43.

28. Blanke. "Librarianship and Political Values." p. 40.

29. Jorge F. Sosa and Michael H. Harris. "Jose Ortega y Gasset and the Role of the Librarian in Post-Industrial America." *Libri*, 41 (March 1991), pp. 19–20; Anne Woodsworth et al., "The Information Job Family: Results of an Exploratory Study." *Library Trends*, 41 (Fall 1992), pp. 250–68.

CHAPTER 11

1. Mason Drukman. *Community and Purpose in America: An Analysis of American Political Culture*. New York: McGraw-Hill, 1971, p. 7.

2. Robert A. Nisbet. *The Sociological Tradition*. New York: Basic Books, 1966, p. 47.

3. Steven Lukes. *Individualism*. Oxford, England: Basil Blackwell, 1973.

4. Ibid., p. 26.

5. Thomas Bender. *Community and Social Change in America*. New Brunswick, N.J.: Rutgers University Press, 1978, pp. 137–42.

6. Robert N. Bellah et al. *The Good Society*. New York: Knopf, 1991, p. 269.

7. Bender. *Community and Social Change in America*, p. 139.

8. Dee Garrison. *Apostles of Culture: The Public Librarian and American Society, 1876–1920*. New York: Macmillan, 1979, pp. 178–79.

9. Ernest L. Boyer. *Ready to Learn: A Mandate for the Nation*. Princeton, N.J.: Carnegie Foundation for the Advancement of Teaching, 1991, p. 4.

10. Ibid., p. 9.

11. Ibid., p. 100.

12. James Quay and James Veninga. National Task Force on Scholarship and the Public Humanities. *Making Connections: the Humanities, Culture, and Community*. New York: American Council of Learned Societies, 1990.

13. Ibid., p. 4.

14. Ibid., p. 7.

15. Ibid., p. 20.

16. Christopher Lasch. "The Communitarian Critique of Liberalism." In *Community in America: The Challenge of "Habits of the Heart."* Edited by Charles H. Reynolds and Ralph V. Norman. Berkeley, Calif.: University of California Press, 1988, p. 175.

17. Ibid., p. 178.

18. Gillian S. Gremmels. "Reference in the Public Interest: An Examination of Ethics." *RQ*, 30 (Spring 1991), pp. 362–69.

19. Robert N. Bellah et al. *Habits of the Heart: Individualism and Commitment in American Life*. New York: Harper, 1985, p. 333.

20. Ralf Dahrendorf, *Life Chances*. Chicago: University of Chicago Press, 1979, p. 33.

21. Ibid., p. 28.

22. Ibid., pp. 31–32.

23. Ibid., p. 43.

24. Charles R. McClure et al. *Planning and Role Setting of Public Libraries: A Manual of Operations and Procedures*. Chicago: American Library Association, 1987, p. 28.

25. Ibid., pp. 32–35.

26. Burton R. Clark. *The Higher Education System*. Berkeley, Calif.: University of California Press, 1983, pp. 269–76.

27. Robert Fishman. *Bourgeois Utopias: The Rise and Fall of Suburbia*. New York: Basic Books, 1987.

28. Anthony Smith. "Technology, Identity, and the Information Machine." *Daedalus*, 115 (Summer 1986), p. 165.

29. James W. Carey. *Communication as Culture*. Boston: Unwin Hyman, 1989, p. 18.

30. Ibid., pp. 18–19.

31. Ibid., pp. 20–21.

32. Ibid., p. 21.

33. Cathy Simon. "Inspiration, Knowledge and Information." In Association of Research Libraries, *Is the Library a Place*? Minutes of the 118th meeting, May 15–17, 1991. Washington, D.C.: Association of Research Libraries, 1991, p. 9.

34. Quoted in Judy Quinn. "California Dreaming: Dowlin & Co. Design a New Main Library." *Library Journal*, 117 (June 1, 1992), p. 56.

35. Simon. "Inspiration." p. 9.

36. Charles R. McClure et al. *Public Libraries and the Internet/NREN: New Challenges, New Opportunities*. Syracuse, N.Y.: Syracuse University, 1992.

CHAPTER 12

1. Michael R. Buckland. *Redesigning Library Services: A Manifesto*. Chicago: American Library Association, 1992.

2. Ibid., p. 76.

3. Beverly T. Watkins. "Many Campuses Start Building Tomorrow's Electronic Library." *Chronicle of Higher Education*, 39 (September 2, 1992), A19–A21.

Bibliography

Abbott, Andrew. *The System of Professions*. Chicago: University of Chicago Press, 1988.

Adams, Guy B., and Virginia H. Ingersoll. "Painting Over Old Works: The Culture of Organization in an Age of Technical Rationality." In *Organizational Symbolism*. Edited by Berry A. Turner. Berlin: Walter de Gruyter, 1990.

Allen, Bryce. "Questions and Answers: Finding Out About Information Needs." *Canadian Library Journal*, 46 (June 1989), 191–93.

American Library Association. *Handbook of Organization and Membership Directory, 1991/92*. Chicago: American Library Association, 1991.

——. Commission on Freedom and Equality of Access to Information. *Freedom and Equality of Access to Information*. Chicago: American Library Association, 1986.

Anderson, James D. et al. "Information Science at Rutgers: Establishing New Inter-Disciplinary Connections." *Journal of the American Society for Information Science*, 39 (September, 1988), 327–30.

Anderson, Lee W. "Reference Librarians and Psychology." *Library Journal*, 81 (May 1, 1956), 1058, 1060.

Apostle, Richard, and Boris Raymond. "Librarianship and the Information Paradigm." *Canadian Library Journal*, 43 (December 1986), 377–84.

Arblaster, Anthony. *The Rise and Decline of Western Liberalism*. Oxford, Britain: Basil Blackwood, 1984.

Arms, Caroline R. Editor. *Campus Strategies for Libraries and Electronic Information*. Rockport, Mass.: Digital Press, 1990.

Arms, William Y. *Electronic Publishing and the Academic Library*. Pittsburgh, Pa.: Carnegie-Mellon University, n.d.

Arms, William Y. et al. "The Design of the Mercury Electronic Library." *EDUCOM Review*, 27 (November/December 1992), 38–41.

Arms, William Y., and Dana S. Scott. *Brief Review of Research on the Electronic Library at Carnegie-Mellon University.* Mercury Technical Report Series No. 2. Pittsburgh, Pa.: Carnegie-Mellon University, 1990.

Arms, William Y., and Thomas J. Michalak. "The Merger of Libraries with Computing at Carnegie-Mellon University." *British Journal of Academic Librarianship* 3 (No. 3, 1988), 153–63.

Ashiem, Lester. "Librarians as Professionals." *Library Trends*, 27 (Winter 1979), 225-57.

Association of Research Libraries. *Is the Library a Place?* Minutes of the 118th Meeting, May 15-17, 1991. Washington, D.C.: Association of Research Libraries, 1991.

Auster, Ethel. "User Satisfaction with the Online Negotiation Interview: Contemporary Concern in Traditional Perspective." *RQ*, 23 (Fall 1983), 47–59.

Bailey, Charles W., Jr. "Integrated Public-Acess Computer Systems: The Heart of the Electronic University." In *Advances in Library Automation and Networking*, Vol. 3, 1989. Greenwich, Conn.: JAI Press, 1989.

———. "Public-Acess Computer Systems: The Next Generation of Library Automation Systems." *Information Technology and Libraries*, 8 (June 1989), 178–85.

Ballard, Thomas. "The Information Age and the Public Library." *Wilson Library Bulletin*, 62 (June 1988), 74–75, 78.

Barber, Benjamin R. *The Conquest of Politics: Liberal Philosophy in Democratic Times.* Princeton, N.J.: Princeton University Press, 1988.

———. *Strong Democracy: Participatory Politics for a New Age.* Berkeley, Calif.: University of California Press, 1984.

Basch, Reva. "Books Online: Visions, Plans, and Perspectives for Electronic Text." *Online*, 15 (July 1991), 13–23.

Battin, Patricia. "The Electronic Library—A Vision for the Future." *EDUCOM Bulletin*, 19 (Summer 1984), 12–17, 34.

Bearman, Toni Carbo. "The Information Society of the 1990s: Blue Sky and Green Pastures?" *Online*, 11 (January 1987), 82–86.

Bedsole, Dan T. "Review of *Libraries of the Future.*" *Special Libraries*, 56 (July–August 1965), 409.

Bell, Daniel. "The Social Framework of the Information Society." In *The Microelectronic Revolution.* Edited by Tom Forester. Oxford, Britain: Basil Blackwell, 1980.

———. *The Coming of Post-Industrial Society.* New York: Basic Books, 1976.

———. *The End of Ideology: On the Exhaustion of Political Ideas in the Fifties.* Rev. Ed. New York: Free Press, 1965.

Bellah, Robert N. et al. *The Good Society.* New York: Knopf, 1991.

———. *Habits of the Heart: Individualism and Commitment in American Life.* New York: Harper, 1985.

Bender, Thomas. *Community and Social Change in America.* New Brunswick, N.J.: Rutgers University Press, 1978.

Bennett, William S., Jr., and Merl C. Hokenstad, Jr. "Full-Time People Workers and Conceptions of the Professional." In *The Sociological Review Monograph*, 20. Edited by Paul Halmos. Keele, Britain: University of Keele, 1973.

Benson, James, and Ruth K. Maloney. "Principles of Searching." *RQ*, 14 (Summer 1975), 316–20.

Berman, Marshall. *All That is Solid Melts into Air: The Experience of Modernity*. New York: Penguin Books, 1988.

Berry, John N. "The Central Library—Beyond Symbolism." *Library Journal*, 115 (June 1, 1990), 7.

Bibliography in an Age of Science. Urbana, Ill.: University of Illinois Press, 1952.

Billings, Harold. "The Bionic Library." *Library Journal*, 116 (October 15, 1991), 38–42.

Binkley, Robert C. *Manual on Methods of Reproducing Research Materials*. Ann Arbor, Mich.: Edwards Brothers, 1936.

Birdsall, William F. The Political Persuasion of Librarianship," *Library Journal*, 113 (June 1, 1988), 75–79.

———. "Public Libraries and Political Culture." *Public Library Quarterly*, 8 (1988), 55–65.

———. "Community, Individualism, and the American Public Library." *Library Journal*, 110 (November 1, 1985), 21–24.

———. "Librarians: Personal Service Professionals?" *Argus*, 11 (May–August, 1982), 53–56.

———. "Librarianship, Professionalism, and Social Change," *Library Journal*, 107 (February 1, 1982), 223–26.

———. "Librarians and Professionalism, Status Measured by Outmoded Models." *Canadian Library Journal*, 37 (June 1980), 145–48.

Blake, Fay M. "Let My People Know: Access to Information in a Post-industrial Society." *Wilson Library Bulletin*, 52 (January 1978), 392–99.

———. "Public Access to Information in the Post-Industrial Society." In *The Information Society: Issues and Answers*. Edited by E. J. Josey. Phoenix, Ariz.: Oryx Press, 1978.

Blake, Virgil P., and Renee Tjoumas. Editors. *Information Literacies for the Twenty-First Century*. Boston: G. K. Hall, 1990.

Blanke, Henry T. "Librarianship and Political Values: Neutrality or Commitment?" *Library Journal*, 114 (July 1989), 39–43.

Bobinski, George S. "Carnegies." *American Libraries*, 21 (April 1990), 296–301.

Boisse, Joseph, and Carla J. Stoffle. "Epilogue: Issues and Answers: The Participants Views." In *The Information Society: Issues and Answers*. Edited by E. J. Josey. Phoenix, Ariz.: Oryx Press, 1978.

Boucher, Virginia. "Non-Verbal Communication and the Reference Interview." *RQ*, 16 (Fall 1976), 27–32.

Bourne, Bill, Udi Eichler, and David Hernan. Editors. *Modernity and Its Discontents (Voices)*. Nottingham, England: Spokesman, 1987.

Boyer, Ernest L. *Ready to Learn: A Mandate for the Nation*. Princeton, N.J.: Carnegie Foundation for the Advancement of Teaching, 1991.

Brantlinger, Patrick. *Bread and Circuses: Theories of Mass Culture as Social Decay*. Ithaca, N. Y.: Cornell University Press, 1983.

Braverman, Miriam. "From Adam Smith to Ronald Reagan: Public Libraries as a Public Good." *Library Journal*, 107 (February 15, 1982), 397–401.

Brindley, Lynne J. Editor. *The Electronic Campus: An Information Strategy*. Boston Spa, U.K.: British Library, 1989.

Briscoe, Peter et al. "Ashurbanipul's Enduring Archetype: Thoughts on the Library's Role in the Future." *College and Research Libraries*, 47 (March 1986), 121–26.

Brown, Doris R. "Three Terminals, a Telefax, and One Dictionary." *College and Research Libraries News*, 46 (November 1985), 536–38.

Brown, George W. et al. *EDUNET: Report of the Summer Study on Information Networks Conducted by the Interuniversity Communications Council (EDUCOM)*. New York: John Wiley, 1967.

Brownrigg, Edwin, and Brett Butler. "An Electronic Library Communications Format: A Definition and Development Proposal for Marc III." *Library Hi Tech*, 8 (1990), 21–26.

Bryan, Alice I. *The Public Librarian*. New York: Columbia University Press, 1952.

_____ . "The Psychology of the Reader." *Library Journal*, 64 (January 1, 1939), 7–12.

Buckland, Michael K. "Emanuel Goldberg, Electronic Document Retrieval, Vannevar Bush's Memex." *Journal of the American Society for Information Science*, 43 (May 1992), 284–94.

_____ . *Redesigning Library Services: A Manifesto*. Chicago: American Library Association, 1992.

_____ . "Foundations of Academic Librarianship." *College and Research Libraries*, 50 (July 1989), 389–96.

_____ . *Library Services in Theory and Practice*, 2nd edn. New York: Pergamon Press, 1988.

_____ . "Looking Ahead—And Around." *Information Reports and Bibliographies*, 7 (1978), 15–17.

Bundy, Mary L., and Paul Wasserman. "Professionalism Reconsidered." *College and Research Libraries*, 29 (January 1968), 5–26.

Bundy, Mary L., Paul Wasserman, and Frederick J. Stielow. Editors. *Activism in American Librarianship 1962–1973*. Chicago: American Library Association, 1987.

Bunge, Charles A. "Interpersonal Dimensions of the Reference Interview: A Historical Review of the Literature." *Drexel Library Quarterly*, 20 (Spring 1984), 4–23.

_____ . "Charting the Reference Query." *RQ*, 8 (Summer 1969), 245–50.

Buschman, John. "Asking the Right Questions About Information Technology. *American Libraries*, 21 (December 1990), 1026–30.

_____ . "A Critique of the Information Broker: Contexts of Reference Services." *Reference Librarian*, 31 (1990), 131–51.

Bush, Vannevar. *Science Is Not Enough*. New York: William Morrow, 1967.

_____ . "Remarks of Vannevar Bush to Project INTREX Planning Conference." In *INTREX: Report of a Planning Conference on Information Transfer Experiments*. Edited by Carl F. J. Overhage and R. Joyce Harmon. Cambridge, Mass.: MIT Press, 1965.

_____ . "As We May Think." *Atlantic Monthly*, 176 (July 1945), 101–108.

Butler, Brett. "The Electronic Library Program: Developing Networked Electronic Library Collections." *Library Hi Tech*, 9 (1991), 21–30.

_____ . "Online Catalogs, Online Reference: An Overview." In *Online Catalogs, Online Reference: Converging Trends*. Edited by Brian Aveney and Brett Butler. Chicago: American Library Association, 1984.

Cady, Susan A. "The Electronic Revolution in Libraries: Microfilm Déja Vu?" *College and Research Libraries*, 51 (July 1990), 374–86.

Carey, James W. *Communication As Culture*. Boston: Unwin Hyman, 1989.

Carey, James W., and John J. Quirk. "The Mythos of the Electronic Revolution." *American Scholar*, 39 (Spring 1970), 219–41; (Summer 1970), 395–424.

Cargill, Jennifer. "The Electronic Reference Desk: Reference Service in an Electronic World." *Library Administration and Management*, 6 (Spring 1992), 82–85.

Carnovsky, Leon, and Lowell Martin. Editors. *The Library in the Community*. Chicago: University of Chicago Press, 1940.

Carter, L. et al. *National Document-Handling Systems for Science and Technology*. New York: John Wiley, 1967.

Casey, Robert S. et al. Editors. *Punched Cards: Their Applications to Science and Industry*, 2nd edn. New York: Reinhold, 1958.

Cherry, Susan S. "Electronic Library Association Born at Columbus Forum." *American Libraries*, 12 (May 1981), 275–76.

Childers, Thomas. "Community and Library: Some Possible Futures." *Library Journal*, 96 (September 15, 1971), 2727–30.

Christian, Roger W. *Electronic Library: Bibliographic Data Bases, 1978–79*. White Plains, N.Y.: Knowledge Industry Publications, 1978.

———. *Electronic Library: Bibliographic Data Bases, 1975–76*. White Plains, N.Y.: Knowledge Industry Publications, 1975.

Clark, Burton R. *The Higher Education System*. Berkeley, Calif.: University of California Press, 1983.

Clecak, Peter. *Crooked Paths: Reflections on Socialism, Conservatism, and the Welfare State*. New York: Harper, 1983.

Cline, Hugh F., and Loraine T. Sinnott. *The Electronic Library: The Impact of Automation on Academic Libraries*. Lexington, Mass.: D. C. Heath, 1983.

Cline, Nancy, "Information Resources and the National Network." *EDUCOM Review*, 25 (Summer 1990), 30–34.

Cohen, Stephen S., and John Sysman. *Manufacturing Matters: The Myth of the Post-Industrial Society*. New York: Basic Books, 1987.

Colson, John C. "Form Against Function: The American Public Library and Contemporary Society." *Journal of Library History*, 18 (Spring 1983), 111–42.

Committee on Scientific and Technical Communication, National Academy of Sciences. *Scientific and Technical Communication: A Pressing Problem and Recommendations for its Solution*. Washington, D.C.: National Academy of Sciences, 1969.

Computer Science and Engineering Board, National Academy of Sciences. *Libraries and Information Technology: A National System Challenge*. Washington, D.C.: National Academy of Sciences, 1972.

Conzen, Michael P. Editor. *The Making of the American Landscape*. Boston: Unwin Hyman, 1990.

Crawford, Susan. "The Origin and Development of a Concept: The Information Society." *Bulletin of the Medical Library Association*, 71 (October 1983), 380–85.

Cronin, Blaise. "There Is no Future for Libraries: There Are Multiple Futures."
    Keynote address, Atlantic Provinces Library Association, Annual Confer-
    ence, May 8, 1992, Halifax, Nova Scotia.
Cuadra, Carlos. *The Coming Era of Local Electronic Libraries*. Bloomington, Ind.:
    School of Library and Information Science, Indiana University, 1983.
Cummings, Anthony M. et al. *University Libraries and Scholarly Communication: A
    Study Prepared for the Andrew W. Mellon Foundation*. Washington, D.C.:
    Association of Research Libraries, 1992.
Dalhousie University Libraries, 1867-1970. Halifax, Nova Scotia: N.p., n.d.
Dahrendorf, Ralf. *Life Chances*. Chicago: University of Chicago Press, 1979.
De Buse, Raymond. "So That's a Book . . . Advance Technology and the Library."
    Information Technology and Libraries, 7 (March 1988), 7–18.
De Gennaro, Richard. "Libraries, Technology, and the Information Marketplace."
    Library Journal, 107 (June 1, 1982), 1045–54.
De Hart, Florence. *The Librarian's Psychological Commitments*. Westport, Conn.:
    Greenwood Press, 1979.
Delaney, Jack. "Interviewing." *Wilson Library Bulletin*, 29 (December 1954), 317–18.
Dennett, Daniel C. "Information, Technology, and the Virtues of Ignorance." *Dae-
    dalus*, 115 (Summer 1986), 135–53.
Derber, Charles. *Professionals as Workers: Mental Labor in Advanced Capitalism*. Bos-
    ton: G. K. Hall, 1982.
Derr, Richard. "Questions: Definitions, Structure, and Classification." *RQ*, 24
    (Winter 1984), 186–90.
Dervin, Brenda, and Patricia Dewdney. "Neutral Questioning: A New Approach
    to the Reference Interview." *RQ*, 25 (Summer 1986), 506–13.
Development Plan for an Electronic Library System: Business Plan. Pittsburgh, Pa.:
    Carnegie-Mellon University, 1991.
Development Plan for an Electronic Library System: Final Report. Pittsburgh, Pa.:
    Carnegie-Mellon University, 1991.
Dickey, William. "Poem Descending a Staircase: Hypertext and the Simultaneity
    of Experience." In *Hypermedia and Literary Studies*. Edited by Paul Delany
    and George P. Landow. Cambridge, Mass.: MIT Press, 1991.
Dickson, David, and David Noble. "By Force of Reason: The Politics of Science and
    Technology Policy." In *The Hidden Election: Politics and Economics in the
    1980 Presidential Campaign*. Edited by Thomas Ferguson and Joel Rogers.
    New York: Pantheon, 1981.
Dillard, Annie. *An American Childhood*. New York: Harper & Row, 1987.
Ditzion, Sidney. *Arsenals of a Democratic Culture*. Chicago: American Library Asso-
    ciation, 1947.
Dizard, Wilson P., Jr. *The Coming Information Age: An Overview of Technology,
    Economics, and Politics*. New York: Longman, 1982.
Dougherty, Richard, and Carol Hughes. *Preferred Futures for Libraries*. Mountain
    View, Calif.: Research Libraries Group, 1992.
Dougherty, Richard, Carol Hughes, and Wendy P. Lougee. "What Will Survive?"
    Library Journal, 110 (February 1, 1985), 41–44.
Dowlin, Kenneth E. "Maggie III: The Prototypical Library System." *Library Hi Tech*,
    4 (1986), 7–21.

———. *The Electronic Library: The Promise and the Process*. New York: Neal-Schuman, 1984.

———. Editor. "The Electronic Library. *Drexel Library Quarterly*, 17 (Fall 1981).

———. "The Electronic Eclectic Library." *Library Journal*, 105 (November 1, 1980), 2265–70.

Drake, Miriam A. "The Online Information System at Georgia Institute of Technology." *Information Technology and Libraries*, 8 (June 1989), 105–9.

Drucker, Peter F. *The Age of Discontinuity*. New York: Harper, 1968.

Drukman, Mason. *Community and Purpose in America: An Analysis of American Political Culture*. New York: McGraw-Hill, 1971.

DuMont, Rosemary R. *Reform and Reaction: The Big City Public Library in American Life*. Westport, Conn.: Greenwood Press, 1977.

Edleman, Hendrik. *Libraries and Information Science in the Electronic Age*. Philadelphia: ISI Press, 1986.

Eichman, Thomas L. "The Complex Nature of Opening Reference Questions." *RQ*, 17 (Spring 1978), 212–22.

Ennis, Philip H. "Technological Change and the Professions: Neither Luddite nor Technocrat." *Library Quarterly*, 32 (July 1962), 189–98.

Estabrook, Leigh. "Productivity, Profit, and Libraries." *Library Journal*, 106 (July 1981), 1377–80.

Evans, Nancy, "Development of the Carnegie-Mellon Library Information Systems." *Information Technology and Libraries*, 8 (June 1989), 110–20.

Evans, Nancy et al. *The Vision of the Electronic Library*. Mercury Technical Report Series No. 1. Pittsburgh, Pa.: Carnegie-Mellon University, 1989.

Evans, Nancy, and Thomas J. Michalak. "Delivering Reference Information Through a Campus Network: Carnegie-Mellon's Library Information System." *Reference Services Review* 15 (Winter 1987), 7–13.

Evans, Richard I. *Carl Rogers: The Man and His Ideas*. New York: Dutton, 1975.

Falgione, Joseph. "Pittsburgh Makes Its Carnegie Work." *American Libraries*, 21 (April 1990), 303.

Farkas-Conn, Irene S. *From Documentation to Information Science*. Westport, Conn.: Greenwood Press, 1990.

Fayen, Emily G. "Beyond Technology: Rethinking 'Librarian.' " *American Libraries*, 17 (April 1986), 240–42.

Fejes, Fred, and James Schwoch. "A Competing Ideology for the Information Age: A Two-Sector Model for the New Information Society." In *The Ideology of the Information Age*. Edited by Jennifer D. Slack and Fred Fejes. Norwood, N.J.: Ablex Publishing, 1987.

Ferkiss, Victor. "Daniel Bell's Concept of Post-Industrial Society: Theory, Myth, and Ideology." *Political Science Reviewer*, 9 (Fall 1979), 61–102.

Fine, Sarah. "The Librarian as Youth Counselor." *Drexel Library Quarterly*, 14 (January 1978), 29–44.

Fink, Deborah. "The Information Society as a 'Hook' for Library Lectures." In *Conceptual Frameworks for Bibliographic Education*. Edited by Mary Reichal and Mary Ann Ramey. Littleton, Colo.: Libraries Unlimited, 1987.

Finks, Lee W. "Values Without Shame." *American Libraries*, 20 (April 1989), 352–54, 356.

Fishman, Robert. *Bourgeois Utopias: The Rise and Fall of Suburbia*. New York: Basic Books, 1987.

Foerster, Heinz Von. "Epistemology of Communication." In *The Myths of Information: Technology and Postindustrial Culture*. Edited by Kathleen Woodward. Madison, Wis.: Coda Press, 1980.

Folk, Hugh. "The Impact of Computers on Book and Journal Publication." In *Economics of Library Automation*. Edited by J. L. Divibiss. Proceedings of the 1976 Clinic on Library Applications of Data Processing. Urbana-Champaign, Ill.: University of Illinois Graduate School of Library Service, 1977.

Forester, Tom. Editor. *The Microelectronics Revolution*. Oxford, England: Basil Blackwell, 1980.

Foskett, D. J. *The Creed of the Librarian: No Politics, No Religion, No Morals*. London: Library Association, 1962.

"Foundations of Library Practice." Charles H. Busha, issue editor. *Drexel Library Quarterly*, 19 (Spring 1983).

Frankel, Charles. "Does Liberalism Have a Future?" In *Relevance of Liberalism*. Edited by the Staff of the Research Institute on International Change. Boulder, Colo.: Westview Press, 1978.

Frankena, Frederick, and Joann Koelln Frankena. "The Politics of Expertise and the Role of the Librarian." *Behavioral and Social Science Librarian*, 61 (Fall/Winter 1986), 37–47.

"The Future is Now: Managing Tomorrow's Virtual Library Today." *Library Administration & Management*, 6 (Spring 1992), entire issue.

Gapen, D. Kaye. "Strategies for Networking in the Next Ten Years." *Journal of Library Administration*, 8 (Fall/Winter 1987), 117–30.

Garceau, Oliver. *The Public Library in the Political Process*. New York: Columbia University Press, 1949.

Garrison, Dee. *Apostles of Culture: The Public Librarian and American Society, 1876-1920*. New York: Macmillan, 1979.

Garrison, Guy. "The Future: Challenges to Information Science Education." *Journal of the American Society for Information Science*, 39 (September 1988), 362–66.

Gaus, Gerald. *The Modern Liberal Theory of Man*. London: Croom Helm, 1983.

Geison, Gerald L. Editor. *Professions and Professional Ideologies in America*. Chapel Hill, N.C.: University of North Carolina Press, 1983.

Geller, Evelyn. *Forbidden Books in American Public Libraries, 1876–1939*. New York: Greenwood Press, 1984.

Getz, Malcolm. *Public Libraries: An Economic View*. Baltimore, Md.: Johns Hopkins, 1980.

Giacoma, Pete. *The Fee or Free Decision*. New York: Neal-Schuman, 1989.

Giuliano, Vincent E. "A Manifesto for Librarians." *Library Journal*, 104 (September 15, 1979), 1837–42.

———. "Electronic Office Information Systems and the Information Manager." *Bulletin of the American Society for Information Science*, 4 (February 1978), 13–15.

———. "The Relationship of Information Science to Librarianship—Problems and Scientific Training." *American Documentation*, 20 (October 1969), 344–45.

Giuliano, Vincent E. et al. *Into the Information Age: A Perspective for Federal Action on Information.* Chicago: American Library Association, 1978.

Glazer, Nathan. "Individualism and Equality in the United States." In *Making America: The Society and Culture of the United States.* Washington, D.C.: U.S. Information Agency, 1987.

Glogoff, Stuart. "Communication Theory's Role in the Reference Interview." *Drexel Library Quarterly,* 19 (Spring 1983), 56–72.

Goldwyn, A. J. "Review of Libraries of the Future." *Library Journal,* 90 (June 15, 1965), 2818–19.

Goode, William J. "The Librarian: From Occupation to Profession?" *Library Quarterly,* 31 (October 1961), 306–20.

Gorman, Michael. Editor. *Convergence: Proceedings of the Second National Conference of the Library and Information Technology Association, October 2–6, 1988.* Chicago: American Library Association, 1990.

Gothberg, Helen. "Communication Patterns in Library Reference and Information Service." *RQ,* 13 (Fall 1973), 7–13.

Gouldner, Alvin. *The Coming Crisis of Western Sociology.* New York: Basic Books, 1970.

Govan, James F. "The Creeping Invisible Hand: Entrepreneurial Librarianship." *Library Journal,* 113 (January 1988), 35–38.

———. "Fluidity and Intangibility: The Stunning Impact of an Expanded Information Base." *Journal of Library Administration,* 8 (Summer 1987), 15–25.

Green, Samuel S. "Personal Relations Between Librarians and Readers." *Library Journal,* 1 (October 1976), 74–81.

Greenberg, Dolores. "Energy, Power, and Perceptions of Social Change in the Early Nineteenth Century." *American Historical Review,* 95 (June 1990), 693–714.

Gremmels, Gillian S. "Reference in the Public Interest: An Examination of Ethics." *RQ,* 30 (Spring 1991), 362–69.

Gusfield, Joseph R. *Community: A Critical Response.* New York: Harper & Row, 1975.

Guskin, Alan E. et al. "Library Future Shock: The Microcomputer Revolution and the New Role of the Library." *College and Research Libraries,* 45 (May 1984), 177–83.

Gutman, Amy. *Liberal Equality.* Cambridge, England: Cambridge University Press, 1980.

Hall, Edward. *The Hidden Dimension.* New York: Doubleday, 1966.

Hall, Peter. *The Organization of American Culture.* New York: New York University Press, 1982.

Halmos, Paul. *The Personal Service Society.* London: Constable, 1970.

———. *The Faith of the Counsellors.* London: Constable, 1965.

Hammer, Donald P. Editor. *The Information Age: Its Development and Impact.* Metuchen, N.J.: Scarecrow Press, 1976.

Hardison, O. B., Jr. *Entering the Maze: Identity and Change in Modern Culture.* New York: Oxford University Press, 1981.

Hardy, Stephen. *How Boston Played: Sports, Recreation, and Community, 1865–1915.* Boston: Northeastern University Press, 1982.

Harr, John M. "The Politics of Information: Libraries and Online Retrieval Systems." *Library Journal*, 111 (February 1, 1986), 40–43.

Harris, Roma M. *Librarianship: The Erosion of a Woman's Profession*. Norwood, N.J.: Ablex, 1992.

_____. "Bibliographic Instruction in Public Libraries: A Question of Philosophy." *RQ*, 29 (Fall 1989), 92–98.

Hartz, Louis. *The Liberal Tradition in America*. New York: Harcourt, Brace & World, 1955.

Hauptman, Robert. *Ethical Challenges in Librarianship*. Phoenix, Ariz.: Oryx, 1988.

Hawkins, Donald T. "The Commodity Nature of Information." *Online*, 11 (January 1987), 67–70.

Hayes, Robert M. Editor. *Libraries and the Information Economy of California*. Los Angeles. Graduate School of Library and Information Science, University of California, Los Angeles, 1985.

Hays, Samuel P. *The Response to Industrialism: 1885–1914*. Chicago: University of Chicago Press, 1957.

Henderson, Hazel. "The Age of Light: Beyond the Information Age." *Futurist*, 20 (July–August 1986), 56.

Hennessy, James A. "Guerrilla Librarianship? A Review Article on the Librarianship of Politics and the Politics of Librarianship." *Journal of Librarianship*, 13 (October 1981), 248–55.

Hennon, Thomas J., Jr. "Public Librarians Take Cool View of the Future: Leadership, Not Technology May Be the Issue." *American Libraries*, 19 (May 1988), 390–92.

Herron, Nancy L. "The Electronic Library." *Library Hi Tech Bibliography*, vol. 2. Ann Arbor, Mich.: Pierian Press, 1987.

Hiss, Tony. *The Experience of Place*. New York: Knopf, 1990.

Hoadley, Irene. "The World That Awaits Us: Libraries of Tomorrow." *Wilson Library Bulletin*, 61 (October 1986), 22–25.

Holland, Barron. "Updating Library Reference Services Through Training for Interpersonal Competence." *RQ*, 17 (Spring 1978), 207–11.

Hopkins, Francis L. "A Century of Bibliographic Instruction: The Historical Claim to Professional and Academic Legitimacy." *College and Research Libraries*, 43 (May 1982), 192–98.

_____. "Bibliographic Instruction: An Emerging Professional Discipline." In *Directions for the Decade: Library Instruction in the 1980s*. Edited by Carolyn A. Kirkendall. Ann Arbor, Mich.: Pierian Press, 1981.

Howard, Helen A. "Innovation in University Organization: The Communication Model." *Journal of Academic Librarianship*, 6 (May 1980), 77–82.

_____. *Administrative Integration of Information Resources and Services in Universities in Canada and the United States: A Report to the Council on Library Resources*. ERIC Document ED 096–945. Arlington, Va.: ERIC Document Reproduction Center, 1974.

Howell, Benita et al. "Fleeting Encounters—A Role Analysis of Reference Librarian-Patron Interaction." *RQ*, 16 (Winter 1976), 124–29.

Hughes, Thomas P. *Networks of Power: Electrification in Western Society, 1880–1930*. Baltimore, Md.: Johns Hopkins University Press, 1983.

Hutchins, Margaret. *Introduction to Reference Work*. Chicago: American Library Association, 1944.

"The 'Information' Market." *Publishers' Weekly*, 195 (April 14, 1969), 64–67.

Ingersoll, Virginia, and Guy B. Adams. "Beyond Organizational Boundaries, Exploring the Managerial Myth." *Administration and Society*, 18 (November 1986), 360–81.

Jahoda, Gerald, and Paul E. Olson. "Models of Reference: Analyzing the Reference Process." *RQ*, 12 (Winter 1972), 148–56.

Jahoda, Gerald, Paul E. Olson, and Judith S. Braunagel. *The Librarian and Reference Queries: A Systematic Approach*. New York: Academic Press, 1980.

Jennerich, Elaine Z. "Before the Answer: Evaluating the Reference Process." *RQ*, 19 (Summer 1980), 360–66.

Jennerich, Elaine Z., and Edward J. Jennerich. *The Reference Interview as a Creative Art*. Littleton, Colo.: Libraries Unlimited, 1987.

Johnson, Kerry, and Marilyn D. White. "The Cognitive Style of Reference Librarians." *RQ*, 21 (Spring 1982), 239–46.

Jonas, Hans. *Philosophical Essays: From Ancient Creed to Technological Man*. Englewood Cliffs, N.J.: Prentice-Hall, 1974.

Jones, C. Lee. "Academic Libraries and Computing: A Time of Change." *EDUCOM Bulletin*, 20 (Spring 1985), 9–12.

Josey, E. J. *Libraries in the Political Process*. Phoenix, Ariz.: Oryx Press, 1980.

Josey, E. J., and Kenneth D. Shearer. Editors. *Politics and the Support of Libraries*. New York: Neal-Schuman, 1990.

Jussim, Estelle. "Review of *Communication Science and Technology Series*." *Library Journal*, 100 (February 15, 1975), 374.

Kaske, Neal, and Nancy P. Sanders. "Networking and the Electronic Library." *Drexel Library Quarterly*, 17 (Fall 1981), 65–76.

Katz, William A. *Introduction to Reference Work: Vol. 2, Reference Services and Reference Processes*. New York: McGraw-Hill, 1992.

Katznelson, Ira. *City Trenches: Urban Politics and the Patterning of Class in the United States*. New York: Pantheon Press, 1981.

Kehoe, Cynthia A. "The Future of Reference III: A Response." *College and Research Libraries News*, 51 (December 1990), 1052–55.

Kemeny, John. "A Library for 2000 A.D." In *Computers and the World of the Future*. Edited by Martin Greenberger. Cambridge, Mass.: MIT Press, 1962.

Kenney, Brigitte L. "Library Information Delivery Systems: Past, Present, and Future." *Drexel Library Quarterly*, 17 (Fall 1981), 36–64.

Kibbey, M., and N. H. Evans. "The Network is the Library." *EDUCOM Bulletin*, 24 (Fall 1989), 15–20.

Kibirige, Harry M. *The Information Dilemma: A Critical Analysis of Information Pricing and the Fees Controversy*. Westport, Conn.: Greenwood Press, 1983.

Kiesler, Sara, et al. "Automating a University Library: Some Effects on Work and Workers." In *Computing and Change on Campus*. Edited by Sara Kiesler and Lee Sproull. New York: Cambridge University Press, 1987.

Kilgour, Frederick. "The Online Catalog Revolution." In *New Trends in Electronic Publishing and Electronic Libraries*. Edited by Ahmed H. Helal and Joachim W. Weiss. Essen, Germany: Gesamthochschulbibliohek Essen, 1984.

King, Geraldine. "Open and Closed Questions: The Reference Interview." *RQ*, 12 (Winter 1972), 157–60.

King, Gilbert W. *Automation and the Library of Congress*. Washington, D.C.: Library of Congress, 1963.

Kleiner, Jane, and Lea Orkiszewski. Editors. *The Electronic Library: Linking People, Information, and Technology*. Chicago: American Library Association, 1992.

Knight, Douglas, and Nourse E. Shipley. Editors. *Libraries at Large*. New York: Bowker, 1969.

Kochen, Manfred, and Joseph C. Donahue. Editors. *Information for the Community*. Chicago: American Library Association, 1976.

Koenig, Michael. Editor. *Managing the Electronic Library*. New York: Special Libraries Association, 1983.

Kranzberg, Melvin. "The Information Age: Evolution or Revolution." *Information Technologies and Social Transformation*. Washington, D.C.: National Academy Press, 1985. Bruce R. Guile. Editor.

Kuhn, Thomas S. *The Structure of Scientific Revolutions*, 2nd edn. Chicago: University of Chicago, 1970.

Kumar, Krishan. *Prophecy and Progress*. Harmondsworth, England: Penguin, 1978.

Kupers, Terry A. *Ending Therapy: The Meaning of Termination*. New York: New York University Press, 1988.

Kurzweil, Edith. *The Freudians: A Comparative Perspective*. New Haven, Conn.: Yale University Press, 1989.

Kusack, James M. "Librarians and the Information Age: Is Reconciliation Possible?" *Bulletin of the American Society for Information Science*, 14 (February/March 1989), 27, 29–30.

―――. "Librarians and the Information Age: An Affair on the Rocks?" *Bulletin of the American Society for Information Science*, 14 (December/January 1988), 26–27.

Kutscher, Ronald, and Valerie A. Personick. "Deindustrialization and the Shift to Services." *Monthly Labor Review*, 109 (June 1986), 3–13.

Lam, R. Errol. "The Reference Interview: Some Intercultural Considerations." *RQ*, 27 (Spring 1988), 390–95.

Lamm, Dottie. "Should the Denver Public Library Be Expanded? Yes." *Denver Post*, August 12, 1990, Section H, 1H, 5H.

Lancaster, Frederick W. "Electronic Publishing." *Library Trends*, 37 (Winter 1989), 316–25.

―――. "Whither Libraries? Or Wither Libraries." *College and Research Libraries*, 39 (September 1978), 345–57. Reprinted 50 (July 1989), 406–19.

―――. "The Impact of Technology on the Use of Information Sources." In *Information Technology and Information Use*. Edited by Peter Ingwersen et al. London: Taylor Graham, 1986.

―――. "The Paperless Society Revisited." *American Libraries*, 16 (September 1985), 553–55.

―――. "Implications for Library and Information Science Education." *Library Trends*, 32 (Winter 1984), 337–48.

―――. "Future Librarianship: Preparing for an Unconventional Career." *Wilson Library Bulletin*, 57 (May 1983), 747–53.

———. "Information Professionals in the Information Age." The Bertha Bassam Lecture in Librarianship, No. 6. Toronto: University of Toronto Faculty of Library and Information Science, 1982.

———. *Libraries and Librarians in an Age of Electronics*. Arlington, Va.: Information Resources Press, 1982.

———. "The Future of the Library in the Age of Telecommunications." In *Telecommunications and Libraries: A Primer for Librarians and Information Managers*. Edited by Donald W. King et al. White Plains, NY: Knowledge Industry Publications, 1981.

———. "The Future of the Librarian Lies Outside the Library." *Catholic Library World*, 51 (April 1980), 388–91.

———. "The Role of the Library in an Electronic Society." In *Role of the Library in an Electronic Society*. Edited by Frederick W. Lancaster. Clinic on Library Applications of Data Processing, 1979. Urbana-Champaign, Ill.: University of Illinois Graduate School of Library Science, 1980.

———. *Information Retrieval Systems: Characteristics, Testing and Evaluation*, 2nd edn. New York: John Wiley, 1979.

———. "Mission Possible—A Future Information System." *Canadian Library Journal*, 36 (December 1979), 339–42.

———. *Toward Paperless Information Systems*. New York: Academic Press, 1978.

———. "The Dissemination of Scientific and Technical Information: Toward a Paperless System." *Occasional Papers*, No. 127 (April 1977). Champaign-Urbana, Ill.: University of Illinois Graduate School of Library Science, 1977.

Lancaster, Frederick W., et al. "The Changing Face of the Library: A Look at Libraries and Librarians in the Year 2001." *Collection Management*, 3 (Spring 1979), 55–77.

Lancaster, Frederick W., and Jana Bradley. "Image 2090: The Brain in Control." *Wilson Library Bulletin*, 63 (June 1989), 50, 52–53.

Lancaster, Frederick W., and E. G. Fayen. *Information Retrieval On-Line*. Los Angeles: Melville Publishing, 1973.

Lane, R. E. "The Decline of Politics and Ideology in a Knowledgeable Society." *American Sociological Review*, 31 (October 1966), 649–62.

Lanham, Richard A. "Electronic Texts and University Structures." In *Scholars and Research Libraries in the 21st Century*. ACLS Occasional Paper No. 14 New York: American Council of Learned Societies, 1990.

Larsen, Svend. "The Idea of an Electronic Library: A Critical Essay." *Libri*, 38 (September 1988), 159–77.

Larson, Mary E. "Connecting to the Electronic Library: A Paradigm Shift in Training Reference Librarians." *The Reference Librarian*, 30 (1990), 97–104.

Lasch, Christopher. "The Communitarian Critique of Liberalism." In *Community in America: The Challenge of "Habits of the Heart."* Charles H. Reynolds and Ralph V. Norman. Editors. Berkeley, Calif.: University of California Press, 1988.

Lears, T. J. Jackson. "From Salvation to Self-Realization: Advertising and the Therapeutic Roots of the Consumer Culture, 1880–1930." In *The Culture of Consumption: Critical Essays in American History, 1880–1980*. Edited by

Richard Wightman Fox and T. J. Jackson Lears. New York: Pantheon Books, 1983.

_____ . *No Place of Grace*. New York: Pantheon Books, 1981.

Leigh, Robert D. *The Public Library in the United States*. New York: Columbia University Press, 1950.

Lewis, David. "Inventing the Electronic University." *College and University Libraries*, 49 (July 1988), 291–304.

Lewis, Dennis A. "Today's Challenge—Tomorrow's Choice: Change or be Changed or the Doomsday Scenario Mk2." *Journal of Information Science*, 2 (September 1980), 59–74.

Ley, David. "Styles of the Times: Liberal and Neo-Conservative Landscapes in Inner Vancouver, 1968–1986." *Journal of Historical Geography*, 13 (January 1987), 40–56.

Licklider, J.C.R. "A Hypothetical Plan for a Library-Information Network." In *Conference on Interlibrary Communications and Information Networks*. Edited by Joseph Becker. Chicago: American Library Association, 1971.

_____ . "Man-Computer Communication." In *Annual Review of Information Science and Technology*, Vol. 3. Edited by Carlos A. Cuadra. Chicago: Encyclopaedia Britannica, 1968.

_____ . "A Crux in Scientific and Technical Communication." *American Psychologist*, 21 (1966), 1044–51.

_____ . *Libraries of the Future*. Cambridge, Mass.: MIT Press,1965.

_____ . "An On-Line Information Network." In *INTREX: Report of a Planning Conference on Information Transfer Experiments*. Edited by Carl F. J. Overhage and R. Joyce Harmon. Cambridge, Mass.: MIT Press, 1965.

Linderman, Winifred B. Editor. *The Present Status and Future Prospects of Reference/Information Service*. Chicago: American Library Association, 1967.

Lipset, Seymour M. *Political Man*. New York: Doubleday, 1963.

Lipsky, Michael. "Street-Level Bureaucracy and the Analysis of Urban Reform." *Urban Affairs Quarterly*, 6 (June 1971), 391–409.

"A Look at Where EDUCOM Now Stands and the Goals it Hopes to Accomplish." *EDUCOM*, 2 (January 1967), 2–3.

Lowi, Theodore J. *The End of Liberalism*, 2nd edn. New York: Norton, 1979.

Lukenbill, W. Bernard. "Teaching the Help Relationship Concepts in the Reference Process." *Journal of Education for Librarianship*, 18 (Fall 1977), 110–20.

Lukes, Steven. *Individualism*. Oxford, England: Basil Blackwell, 1973.

Lynch, Beverly P. "Libraries as Bureaucracies." *Library Trends*, 27 (Winter 1979), 259–67.

Lynch, Kevin. *The Image of the City*. Cambridge, Mass.: MIT Press, 1960.

Lyon, David. *The Information Society: Issues and Illusions*. Cambridge, England: Polity Press, 1988.

MacCann, Donnarae. Editor. *Social Responsibility in Librarianship: Essays on Equality*. Jefferson, N.C.: McFarland, 1989.

Machlup, Fritz. *The Production and Distribution of Knowledge in the United States*. Princeton, N.J.: Princeton University Press, 1962.

MacIntyre, Alasdair. *After Virtue*. Notre Dame, Ind.: University of Notre Dame Press, 1981.

MacLeish, Archibald. "The Premise of Meaning." In *The University—The Library*. Edited by Samuel Rothstein. Oxford: Shakespeare Head Press, 1972.

Malinconico, Michael. "Information's Brave New World." *Library Journal*, 117 (May 1, 1992), 36–40.

Malyshev, Nina A. "Concept and Reality: Managing Pikes Peak Library District's Community Resource and Information System." *Reference Services Review*, 16 (November. 4, 1988), 7–12.

Marchand, Philip. *Marshall McLuhan: The Medium and the Messager*. Toronto: Random House, 1989.

Markuson, Barbara E. Editor. *Libraries and Automation*. Washington, D.C.: Library of Congress, 1964.

Martin, Bernice. *A Sociology of Contemporary Cultural Change*. New York: St. Martin's Press, 1981.

Martin, Gordon, and Irving Lieberman. "Library 21: ALA's Exhibit at the World's Fair." *ALA Bulletin*, 56 (March 1962), 230–32.

Martin, Marilyn J. "Academic Libraries and Computing Centers: Opportunities for Leadership." *Library Administration and Management*, 6 (Spring 1992), 77–81.

Martin, Susan K. "Library Networks: Trends and Issues." *Journal of Library Administration*, 8 (Summer 1987), 27–33.

Masson, Jeffrey M. *Against Therapy*. London: Fontana, 1990.

Maxfield, David K. *Counselor Librarianship: A New Departure*. Occasional Papers No. 38 (March 1954). Champaign-Urbana, Ill.: University of Illinois Library School, 1954.

———. "Counselor Librarianship at U.I.C." *College and Research Libraries*, 15 (April 1954), 161–66, 179.

May, James. "Computer Technology and Library Information Systems." *Cause/Effect* (Spring 1990).

May, Rollo R. "Therapy in Our Day." In *The Evolution of Psychotherapy*. Edited by Jeffrey K. Zeig. New York: Brunner/Mazel, 1987.

Mayer, Michael. "The Transformation of Librarianship." *Canadian Library Journal*, 47 (August 1990), 233–35.

Mazlish, Bruce. *A New Science: The Breakdown of Connections and the Birth of Sociology*. New York: Oxford University Press, 1989.

McClure, Charles R. et al. *Public Libraries and the Internet/NREN: New Challenges, New Opportunities*. Syracuse, N.Y.: Syracuse University, 1992.

——— et al. *The National Research and Education Network (NREN)*. Norwood, N.J.: Ablex Publishing, 1991.

——— et al. *Planning and Role Setting of Public Libraries: A Manual of Options and Procedures*. Chicago: American Library Association, 1987.

McGarry, K. J. *Communication, Knowledge, and the Librarian*. London: Clive Bingley, 1975.

McKinlay, John B. "Toward the Proletarianization of Physicians." In *Professionals as Workers: Mental Labor in Advanced Capitalism*. Edited by Charles Derber. Boston: G. K. Hall, 1982.

McNeill, William H. *Mythistory and Other Essays*. Chicago: University of Chicago Press, 1986.

Mellon, Constance. Editor. *Bibliographic Instruction: The Second Generation*. Littleton, Colo.: Libraries Unlimited, 1987.

Merikangas, Robert J. "Librarian and Client: Who's in Charge?" In *Options for the 80s: Proceedings of the Second National Conference of the Association of College and Research Libraries.* Edited by Michael D. Kathman and Virgil F. Massman. Greenwich, Conn.: JAI Press, 1981.

Meyrowitz, Joshua. *No Sense of Place: The Impact of Electronic Media on Social Behavior.* New York: Oxford University Press, 1985.

Michalak, Thomas J. "An Experiment in Enhancing Catalog Records at Carnegie-Mellon University." *Library Hi Tech,* 8 (1990), 33–41.

Miles, Ian. *Mapping and Measuring the Information Economy.* London: British Library Research and Development Department, 1989.

Miller, Constance, and James Rettig. "Reference Obsolescence." *RQ,* 25 (Fall 1985), 52–58.

Miller, Constance, James Rettig, and Patricia Tegler. "In Pursuit of Windmills: Librarians and the Determination to Instruct." *Reference Librarian,* 18 (Summer 1987), 119–34.

Molholt, Pat. "The Future of Reference III: A Paradigm Shift for Information Services." *College and Research Libraries,* 5 (December 1990), 1045–51.

———. "What Happened to the Merger Debate?" *Libraries and Computing Centers,* No. 13 (May 1989), n.p. Insert in *Journal of Academic Librarianship,* 15 (May 1989).

———. "On Converging Paths: The Computing Center and the Library." *Libraries and Computing Centers,* No. 1 (March 1987). Insert in *Journal of Academic Librarianship,* 13 (March 1987).

———. "The Information Machine: A New Challenge for Librarians." *Library Journal,* 111 (October 1, 1986), 47–52.

———. "On Converging Paths: The Computer Center and the Library." *Journal of Academic Librarianship,* 11 (November 1985), 284–88.

Molz, R. Kathleen. *The Knowledge Institutions in the Information Age: The Case of the Public Library.* Washington, D.C.: Library of Congress, 1988.

Moran, Barbara B. et al. "The Electronic Campus: The Impact of the Scholar's Workstation Project on the Libraries at Brown." *College and Research Libraries,* 48 (January 1987), 5–16.

Mumford, Lewis. *The City in History.* New York: Harcourt, Brace & World, 1961.

Munoz, Joanna L. "The Significance of Nonverbal Communication in the Reference Interview." *RQ,* 16 (Spring 1977), 220–24.

Myrdal, Gunnar. *An American Dilemma.* New York: Harper, 1944.

Nauratil, Marcia J. *The Alienated Librarian.* New York: Greenwood Press, 1989.

Neff, Raymond K. "Merging Libraries and Computer Centers: Manifest Destiny or Manifestly Deranged?" *EDUCOM Bulletin,* 20 (Winter 1985), 8–12, 16.

Neill, S. D. "The Drift from Art to Science: A Profession in Transition: The Case of Collection Development." In *Information Literacies for the Twenty-First Century.* Edited by Virgil P. Blake and Renee Tjoumas. Boston: G. K. Hall, 1990.

Nemeyer, Carol A. "The Center for the Book." In *Books, Libraries and Electronics: Essays on the Future of Written Communication.* Edited by Efrem Sigel et al. White Plains, N.Y.: Knowledge Industry Publications, 1982.

Neubauer, Karl W. "Electronic Library? The Consequences of Micros on Data Processing Systems in Libraries in the Age of CD-ROM." In *The Impact of*

CD-ROM on Library Operations and Universal Availability of Information. Edited by Ahmed H. Lelal and Joachim W. Weiss. Essen, Germany: Universitatsbibliothek Essen, 1989.

New Information Technologies—New Opportunities. Edited by Linda C. Smith. Clinic on Library Applications of Data Processing, 1981. Urbana-Champaign, Ill.: Graduate School of Library and Information Science, 1982.

Nickum, Marj. "Should the Denver Public Library Be Expanded? No." *Denver Post,* August 12, 1990, Section H, 1H, 5H.

Nielsen, Brian. "The Role of the Public Services Librarian: The New Revolution." In *Rethinking the Library in the Information Age. Vol. 3: Issues in Library Research: Proposals for the 1990s.* Washington, D.C.: U.S. Department of Education, Government Printing Office, 1989.

———. "Teacher or Intermediary: Alternative Professional Models in the Information Age." *College and Research Libraries,* 43 (May 1982), 183–91.

———. "Technological Change and Professional Identity." In *New Information Technologies—New Opportunities.* Edited by Linda C. Smith. Clinic on Library Applications of Data Processing, 1981. Urbana-Champaign, Ill.: Graduate School of Library and Information Science, 1982.

Nisbet, Robert A. *Community and Power.* London: Oxford University Press, 1968. (Originally published as *The Quest for Community,* 1953.)

———. *The Sociological Tradition.* New York: Basic Books, 1966.

Nyce, James M., and Paul Kahn. "Innovation, Pragmaticism, and Technological Continuity: Vannevar Bush's Memex." *Journal of the American Society for Information Science,* 40 (May 1989), 214–20.

Nye, David E. *Electrifying America: Social Meaning of a New Technology, 1880–1940.* Cambridge, Mass.: MIT Press, 1990.

———. *Image Worlds: Corporate Identities at General Electric, 1850–1930.* Cambridge, Mass.: MIT Press, 1985.

Online Computer Library Center, Inc. *OCLC Annual Report, 1990/91.* Dublin, Ohio: OCLC, 1991.

Orr, J. M. *Libraries as Communication Systems.* Westport, Conn.: Greenwood Press, 1977.

Overhage, Carl F. J., and R. Joyce Harmon. *INTREX: Report of a Planning Conference on Information Transfer Experiments.* Cambridge, Mass.: MIT Press, 1965.

Palmour, Vernon E. et al. "A Planning Process for Public Libraries: Introduction and Overview." In *Public Librarianship: A Reader.* Edited by Jane Robbins-Carter. Littleton, Colo.: Libraries Unlimited, 1983.

Parker, Edwin B. "Information and Society." In *Annual Review of Information Science and Technology,* Vol. 8. Edited by Carlos A. Cuadra. Washington, D.C.: American Society for Information Science, 1973.

———. "Potential Interrelationships Between Library and Other Mass Media Systems." In *Conference on Interlibrary Communications and Information Networks.* Edited by Joseph Becker. Chicago: American Library Association, 1971.

———. "The New Communication Media." In *Toward Century 21: Technology, Society, and Human Values.* Edited by C. S. Wallia. New York: Basic Books, 1970.

———. "Developing a Campus Information Retrieval System." *Proceedings of a Conference Held at Stanford University Libraries October 4–5, 1968.* Edited by

Allen B. Veaner and Paul J. Fasana. Stanford, Calif.: Stanford University Libraries, 1969.

Parker, Edwin B., and W. J. Paisley, "Research for Psychologists at the Interface of the Scientist and His Information System." *American Psychologist*, 21 (1966), 1061–71.

Parkhurst, Carola. Editor. *Library Perspectives on NREN: The National Research and Education Network*. Chicago: Library and Information Technology Association, 1990.

Patterson, Franklin, and Charles R. Longsworth. *The Making of a College: Plans for a New Departure in Higher Education*. Cambridge, Mass.: MIT Press, 1966.

Peck, Theodore P. "Counseling Skills Applied to Reference Services." *RQ*, 14 (Spring 1975), 233–35.

Penland, Patrick R. *Communication for Librarians*. Pittsburgh: University of Pittsburgh, 1971.

———. "Counselor Librarianship." In *Encyclopedia of Library and Information Science*, Vol. 6. New York: Marcel Dekker, 1971.

———. *Interviewing for Counselor and Reference Librarians*. Pittsburgh: University of Pittsburgh, 1970.

———. *Advisory Counseling for Librarians*. Pittsburgh: University of Pittsburgh, 1969.

Penland, Patrick R., and Aleyamma Mathai. *Interpersonal Communication*. New York: Marcel Dekker, 1974.

Perrolle, Judith A. *Computers and Social Change*. Belmont, Calif.: Wadsworth, 1987.

Pfaffenberger, Bryan. *Democratizing Information: Online Databases and the Rise of End-User Searching*. Boston: G. K. Hall, 1990.

Plotnik, Art. "Chicago to Build Nation's Largest Municipal Library: Classical Design Triumphs in International Competition." *American Libraries*, 19 (July/August 1988), 565–66.

Plunkett, Lois M. "The 1980's: A Decade of Job Growth and Industry Shifts." *Monthly Labor Review*, 113 (September 1990), 3–16.

Porat, Marc U. "Global Implications of the Information Society." *Journal of Communication*, 28 (Winter 1978), 70–80.

Powell, Judith W., and Robert B. Lelieuvre. *Peoplework: Communications Dynamics for Librarians*. Chicago: American Library Association, 1979.

President's Science Advisory Committee. *Science, Government, and Information: The Responsibilities of the Technical Community and the Government in the Transfer of Information*. Washington, D.C.: The White House, 1963.

———. *Improving the Availability of Scientific and Technical Information in the United States*. Washington, D.C.: The White House, 1958.

Public Library Association. *The Library Connection: Essays Written in Praise of Public Libraries*. Chicago: American Library Association, 1977.

Quay, James, and James Veninga. *National Task Force on Scholarship and the Public Humanities: Making Connections, the Humanities, Culture, and Community*. New York: American Council of Learned Societies, 1990.

Quinn, Judy. "California Dreaming: Dowlin & Co. Design a New Main Library." *Library Journal*, 117 (June 1, 1992), 55–58.

Quinn, Judy, and Michael Rogers. "ARL Libraries Fight for Their 'Place' on Campus." *Library Journal*, 116 (June 15, 1991), 16–17.

Raelin, Joseph A. *The Clash of Cultures*. Boston: Harvard Business School Press, 1986.

Rawlinson, Nora. "The Central Library—A Fatal Attraction." *Library Journal*, 115 (June 1, 1990), 6.

Ray, Ron. "Crucial Critics for the Information Age." *Library Journal*, 118 (April 1, 1993), 46–49.

Rayward, W. Boyd. "Library and Information Science: An Historical Perspective." *Journal of Library History*, 20 (Spring 1985), 120–36.

Reagan, Ronald. "Inaugural Address, January 20, 1981." *Public Papers of the Presidents of the United States, Ronald Reagan, 1981*. Washington, D.C.: U.S. Government Printing Office, 1982.

The Relevance of Liberalism. Edited by the Research Institute on International Change, Columbia University. Boulder, Colo.: Westview Press, 1978.

Relph, Edward. *Place and Placelessness*. London: Pion Limited, 1976.

Rethinking the Library in the Information Age. Vol. 3: Issues in Library Research: Proposals for the 1990s. Washington, D.C.: Office of Educational Research and Improvement, Government Printing Office, 1989.

Rettig, James. "A Theoretical Model and Definition of the Reference Process." *RQ*, 18 (Fall 1978), 19–29.

Reynolds, Charles H., and Ralph V. Norman. Editors. *Community in America: The Challenge of "Habits of the Heart."* Berkeley, Calif.: University of California Press, 1988.

Rice, James G. "The Dream of the Memex." *American Libraries*, 19 (January 1988), 14–17.

Rider, Fremont. *The Scholar and the Future of the Research Library*. New York: Hadham Press, 1944.

Rieff, Philip. *The Triumph of the Therapeutic*. London: Chatto and Windus, 1966.

Riggs, Donald E., and Gordon A. Sabine. *Libraries in the '90s: What the Leaders Expect*. Phoenix, Ariz.: Oryx Press, 1988.

Robbins, Jane. "The Reference Librarian: A Street-Level Bureaucrat?" *Library Journal*, 97 (April 15, 1972), 1389–92.

Robbins-Carter, Jane. "Political Science: Utility for Research in Librarianship." *Library Trends*, 32 (Spring 1984), 425–39.

Robins, Kevin, and Frank Webster. "Information as Capital: A Critique of Daniel Bell." In *The Ideology of the Information Age*. Edited by Jennifer D. Slack and Fred Fejes. Norwood, N.J.: Ablex Publishing, 1987, 95–117.

Robinson, Barbara. "Reference Services: A Model of Question Handling." *RQ*, 29 (Fall 1989), 48–61.

Robinson, Charles. "The Public Library Vanishes." *Library Journal*, 117 (March 15, 1992), 51–54.

Rochell, Carlton. *Dreams Betrayed: Working in the Technological Age*. Lexington, Mass.: Lexington Books, 1987.

———. *Wheeler and Goldhor's Practical Administration of Public Libraries*. New York: Harper, 1981.

Rose, Ernestine. *The Public Library in American Life*. New York: Columbia University Press, 1954.

Rosenblum, Nancy L. *Liberalism and the Moral Life*. Cambridge, Mass.: Harvard University Press, 1989.

Roszak, Theodore. *The Cult of Information*. New York: Pantheon, 1986.

Rothstein, Samuel. "Across the Desk: A Hundred Years of Reference Encounters." In *Symposium on the Reference Interview: Proceedings of the CACUL Symposium on the Reference Interview*. Ottawa: Canadian Library Association, 1979.

———. *The Development of Reference Services Through Academic Traditions, Public Library Practice and Special Librarianship*. ACRL Monographs No. 14. Chicago: Association of College and Reference Libraries, 1955.

Rowe, Richard R. "You, the CIO." *American Libraries*, 18 (April 1987), 297.

Rubin, Brent D. "The Communication-Information Relationship in System-Theoretic Perspective." *Journal of the American Society for Information Science*, 43 (January 1992), 15–27.

Rubin, Michael R. "The Emerging World-Wide Information Economy." *Library Hi Tech*, 4 (Winter 1986), 79–86.

Rubin, Michael R. et al. *The Knowledge Industry in the United States, 1960–1980*. Princeton, N.J.: Princeton University Press, 1986.

Rueschemeyer, Dietrich. "Doctors and Lawyers: A Comment on the Theory of Professions." *Canadian Review of Sociology and Anthropology*, 1 (February 1964), 17–30.

Sack, John R. "Open Systems for Open Minds: Building the Library Without Walls." *College and Research Libraries*, 47 (November 1986), 535–44.

Saunders, Laverna M. "The Virtual Library Today." *Library Administration and Management*, 6 (Spring 1992), 66–70.

———. Editor. *The Virtual Library: Visions and Realities*. Westport, Conn.: Meckler, 1992.

Schiller, Anita R. "Instruction or Information: What's Changed." *Reference Librarian*, 1/2 (Fall/Winter 1981), 3–11.

———. "Reference Service: Instruction or Information." *Library Quarterly*, 35 (January 1965), 52–60.

Schiller, Herbert I. *Who Knows: Information in the Age of the Fortune 500*. Norwood, N.J.: Ablex Publishing, 1981.

Schultheiss, Louis A., et al. *Advanced Data Processing in the University Library*. New York: Scarecrow Press, 1962.

Schuman, Patricia G. "Reclaiming Our Technological Future." *Library Journal*, 115 (March 1, 1990), 34–38.

Segal, Howard P. *Technological Utopianism in American Culture*. Chicago: University of Chicago Press, 1985.

Shaughnessy, T. W. "Technology and Structure of Libraries." *Libri*, 32 (June 1982), 149–55.

Shera, Jesse H. *The Foundations of Education for Librarianship*. New York: John Wiley, 1972.

———. *Foundations of the Public Library*. Chicago: University of Chicago, 1949.

Shils, Edward. "The Antinomies of Liberalism." In *The Relevance of Liberalism*. Edited by the Staff of the Research Institute on International Change, Columbia University. Boulder, Colo.: Westview Press, 1978.

Shuman, Bruce A. *The Library of the Future*. Englewood, Colo.: Libraries Unlimited, 1989.

Sigel, Efram et al. *Books, Libraries and Electronics: Essays on the Future of Written Communication*. White Plains, N.Y.: Knowledge Industry Publications, 1982.

Silvestri, George, and John Lukasiewicz. "Projections of Occupational Employ-
    ment, 1988–2000." *Monthly Labor Review*, 112 (November 1989), 42–65.
Simon, Cathy. "Inspiration, Knowledge and Information." In *Is the Library a Place?*
    Association of Research Libraries Minutes of the 118th Meeting, May
    15–17, 1991. Washington, D.C.: Association of Research Libraries, 1991.
Slack, Jennifer D., and Fred Fejes. Editors. *The Ideology of the Information Age*.
    Norwood, N.J.: Ablex Publishing, 1987.
Smail, David. *Taking Care: An Alternative to Therapy*. London: Dent, 1987.
Smith, Anthony. "Technology, Identity, and the Information Machine." *Daedalus*,
    115 (Summer 1986), 155–69.
Smith, Eldred. *The Librarian, the Scholar, and the Future of the Research Library*. New
    York: Greenwood Press, 1990.
Smith, Linda C. Editor. *Professional Competencies—Technology and the Librarian*.
    Clinic on Library Applications of Data Processing, 1983. Urbana-Cham-
    paign, Ill.: University of Illinois Graduate School of Library and Informa-
    tion Science, 1983.
_____. " 'Memex' as an Image of Potentiality in Information Retrieval Research
    and Development." In *Information Retrieval Research*. Edited by R. N.
    Oddy et al. London: Butterworths, 1981.
Smith, Lisa L. "Evaluating the Reference Interview: A Theoretical Discussion of
    the Desirability and Achievability of Evaluation." *RQ*, 31 (Fall 1991),
    75–79.
Smith, Robert F. "A Funny Thing is Happening to the Library on Its Way to the
    Future." *The Futurist*, 12 (April 1978), 85–91.
Sosa, Jorge F., and Michael H. Harris. "Jose Ortega y Gasset and the Role of the
    Librarian in Post-industrial America." *Libri*, 41 (March 1991), 3–21.
Starr, Paul. *The Social Transformation of American Medicine*. New York: Basic Books,
    1982.
Stearns, Peter. "The Idea of Postindustrial Society: Some Problems." *Journal of
    Social History*, 17 (Summer 1984), 685–93.
Steele, Timothy. "The Library." *Poetry*, 143 (December 1983), 129.
Steig, Margaret F. *Change and Challenge in Library and Information Science Education*
    Chicago: American Library Association, 1992.
_____. "Technology and the Concept of Reference or What Will Happen to the
    Milkman's Cow." *Library Journal*, 115 (April 15, 1990), 45–49.
Suprenant, Thomas. "Future Libraries: The Electronic Environment." *Wilson Li-
    brary Bulletin*, 56 (January 1982), 336–41.
Suprenant, Thomas, and Claude Perry-Holmes. "The Reference Librarian of the
    Future: A Scenario." *RQ*, 25 (Winter 1985), 234–38.
Susman, Warren I. *Culture as History*. New York: Pantheon, 1985.
Svenonius, Elaine. "Review of *Libraries of the Future*." *Library Quarterly*, 35 (October
    1965), 397.
"The Talk of the Town." *The New Yorker* (February 18, 1990), 21–22.
Taube, Mortimer. "The Coming Age of Information Technology." *Bulletin of the
    Medical Library Association*, 52 (January 1964), 120–27.
Taylor, Robert S. "Chance, Change and the Future in the Information Profession."
    Bulletin of the American Society for Information Science." 19 (Decem-
    ber/January 1993), 16–18.

————. "Value-Added Processes in the Information Life Cycle." *Journal of the American Society for Information Science*, 33 (September 1982), 341–46.

————. "Reminiscing About the Future: Professional Education and the Information Environment." *Library Journal*, 104 (September 15, 1979), 1871–75.

————. "Patterns Toward a User-Centered Academic Library." In *New Dimensions for Academic Library Service*. Edited by E. J. Josey. Metuchen, N.J.: Scarecrow Press, 1975.

————. *The Making of a Library*. New York: Becker and Hayes, 1972.

————. "Technology and Libraries." *EDUCOM Bulletin*, 5 (May 1970), 4–5.

————. "Toward the Design of a College Library for the Seventies." *Wilson Library Bulletin*, 43 (September 1968), 41–51.

————. "Question Negotiation and Information Seeking in Libraries." *College and Research Libraries*, 29 (May 1968), 178–94.

————. "The Interfaces Between Librarianship and Information Science and Engineering." *Special Libraries*, 58 (January 1967), 45–48.

————. "Review of *Libraries of the Future*." *College and Research Libraries*, 26 (September 1965), 406–407.

————. "The Process of Asking Questions." *American Documentation*, 13 (October 1962), 391–96.

Thigpen, Robert B., and Lyle A. Downing. "Liberal and Communitarian Approaches to Justification." *Review of Politics*, 51 (Fall 1989), 533–50.

Thompson, James. *The End of Libraries*. London: Clive Bingley, 1982.

Tinder, Glenn. "Community: The Tragic Ideal." *Yale Review*, 65 (Summer 1976), 550–64.

Toffler, Alvin. *The Third Wave*. New York: Morrow, 1980.

————. *Future Shock*. New York: Random House. 1970.

Tongate, John. "The Future of Reference III: Discussion Summary." *College and Research Libraries News*, 51 (December 1990), 1057–58.

Toth, Susan Allen, and John Coughan. Editors. *Reading Rooms*. New York: Doubleday, 1991.

Trani, Eugene P. Editor. *The Future of the Academic Library*. Occasional Papers Nos. 188 and 189 (January 1991). Urbana-Champaign, Ill.: Graduate School of Library and Information Science, 1991.

Troll, Denise A. "Information Technologies at Carnegie-Mellon." *Library Administration and Management*, 6 (Spring 1992), 91–99.

Trombatore, Dennis. "The Future of Reference III: Another Response." *College and Research Libraries News*, 51 (December 1990), 1055–56.

Tucker, John M. "User Education in Academic Libraries: A Century in Retrospect." *Library Trends*, 29 (Summer 1980), 9–27.

Turner, Berry A. Editor. *Organizational Symbolism*. Berlin: Walter de Gruyter, 1990.

Ulveling, Ralph A. "The Public Library in the Large Community." In *The Library in the Community*. Edited by Leon Carnovsky. Chicago: University of Chicago Press, 1940, 23–37.

United States Department of Commerce. *The Information Economy*, 9 volumes. Office of Telecommunications Special Publication 77–12, 1977. Washington, D.C.: Government Printing Office, 1977.

Van House, Nancy A. *Public Library User Fees*. Westport, Conn.: Greenwood Press, 1983.

Vavrek, Bernard F. "The Nature of Reference Librarianship." *RQ*, 13 (Spring 1974), 213–17.

———. "Emergence of a New Reference?" *Journal of Education for Librarianship*, 10 (Fall 1969), 109–15.

———. "A Theory of Reference Service." *College and Research Libraries*, 29 (November 1968), 508–10.

———. "The Reference Librarian as a Technician." *RQ*, 7 (Fall 1967), 5–8.

Veroff, Joseph et al. *The Inner American: A Self-Portrait from 1957–1976*. New York: Basic Books, 1981.

Von Seggern, Marilyn. "Evaluating the Interview." *RQ*, 29 (Winter 1989), 260–65.

Wagers, Robert. "American Reference Theory and Information Dogma." *Journal of Library History*, 13 (Summer 1978), 265–81.

Ward, John William. *Red, White, and Blue: Men, Books, and Ideas in American Culture*. New York: Oxford University Press, 1969.

Warntz, Chris. "Some Promises Kept: The Peterborough Town Library." *Wilson Library Bulletin*, 56 (January 1982), 342–46.

Watkins, Beverly T. "Many Campuses Start Building Tomorrow's Electronic Library." *Chronicle of Higher Education*, 39 (September 2, 1992), A19–A21.

Watts, Spencer E., and Alan R. Samuels. "What Business Are We In? Perceptions of the Roles and Purposes of the Public Library in Professional Literature." *Public Libraries*, 23 (Winter 1984), 131–34.

Weiskel, Timothy C. "The Electronic Library: Changing the Character of Research." *Change*, 20 (November/December 1988), 38–47.

Weizenbaum, Joseph. *Computer Power and Human Reason: From Judgment to Calculation*. San Francisco: W. H. Freeman, 1976.

West, Richard P., and Richard N. Katz. "Implementing the Vision: A Framework and an Agenda for Investing in Academic Computing." *EDUCOM Review*, 25 (Winter 1990), 32–37.

Westin, Alan F., and Anne L. Finger. *Using the Public Library in the Computer Age*. Chicago: American Library Association, 1991.

Wheeler, Joseph L., and Alford M. Githens. *The American Public Library Building*. New York: C. Scribner's, 1941.

White, Herbert S. "Bibliographic Instruction, Information Literacy, and Information Empowerment." *Library Journal*, 117 (January 1992), 76, 78.

———. *Librarians and the Awakening from Innocence*. Boston: G. K. Hall, 1989.

White, Lawrence J. *Public Library in the 1980s*. Lexington, Mass.: Lexington Books, 1983.

White, Marilyn D. "Evaluation of the Reference Interview." *RQ*, 25 (Fall 1985), 76–84.

———. "The Reference Encounter Model." *Drexel Library Quarterly*, 19 (Spring 1983), 38–55.

———. "The Dimensions of the Reference Interview." *RQ*, 20 (Summer 1981), 373–81.

White House Conference on Library and Information Services. *Summary, March 1980*. Washington, D.C.: Government Printing Office, 1980.

Whitlatch, Jo Bell. *The Role of the Academic Reference Librarian*. New York: Greenwood Press, 1990.

Whyte, William H. *City: Rediscovering the Center*. New York: Doubleday, 1988.

Wicklein, John. "Will the New Technologies Kill the Public Library?" In *Crossroads: Library and Information Technology Association National Conference, 1983*. Edited by Michael Gorman. Chicago: American Library Association, 1984.

Wiebe, Robert H. *The Search for Order, 1877–1920*. New York: Hill and Wang, 1967.

Wiener, Norbert. *Cybernetics or Control and Communication in the Animal and the Machine*, 2nd edn. Cambridge, Mass.: MIT Press, 1961.

Wilensky, Harold L. "The Professionalization of Everyone?" *American Journal of Sociology*, 70 (September 1964), 137–58.

Williams, Patrick. *The American Public Library and the Problem of Purpose*. New York: Greenwood Press, 1988.

Williams, Raymond. *Television: Technology and Cultural Form*. New York: Schocken Books, 1975.

Wilson, Patrick. "The Second Objective." In *The Conceptual Foundations of Descriptive Cataloguing*. Edited by Elaine Svenonius. San Diego, Calif.: Academic Press, 1989.

———. "The Face Value Rule in Reference work." *RQ*, 25 (Summer 1986), 468–75.

Wilson, Pauline E. *Stereotype and Status: Librarians in the United States*. Westport, Conn.: Greenwood Press, 1982.

Winner, Langdon. *The Whale and the Reactor*. Chicago: University of Chicago Press, 1986.

———. "Mythinformation in the High-Tech Era." *IEEE Spectrum*, 21 (June 1984), 80–84.

———. *Autonomous Technology: Technics-Out-Of-Control as a Theme in Political Thought*. Cambridge, Mass.: MIT Press, 1977.

Winter, Michael F. *The Culture and Control of Expertise*. New York: Greenwood Press, 1988.

Wolff, Robert P. *The Poverty of Liberalism*. Boston: Beacon Press, 1968.

Woodsworth, Anne. *Patterns for Managing Information Technology on Campus*. Chicago: American Library Association, 1991.

Woodsworth, Anne, et al. "The Information Job Family: Results of an Exploratory Study." *Library Trends*, 41 (Fall 1992), 250–68.

———. "The Model Research Library: Planning for the Future." *Journal of Academic Librarianship*, 15 (July 1989), 132–38.

———. "Chief Information Officers on Campus." *EDUCOM Bulletin*, 22 (Summer 1987), 2–4.

Woodward, Kathleen. Editor. *The Myths of Information: Technology and Post-Industrial Culture*. Madison, Wis.: Coda Press, 1980.

Wright, Karen. "The Road to the Global Village." *Scientific American*, 262 (March 1990), 83–94.

Wurman, Richard S. *Information Anxiety*. New York: Doubleday, 1989.

Wyer, James I. *Reference Work: A Textbook for Students of Library Work and Librarians*. Chicago: American Library Association, 1930.

Yankelovich, Daniel. *New Rules: Searching for Self-Fulfillment in a World Turned Upside Down*. New York: Random House, 1981.

Zeig, Jeffrey K. *The Evolution of Psychotherapy*. New York: Brunner/Mazel, 1987.

Zeleny, Milan. "The Self-Service Society: A New Scenario of the Future." *Planning Review*, 7 (May 1979), 3–7, 37–38.

Index

About the Author

WILLIAM F. BIRDSALL is University Librarian at Dalhousie University in Halifax, Nova Scotia. He has previously held positions at Iowa State University, the University of Wisconsin-LaCrosse, and the University of Manitoba. His publications include articles in: *Library Journal, Canadian Library Journal, Journal of Academic Librarianship, The American Archivist,* and *Journal of Library History.*

ISBN 0-313-29210-8

90000>

EAN

9 780313 292101

HARDCOVER BAR CODE